Great Places

TO STAY

For special breaks and celebrations

Welcome ...

Indulge yourself at tempting hotels, B&Bs and self-catering homes

A warm welcome to this the first edition of Great Places to Stay, produced by VisitBritain.

Looking for the very best romantic retreats, hidden gems and places to unwind that Great Britain has to offer? From VisitBritain Silver and Gold Award-winning accommodation to 4 and 5 Star, this is the pick of the crop when it comes to fulfiling your leisure needs.

Indulge yourself on bumper breakfasts of locally-sourced produce accompanied by home-made bread and preserves, or relax next to an open log fire with a book in one hand and a glass or cup of something warming in the other; pamper yourself with soothing spa treatments or experience the exhilaration of hitting the fairway-splitting drive on a top golf course. And let's not forget that many of those featured in this book offer a great venue for get-togethers or re-unions with family and/or friends.

There are castles, stately homes, farmhouses, and cosy cottages, many with marvellous views of countryside or coastline. Those who like to go on shopping sprees or visit places of historical interest can opt for a top hotel in cities like London and Edinburgh, or choose a country house within a short drive of cities such as Bath, Carlisle and Newcastle.

Become a castaway on your own terms on a visit to the Isle of Wight or the Isles of Scilly or even on a privately-owned Scottish island.

Whatever and wherever it is that helps you switch off and enjoy your leisure time you'll find them in these pages. Keep this book handy and you'll never be short of ideas for surprise weekend breaks or planned long vacations.

For more great ideas go to visitbritain.com

Swinton Park

Matfen Hall

Blaize Cottages

How to ...

... USE THIS BOOK

There are two ways to pinpoint the places that are just right for you. By location – use the map on pages 6 and 7 to find what is available in the part of the country you most wish to visit. By speciality – turn to the indexes on page 265 to help you find the right place to stay if you have a particular requirement such as organising a reunion, wedding reception or you need Internet access.

Star ratings

Establishments are awarded a rating 1-5 Stars based on a combination of quality of facilities and services provided. The more stars, the higher the quality and the greater the range of facilities and level of service. The process to arrive at a Star rating is very thorough to ensure that when you book accommodation you can be confident it will meet your expectations. Professional assessors visit establishments annually and work to strict criteria to rate the available facilities and service.

A quality score is awarded for every aspect of the experience. For hotels and B&B accommodation this includes the comfort of the bed, the quality of the breakfast and dinner and, most importantly, the cleanliness. For self-catering properties the assessors also take into consideration the layout and design of the accommodation, the ease of use of all appliances, the range and quality of the kitchen equipment, and the variety and presentation of the visitor information provided. The warmth of welcome and the level of care that each establishment offers its guests are noted, and places that go the extra mile to make every stay a special one will be rewarded with high scores for quality.

All the national assessing bodies (VisitBritain, VisitScotland, VisitWales and the AA) now operate to a common set of standards for rating each category of accommodation, giving holidaymakers and travellers a clear guide on what to expect.

Ratings made easy

★★★	Good level of quality and comfort
★★★★	Excellent standard throughout
★★★★★	Exceptional with a degree of luxury

For details on the quality rating schemes, go to visitbritain.co.uk/accommodation/qas.aspx

Gold and Silver Awards

These awards from VisitBritain are highly prized by proprietors and are given to accommodation offering the highest level of quality within their star rating, particularly in housekeeping, service and hospitality, bedrooms, bathrooms and food.

Designators explained

Hotel: A minimum of six bedrooms, but more likely to have more than 20.

Small Hotel: A maximum of 20 bedrooms and likely to be more personally run.

Country House Hotel: Set in ample grounds or gardens, in a rural or semi-rural location, with the emphasis on peace and quiet.

Guest Accommodation: Encompassing a wide range of establishments from one room B&Bs to larger properties which may offer dinner and hold an alcohol licence.

B&B: Accommodating no more than six people, the owners of these establishments welcome you into their own home as a special guest.

Guest House: Generally comprising more than three rooms. Dinner is unlikely to be available. May be licensed.

Farmhouse: B&B, and sometimes dinner, but always on a farm.

Inn: Pub with rooms – many with restaurants, too.

Restaurant with Rooms: A licensed restaurant is the main business but there will be a small number of bedrooms, with all the facilities you would expect, and breakfast the following morning.

Self-Catering: Chose from cosy country cottages, smart town-centre apartments, seaside villas, grand country houses for large family gatherings. Most take bookings by the week, generally from a Friday or Saturday, but short breaks are increasingly offered, particularly outside the main season.

Camping, Touring and Holiday Park: These will allow you to bring your own caravan, motor home or tent. Also you can hire a caravan holiday home for a short break or longer holiday. They range from small, rural sites to large parks with all the added extras such as a pool.

Web and email

Please note that all web addresses throughout this book are printed without the www. prefix. Where a long web or email address requires two lines please do *not* insert a space where it breaks on to the second line. Where a hyphen or full stop is shown at the end of the first line it *should* be inserted when typing the address into your browser.

Contents

For a Who's Who of accommodation and where to find them on the map see pages 6-7. For some great ideas on how to enjoy your leisure time see pages 8-13. Want to check out the specialities of the listed properties? Turn to Indexes starting on page 265.

MAP REF	Accommodation	PAGE NO
1	**17 Northgate,** Oakham, Rutland	14
2	**33/2 Queen Street,** Edinburgh	15
3	**40 York Road,** Tunbridge Wells, Kent	16
4	**6 & 15 Stonegate Court,** York, N Yorkshire	17
5	**8 Clarendon Crescent,** Leamington Spa, Warwickshire	18
6	**Abbey Court,** Shrewsbury, Shropshire	21
7	**Alliblaster House,** Rudgwick, West Sussex	22
8	**Allt y Golau,** Felingwm Uchaf, Carmarthenshire	24
9	**Alma Mater,** Lymington, Hampshire	26
10	**The Apartments,** SW London	27
11	**The Apartments – Oxford,** Oxfordshire	28
12	**Armsyde,** Padstow, Cornwall	30
13	**Artizana Suite,** Prestbury, Cheshire	31
14	**Ascot House,** York, N Yorkshire	32
15	**Atlantic House,** Lizard, Cornwall	33
16	**The Ayrlington,** Bath, Somerset	34
17	**Barbican House,** York, N Yorkshire	36
18	**Barncastle,** Stroud, Gloucestershire	38
19	**Battlesteads Hotel,** Hexham, Northumberland	39
20	**Beacon Hill Farm,** Morpeth, Northumberland	40
21	**Beech Farm Cottages,** Tetney, Lincolnshire	42
22	**Beech House,** Kendal, Cumbria	43
23	**The Bentley Kempinski Hotel,** London	44
24	**Berkeley House,** Tetbury, Gloucestershire	45
25	**Bethany House,** Tunbridge Wells, Kent	46
26	**Bidwell Farm Cottages,** Upottery, Devon	47
27	**Black Boys Inn,** Hurley, Berkshire	48
28	**Blaize Cottages,** Lavenham, Suffolk	49
29	**Blenheim Lodge,** Bowness-on-Windermere, Cumbria	50
30	**Blue Hayes Private Hotel,** St Ives, Cornwall	51
31	**The Blue Rooms,** Fossgate, York	52
32	**Bowling Green Hotel,** Plymouth, Devon	54
33	**Brayscroft House,** Eastbourne, Sussex	55
34	**Brighton Marina Holiday Apartments,** Brighton, East Sussex	56
35	**Brills Farm,** Norton Disney, Lincolnshire	58
36	**Broadoaks Country House,** Windermere, Cumbria	59
37	**Bruern Stables,** Chipping Norton, Oxfordshire	60
38	**Bush Nook Country Guest House,** Gilsland, Cumbria	61
39	**Buxton's Victorian Guest House,** Buxton, Derbyshire	62
40	**Camelot Lodge,** Eastbourne, East Sussex	64
41	**Carlyon Bay Hotel,** St Austell, Cornwall	66
42	**Carnoustie Golf Hotel,** Carnoustie, Angus	68
43	**The Cedars,** Grantham, Lincolnshire	69
44	**Chequer Cottage,** Horseheath, Cambridgeshire	70
45	**Cheriton House,** Huntingdon, Cambridgeshire	71
46	**Cherrygarth Cottages,** Slingsby, Yorkshire	72
47	**Church Farm Country Cottages,** Bradford on Avon, Wiltshire	73
48	**Cliff Barns,** Narborough, Norfolk	74
49	**Clow Beck House,** Darlington, Co Durham	76
50	**Coach House at Crookham,** Cornhill-on-Tweed, Northumberland	78
51	**Cofton Country Holidays,** Starcross, nr Dawlish, South Devon	80
52	**Coldbeck House,** Kirkby Stephen, Cumbria	82
53	**The Colonnade,** London	83
54	**Compton Pool Farm,** Marldon, Devon	84
55	**Cossington Park,** Bridgwater, Somerset	86
56	**The Courthouse Kempinski,** London	88
57	**The Cove,** Penzance, Cornwall	89
58	**Cressbrook Hall,** Buxton, Derbyshire	90
59	**Crich House,** Barnard Castle, Co Durham	91
60	**The Crown Inn,** Playhatch, Berkshire	92
61	**Damerons Farm Holidays,** Ipswich, Suffolk	93
62	**Dannah Farm Country House,** Belper, Derbyshire	94
63	**De Grey's Town House,** Ludlow, Shropshire	96
64	**Dolphin Quays,** Poole, Dorset	97
65	**Domineys Cottages,** Dorchester, Dorset	98
66	**Draycott Hotel,** London	99
67	**Dunsley Hall,** Whitby, N Yorkshire	100
68	**Emsworth House,** Bradfield, Essex	101
69	**Enchanted Manor,** Niton, Isle of Wight	103
70	**Eshott Hall,** Morpeth, Northumberland	104
71	**Fairfield Garden Guest House,** Bowness-on-Windermere, Cumbria	105
72	**Faweather Grange,** High Eldwick, Yorkshire	106
73	**Fern Cottage,** Pucklechurch, South Gloucestershire	107
74	**The Firs,** Bath, Somerset	108
75	**Foxes Reach,** Catbrook, Monmouthshire	109
76	**Foxgloves,** Wigton, Cumbria	110
77	**Friary Close,** Chichester, West Sussex	111
78	**Gallon House,** Knaresborough, N Yorkshire	112
79	**Garden Lodge,** Folkestone, Kent	113
80	**Glebe House,** Chippenham, Wiltshire	114
81	**Godshill Park Farmhouse,** Isle of Wight	115
82	**Grand Hotel,** Kenilworth, Warwickshire	116
83	**The Grange,** Shanklin, Isle of Wight	117
84	**The Grange Hotel,** Newark, Nottinghamshire	118
85	**The Green Hotel,** Kinross, Perthshire	119
86	**Green Lawns Hotel,** Falmouth, Cornwall	120
87	**Grendon Guest House,** Buxton, Derbyshire	121
88	**Grimblethorpe Hall Country Cottages,** nr Louth, Lincolnshire	122
89	**Groomes Country House,** Bordon, Hampshire	123
90	**Halfway Bridge Inn,** nr Petworth, W Sussex	124
91	**Halsteads Barn,** nr Lancaster, N Yorkshire	125
92	**The Hampshire Court,** Basingstoke, Hampshire	126
93	**Harbour Heights,** Dartmouth, Devon	127
94	**Hayden's,** Rye, East Sussex	128

95	Heatherly Cottage, nr Corsham, Wiltshire	130
96	Hell Bay, Isles of Scilly	131
97	Highcliffe House, Lynton, Devon	133
98	Higher Wiscombe, Colyton, Devon,	134
99	Highgate House, Creaton, Northampton	135
100	Hob Green Hotel, Harrogate, N Yorkshire	136
101	Holiday Inn Ashford North, Ashford, Kent	137
102	Holme House, Hebden Bridge, W Yorkshire	138
103	Hope Farm House, Alstonefield, Derbyshire	140
104	Hornby Hall, Penrith, Cumbria	142
105	The Island Hotel, Tresco, Isles of Scilly	143
106	Isle of Eriska Hotel, by Oban, Argyll	144
107	Jeakes House, Rye, East Sussex	145
108	Jinlye, Church Stretton, Shropshire	146
109	Kasbah, Ryde, Isle of Wight	147
110	Kildonan Lodge Hotel, Edinburgh	148
111	Kingfisher Barn, Abingdon, Oxfordshire	149
112	Kingston Estate, Totnes, Devon	150
113	Kingston House, Totnes, Devon	152
114	Lakelovers, Bowness-on-Windermere, Cumbria	155
115	Langdale Hotel, nr Ambleside, Cumbria	156
116	Langley Castle Hotel, Hexham, Northumberland	157
117	The Leconfield, Ventnor, Isle of Wight	158
118	Linthwaite House Hotel, Windermere, Cumbria	159
119	Little Holtby, Northallerton, N Yorkshire	160
120	Llwyndu Farmhouse, Barmouth, Gwynedd	161
121	Lonmay Old Manse, by Fraserburgh, Aberdeenshire	162
122	Lonsdale Hotel, Bowness-on-Windermere, Cumbria	163
123	Macdonald Holyrood Hotel, Edinburgh	164
124	Magnolia House, Canterbury, Kent	165
125	Manorhouse, nr Bury St Edmunds, Suffolk	166
126	Manor House Farm, Uttoxeter, Staffordshire	167
127	Mansefield B&B, Greenlaw, Berwickshire	168
128	Mansefield House, Loch Long, Argyll and Bute	169
129	MapleLeaf Middlewick Holiday Cottages & B&B, Glastonbury, Somerset	170
130	Marlborough House, Bath, Somerset	171
131	Matfen Hall, Matfen, Newcastle upon Tyne	172
132	Melrose House, London	173
133	Mill of Blackhall, Menmuir, Angus	174
134	Millness Croft Cottages, Inverness, Inverness-shire	175
135	Millstream Hotel, Chichester, W Sussex	176
136	Mitchell's of Chester, Chester, Cheshire	177
137	Nailey Cottages, Bath, Somerset	178
138	New Inn, Tresco, Isles of Scilly	179
139	Oak Farm Barn, Bury St Edmunds, Suffolk	180
140	Ocklynge Manor, Eastbourne, E Sussex	182
141	Old Bridge Hotel, Huntingdon, Cambridgeshire	183
142	Old Farm Cottages, Norwich, Norfolk	184
143	The Old Farmhouse & The Granary, Penzance, Cornwall	186
144	The Old Vicarage, Pickering, N Yorkshire	189
145	Outchester and Ross Farm Cottages, Bamburgh, Northumberland	190
146	Park Farm, Saxmundham, Suffolk	192
147	Park Farm Cottages, Saxmundham, Suffolk	193
148	Park House Hotel, Midhurst, W Sussex	194
149	Pelham House, Lewes, E Sussex	196
150	Pentre Mawr Country House, Llandrynog, Denbigh	197
151	The Pheasant Inn, Falstone, Northumberland	198
152	Raffles, Blackpool, Lancashire	199
153	The Relish, Folkestone, Kent	201
154	The Residence, Bath, Somerset	202
155	Hotel Riviera, Sidmouth, Devon	204
156	Rooke Country Cottages, Wadebridge, Cornwall	206
157	Rothay Manor, Ambleside, Cumbria	208
158	The Roxburghe Hotel, Edinburgh	209
159	Royal Duchy Hotel, Falmouth, Cornwall	210
160	Royal Lancaster Hotel, London	212
161	The Royal Oak, Chichester, W Sussex	213
162	Rye Lodge, Rye, E Sussex	214
163	Saunton Sands Hotel, nr Braunton, Devon	216
164	Sea Tree House, Lyme Regis, Dorset	218
165	Spanhoe Lodge, Harringworth, Northamptonshire	219
166	The Stables, Shrewsbury, Shropshire	220
167	Steele's Mill, Penrith, Cumbria	221
168	Strathdon Hotel, Blackpool, Lancashire	222
169	Swan Hotel, Lavenham, Suffolk	223
170	Swinton Park, Masham, N Yorkshire	224
171	Sychnant Pass Country House, Conwy	227
172	Ta Mill, Launceston, Cornwall	228
173	Tall Ships, Charlestown, Cornwall	230
174	Thirty Two, Cheltenham, Gloucestershire	231
175	Thornham Hall, Eye, Suffolk	232
176	Three Chimneys Farm, Goudhurst, Kent	233
177	Tides Reach Hotel, Salcombe, Devon	234
178	Tom's Barn, Ashbourne, Derbyshire	235
179	Tone Dale House, Wellington, Somerset	236
180	Tower House 1066, St Leonards-on-Sea, E Sussex	238
181	Trafford Bank Guest House, Inverness	239
182	Treverbyn Vean Manor, Liskeard, Cornwall	240
183	Ty'n Rhos Country House, Caernarfon, Gwynedd	241
184	Underleigh House, Hope Valley, Derbyshire	242
185	The Valley, Truro, Cornwall	243
186	Vanilla Cottage, nr Usk, Monmouthshire	244
187	Venn Farm, Plymouth, South Devon	246
188	Waitby School, Kirkby Stephen, Cumbria	247
189	Wallett's Court Country House Hotel, Restaurant and Spa, Dover, Kent	248
190	Waren Lea Hall, Bamburgh, Northumberland	250
191	The Washington Mayfair, London	252
192	The Weary at Castle Carrock, nr Carlisle, Cumbria	254
193	Westcott Barton, Barnstaple, North Devon	255
194	Wethele Manor, nr Leamington Spa, Warwickshire	256
195	Witch Hazel, Wymondham, Norfolk	258
196	Woodlands Country House, Padstow, Cornwall	260
197	Woodlands Country House, Ireby, Cumbria	261
198	Yellowtop Country Park, Foggathorpe, E Yorkshire	262
199	Yewfield, Ambleside, Cumbria	263
200	Yorke Lodge, Canterbury, Kent	264

PICK YOUR SPOT THEN CHECK OUT A TOP ACCOMMODATION THERE

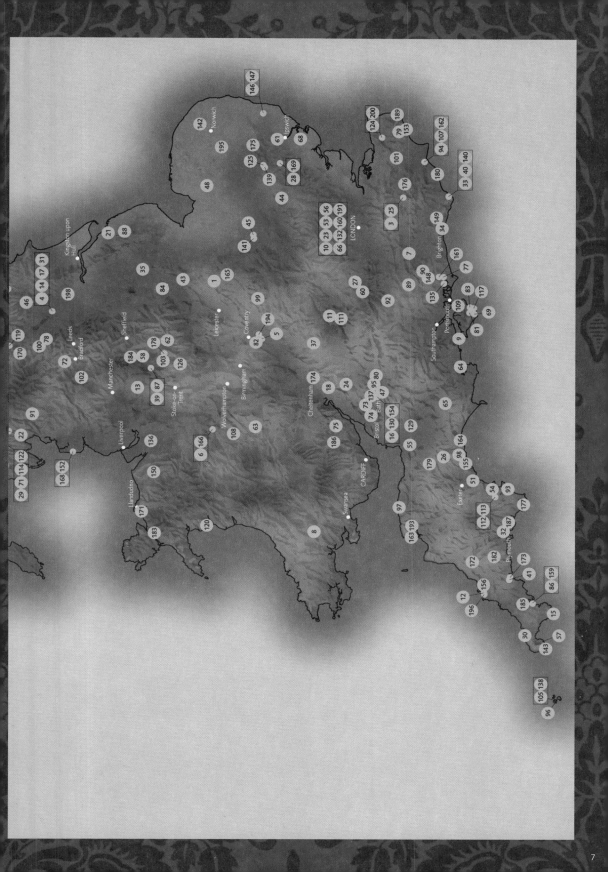

Stylish dining

Dress up and head to the city for a night of exquisite delicacies and fine wine...

Celtic Manor

Find excellent service, mouth-watering food and a relaxing ambience in stylish settings all over England that will help you forget your worries and leave you feeling totally pampered.

London boasts a huge range of cuisines, from good old English to French, Indian, Chinese, Thai, American... whatever takes your fancy really.

With such an amazing selection, why not try something new or different? You could try the 1880 at The Bentley Kempinski Hotel, tucked away in chic Chelsea, or the Boisdale of Belgravia, a short stroll from Victoria. For that extra special romantic evening hidden away from everyone, why not visit Babylon Restaurant at The Roof Gardens, 100ft above Kensington High Street with its amazing views of the city's skyline. Why not put your best clothes on and join friends or family for a special evening in a top restaurant? Spoil yourself in Edinburgh at The Witchery close to the castle or at The London Carriage Works in Liverpool or Hibiscus Restaurant in Ludlow. As an alternative head out to the Olive Tree Restaurant at Newport's Celtic Manor, golf's next European Ryder Cup venue.

In today's world, many of us have to watch what we eat but that doesn't mean you can't enjoy gorgeous food. Most restaurants cater for different diets so don't be afraid to ask. For more food for thought, Food for Friends in Brighton or The Greenhouse in Norwich offer a fantastic vegetarian menu. Rest easy in knowing you've had a relaxing night out and there is no washing up to do! Ω

Pleasures of dining in the big city

The Witchery

Indulge in fresh seafood

Country living

Savour local, organic produce to recharge the body and enliven the taste buds.

Feast in local produce

Organic food and local produce are the new buzz words in the food industry so why not head out to the country for a hearty meal? You can enjoy a scrumptious meal that you know hasn't travelled miles to reach you plate.

And when you find you can't move because you've eaten so much, you can stay the night and eat more in the morning! If Highland air is for you there's The Cross at Kingussie which is rated a one of the top half dozen restaurants in the Cairngorms. Jesmond Dene House, close to Newcastle, offers a range of local specialities or you could stay at The Ponsbourne Park Hotel and Restaurant, set in gorgeous Hertfordshire countryside. Or head to Bedruthan Steps Hotel on the North Cornwall coast for the sea air that's sure to give you an appetite.

If pub grub is what you're after then you're sure to find something to satisfy that grumbling stomach. Cosy pubs, stylish pubs, busy pubs, quiet pubs, it's entirely up to you where you decide to stop. The friendly staff and informal atmosphere make a pub meal all the more enjoyable. You could try The Olive Branch in Rutland, The Star Inn at Harome in the glorious North York Moors National Park, or The Holly Bush Inn in Staffordshire. Then there's The Aleppo Merchant Inn in mid-Wales, named by a retired sea captain after his ship and opposite the church which is the final resting place of fashion designer Laura Ashley.

Whether it's traditional bangers and mash or salmon en croute with a dill butter and pea watercress puree, enjoy your pint around a warm fire or under a sun umbrella in any season! Ω

Ripley Castle, North Yorkshire

A tasty pub meal in the countryside

Jesmond Dene House, Newcastle upon Tyne

Step back in time

Lose yourself in a world of enchanted forests, secret gardens and a different era...

Tatton Gardens, Cheshire

The Eden Project

York Minster

Blenheim Palace

Imagine living in a time when Mr Darcy was gallivanting around (or indeed Elizabeth Bennet), where your home had four kitchens and 10 bedrooms and you were waited on hand and foot. Step back in time and escape into a world of lavish interiors and magnificent paintings in one of the UK's stunning stately homes. Visit Blenheim Palace in Oxfordshire for breathtaking grandeur or Chatsworth in Derbyshire to relive 18th century England at its finest.

Take a stroll around beautifully manicured lawns and spectacular blooms or get lost in a maze like the one at Hampton Court Palace in Surrey, or Tatton Park in Cheshire. You could fly through the trees on a giant swing at Groombridge Place Gardens in Kent, walk through Northumberland's beautiful Alnwick Garden or visit the organic kitchen garden at Audley End House and Gardens in Essex or Edinburgh's Royal Botanic Garden.

Or why not get lost in the jungle at the award-winning Eden Project in Cornwall where you can explore the flora and fauna and feel like you're a world away from home?

For peace and tranquillity, you could spend some time reflecting in a beautiful cathedral. The relaxing tones of the organ and the hushed silence will help you gather your thoughts so you're ready to take on the world again. From St Paul's in London and Gothic York Minster in York to Wales' St David's Cathedral in the UK's smallest city you can admire the beauty of stained glass at its finest and experience an overwhelming sense of peace. Ω

Nature's best

Wherever you live, rolling hills and breathtaking scenery are within reach. Take some time out and immerse yourself in natural beauty...

Lake District, Cumbria

The UK boasts numerous National Parks, protected areas bursting with natural beauty, wildlife and cultural heritage. From wild, expansive moors to stunning coastline and rugged cliffs, the parks offer an array of activities to enjoy. Meander through the winding roads of the Yorkshire Dales, or enjoy the sea breeze and spectacular views of Exmoor. There's so much to see and do, why not book into a hotel and spend a weekend exploring a park?

There are also thousands of different walks and trails just waiting to be discovered. So get outside and take a well-earned walk to clear your mind and help you refocus. You could visit the Wye Valley straddling the border between England and Wales which is renowned as one of the most dramatic and scenic landscape areas in southern Britain. Or you could take the Tolkien Trail in the Ribble Valley or explore the Forest of Bowland in Lancashire or the Forest of Marston in Bedfordshire. If you're in search of the ocean, you could head to Beesands Beach in Devon or if you fancy a spot of birdwatching, keep your eyes open at Minsmere on the Suffolk coast. Whether you need a brisk walk, or a leisurely ramble, the UK offers some great places for you to escape to.

And if you want the views without the exercise (sometimes being lazy is the best remedy for stress!) why not soar above the clouds in a hot air balloon or even a helicopter? Leave your cares far behind you as you fly above a stunning city such as Bath or Edinburgh or over the spectacular North Pennines Area of Outstanding Natural Beauty. Ω

Beach at Gibraltar Point, Lincolnshire

Ilkley, West Yorkshire

Castaway

Unspoilt beaches and ocean views.
To escape, head to a beautiful island…

Holy Island of Lindisfarne, Northumberland

The UK has a number of island retreats where you can escape the pressures of modern life and settle down to some unadulterated 'me' time.

Experience the exclusivity of staying on the privately-owned Isle of Eriska with its own six-hole golf course 12 miles north of Oban off Scotland's west coast. Gain inner peace surrounded by the beauty and spirituality of the Holy Island of Lindisfarne. Let the 'Pilgrims Way' guide you through the hills to the secluded Norman Priory where you can wander around the magnificent columns and arches and soak in the breathtaking scenery overlooking the gleaming blue ocean.

Those seeking an Area of Outstanding Natural Beauty will find it off the North Wales coast on the island of Anglesey where a path covers more than 100 miles of superb coastline. From Holyhead Mountain you can see Ireland on the horizon.

For a milder climate, only two hours away from London is the beautiful Isle of Wight. Meander through the thatched villages or follow one of the stunning coastal trails. There's something for everyone's taste on this island, whether you want to try a spot of sailing or relax with a cup of tea in one of the quaint tearooms.

If what you are after is a more tropical island experience, treat yourself to a break on the Isles of Scilly, just off the coast of Cornwall. The breezes of the Gulf Stream warm the beaches and encourage sub-tropical plants to grow, creating an atmosphere that feels a million miles away. Ω

Cast yourself away and find a deserted beach

Freshwater Bay, Isle of Wight

Get yourself going

Re-energise yourself and feel the wind in your hair as you horse-ride, cycle or walk through some of the most gorgeous parts of the UK...

Cycling in Snowdonia

Discover some of the UK's secrets as you walk along ancient trails and rugged cliff tops. Make a weekend of it and join a walking holiday. Foot Trails organise walking holidays in the South West of England where you can either go along with others or take a walk on your own.

A great way to see more of the countryside is on horseback. Whether you fancy an exhilarating gallop or a peaceful trot, there are plenty of horse-riding stables offering treks for all ages and standards, in the city and in the countryside. Hyde Park and Kensington Stables in London offer a variety of treks and lessons or you could visit Freshfields Equestrian Centre in Shropshire. Looking farther North? Try a two-day luxury horse-riding holiday in Galloway, in the untouched south west of Scotland.

Or why not try cycling along some of the fantastic car-free cycle paths? Make sure you stop off along the way and enjoy a pub lunch, taking time to enjoy the area around you. You could follow the Cider Cycling Route in Herefordshire, discovering how traditional cider is made, or why not spend a weekend cycling around the North York Moors, on a route organised by Special Places Tours soaking up the clean fresh air? In Wales the Celtic Trail cycling and walking route lets you explore golden sandy beaches, picturesque seaside towns and lush rolling hills between Swansea and Fishguard.

If you like the idea of the wind in your hair but think that flexing a foot may be enough exercise for you, then hire a classic car for a spin through some of England's most beautiful villages. Cornwall Classic Car Hire offers a range of classic British sportscars for rent within the stunning counties of Cornwall and Devon. Or you could live the life of a silver-screen star for a day with The Grand Touring Club in Suffolk who'll hire you a classic car and help you put together a tour.

Alternatively, if you fancy a slower pace, you could drift down the river listening to the simple clip-clop of your horse-drawn barge with the Kennet Horse Boat Company in Berkshire. Ω

Holkham Hall Estate, Northumberland

Walking in the Peak District

17 Northgate

OAKHAM, RUTLAND 4 STAR B&B

Great base from which to discover the delights of Hidden England

This 300-year-old thatched farmhouse in gently-rolling countryside in Hidden England is located in the centre of a small, traditional town just 10 minutes from the plethora of wildlife and outdoor activities at Rutland Water.

Two purpose-built B&B rooms were added to the Listed main house as part of a major renovation project completed in 2004. There is one double room with king-size bed and one twin-bedded room, both with en suite facilities, including large, walk-in showers. Each room has its own TV, patio with French table and chairs and private entrance off the gravel drive where off-street parking is available.

An excellent, large breakfast with home-made preserves is served in the garden room. The varied menu includes a range of options from a traditional, full English and porridge to smoked salmon and, on special occasions, a champagne breakfast.

For those wishing to explore the rural beauties of England's smallest county and its large lake, 17 Northgate provides an ideal base. Ω

Matter of facts

CONTACT
Dane Gould
T +44 (0)1572 759271
E dane@
danegould.wanadoo.co.uk
W 17northgate.co.uk
Address 17 Northgate,
Oakham,
Rutland LE15 6QR

RATING
VisitBritain 4 Star B&B

SLEEPING
One double room and one twin room, both en suite.

FOR THE FAMILY
Highchair, travel cot and folding bed available.

FACILITIES
Guest rooms have separate entrances and patios with tables and chairs; off-street parking.

NEAREST SHOPS, PUBS AND RESTAURANTS
All within five-minute walk in Oakham High Street; twice-weekly market and monthly farmers' market.

OUT AND ABOUT
Rutland Water for fishing, bird watching, walking, sailing and cycling; Geoff Hamilton's Barnsdale Garden; stately homes, including Belvoir and Rockingham castles, Belton House and Burghley House.

PRICES PER ROOM PER NIGHT AND WHAT'S INCLUDED
Double occupancy £75.00-£85.00; single occupancy £50.00-£60.00. Includes breakfast. Reductions for stays of three nights or more.

33/2 Queen Street

EDINBURGH 5 STAR SELF-CATERING

Townhouse mixes modern amenities with elegant period features

This elegant, Grade A Listed Georgian townhouse, built around 1790, occupies a superb location in the centre of the Scottish capital. It is a magnificent, triple-windowed drawing room apartment with views over the private residents' gardens to which guests have a key.

Although the one-bedroom property contains many elegant period features, it has a high-tech specification which includes a 43-in plasma TV with 30+ digital channels and integrated Bose sound system fed into every room. Consequently, it is ideal for entertaining.

The bedroom has a queen-size bed, large fitted wardrobe, dressing table and wall-mounted 22-in LCD TV. Two sofas in the drawing room can be converted into beds should guests be staying over. The galley-style kitchen is fully fitted with a host of appliances and the shower room/WC features a superb power shower with ceiling-mounted drench head and four body jets. Ω

Matter of facts

CONTACT
Francois Boissière
T +44 (0)7973 345559
E info@
edinburghflats.co.uk
W edinburghflats.co.uk
Address Flat No 2,
33 Queen Street,
Edinburgh EH2 1JK
Booking address
27 Queen Street,
Edinburgh EH2 1JK

RATING
VisitScotland 5 Star
Self Catering

SLEEPING
One bedroom with queen-size bed; two sofas in drawing room can be converted into beds.

FOR THE FAMILY
Cot, pushchair and highchair available on request.

FACILITIES
Broadband Internet access, housemaid services and garaging on request. Round-the-clock assistance available from owner's representative living just a few doors away.

NEAREST SHOPS, PUBS AND RESTAURANTS
Numerous establishments a short walk away in the centre of Edinburgh.

OUT AND ABOUT
Historic Edinburgh with its many attractions and famous castle is on the doorstep.

PRICES PER WEEK AND WHAT'S INCLUDED
£420.00-£950.00.
Nightly rates are available (three nights minimum).
Includes bed linen/towels.

40 York Road

TUNBRIDGE WELLS, KENT 4 STAR B&B

Country charm and elegance within striking distance of London's bustle

An attractive, Grade II Listed Regency townhouse in the centre of Tunbridge Wells, 40 York Road is conveniently located for the town's many shops and restaurants and for Kent's major tourist attractions.

The house features the original staircase from the hall to the first-floor bedrooms and cloakroom and all rooms contain the original, open fireplaces. Guests have access to a sitting room, dining room and garden room. The two bedrooms can be either doubles or twins. Both have en suite facilities and are equipped with TVs, wireless Internet access, hospitality trays and hairdryers. Ironing facilities are also available.

Outside there is a small front garden with climbers reaching the balcony and a courtyard back garden where breakfast can be served in fine weather.

Retaining much of the charm and elegance of its Georgian heyday, Royal Tunbridge Wells and the surrounding area today remains a favoured destination for those who want to enjoy elegant surroundings in the countryside and yet be just a short distance from London's hustle and bustle. Ω

Matter of facts

CONTACT
Mrs P Lobo
T +44 (0)1892 531342
E yorkroad@tiscali.co.uk
W yorkroad.co.uk
Address 40 York Road, Tunbridge Wells, Kent TN1 1JY

RATING
VisitBritain 4 Star B&B

SLEEPING
Two double/twin rooms, both en suite.

FOR THE FAMILY
Unsuitable for children under 12.

FACILITIES
Sitting room; dining room; garden room; courtyard garden; wireless Internet access; restricted on-street parking and 24-hour car park at £3.60 a day available nearby.

NEAREST SHOPS, PUBS AND RESTAURANTS
Minutes away in Tunbridge Wells town centre; many restaurants include Michelin star Carluccio's, Petit Blanc, Wagamama, Prezzo and Sankeys (fish).

OUT AND ABOUT
The Pantiles; High Rocks; Hever Castle; Sissinghurst; Bodiam Castle; Leeds Castle; Scotney Castle; Chartwell; Knole; Great Dixter house and gardens; Groombridge Place; Wakehurst Place; Glyndebourne.

PRICES PER NIGHT AND WHAT'S INCLUDED
Double occupancy £65.00; single occupancy £38.00. Includes breakfast. Dinner available at £25.00 per person.

6 & 15 Stonegate Court

YORK 5 STAR SELF-CATERING

Award-winning apartments just a stone's throw from York Minster

Nestling in the shadow of York Minster, these two five star, self-catering apartments have earned many accolades, including VisitBritain's Best Self Catering Holiday in England 2006 award. The discreet and private location in a beautiful courtyard surrounded by Georgian, Tudor and Stuart buildings is just moments away from York's bustling ancient streets.

The luxurious apartments have their own private terraces in which to sit back and listen to the birds in the Minster gardens beyond. No 15 has two double bedrooms, one of which is en suite, and a large living/dining room. The split-level No 6 has a beautiful, galleried bedroom with king-size bed overlooking the wonderful living/dining room.

Both apartments contain a pristine family bathroom and fully-equipped designer kitchen with cooker and hob, microwave, fridge, freezer, washer-dryer, dishwasher and slow-cooker, together with everything else to make your stay easy and restful. They also have a TV-combination, including Freeview, with videos and DVDs, together with a wide choice of CDs to play on the high-quality sound system. Ω

Matter of facts

CONTACT
Malcolm and Susan Kitchener
T +44 (0)1904 766789 or +44 (0)7746 552478
E sue@yorkluxuryholidays.co.uk
W yorkluxuryholidays.co.uk
Booking address
11 Earswick Chase, Old Earswick, York YO32 9FZ

RATING
VisitBritain 5 Star Self-Catering

SLEEPING
6 Stonegate Court – one galleried double bedroom overlooking the living accommodation;
15 Stonegate Court – two double bedrooms, one of which is en suite and with access to a terrace.

FOR THE FAMILY
Children welcome; cot, highchair, DVDs, games, books available.

FACILITIES
Welcome basket, wine, flowers, sweets, tea, coffee, milk and a gift; free city centre car parking (first come, first served); telephone; free wireless broadband Internet; Freeview; digital safe.

NEAREST SHOPS, PUBS AND RESTAURANTS
All less than a one-minute walk away in city centre.

OUT AND ABOUT
Within walking distance are York Minster; St William's College; Treasurers House; National Railway Museum; Merchant Tailors' Hall; Merchant Adventurers' Hall; Museum Gardens; Yorkshire Museum; King's Manor; York Art Gallery; Impressions Gallery; Jorvik; Clifford's Tower; York Castle Museum; York Dungeon; Guildhall; Barley Hall; Fairfax House; The Arc. York Racecourse is one mile away.

PRICES PER WEEK AND WHAT'S INCLUDED
6 Stonegate Court (one bedroom) – £721.00; 15 Stonegate Court (two bedrooms) – £1,085.00. Guests can arrive any day and stay two nights or more. Includes utilities, luxury bedding, towels, robes, hot drinks, milk, wine, fresh flowers, gift and welcome basket of fruit or Yorkshire fare.

8 Clarendon Crescent

LEAMINGTON SPA, WARWICKSHIRE 4 STAR SILVER AWARD B&B

Hosts make every effort to ensure guests make best of Spa town visit

Overlooking a private dell in a quiet backwater of picturesque Leamington Spa, this is a splendid Grade II Listed Regency house elegantly furnished with antiques. The property is a haven of peace and tranquillity with four tastefully-decorated, individually-designed bedrooms, each with TV, tea and coffee-making facilities and en suite or private bathroom.

Hosts David and Christine Lawson have created an environment with a warm, relaxing, informal atmosphere and are on hand to recommend the pick of Leamington Spa's many splendid restaurants and suggest places of interest to visit.

A delicious breakfast is cooked to order with home-made bread and preserves while special diets are catered for. Relax in the drawing room, saunter around the south-facing garden or take a five-minute stroll to the town centre where you will find many shops, restaurants and tourist attractions, including the Pump rooms and garden. Ω

Matter of facts

CONTACT
David and Christine Lawson
T +44 (0)1926 429840
E lawson@lawson71.fsnet.co.uk
W 8clarendoncrescent.co.uk
Address
8 Clarendon Crescent, Leamington Spa, Warwickshire CV32 5NR

RATING
Visit Britain 4 Star Silver Award B&B

SLEEPING
Two double, one twin and one single bedroom. Three have en suites and one has a private bathroom.

FACILITIES
Drawing room and garden; TV and tea and coffee in all bedrooms.

NEAREST SHOPS, PUBS AND RESTAURANTS
Many in the centre of Leamington Spa, a five-minute walk away.

OUT AND ABOUT
Warwick, famous for its castle, is two miles away. Convenient for Stratford-upon-Avon, the Cotswolds, National Agricultural Centre, Warwick University, the National Exhibition Centre and Birmingham Airport.

PRICES PER NIGHT AND WHAT'S INCLUDED
Double occupancy £75.00, single occupancy £45.00. Includes breakfast. No surcharge for single occupancy of double rooms; 10% discount for four nights or more.

The statue of Waterloo General
Lord Rowland Hill in Shrewsbury.

Abbey Court House

SHREWSBURY, SHROPSHIRE 4 STAR GUEST HOUSE

Abbey Court – a perfect base for exploring historic Shrewsbury

Abbey Court House is situated in a pleasant area of Shrewsbury only a short walk from the town centre. It is a perfect base for exploring the historic town with its many attractions. This rather special guest house is a 150-year-old Grade II Listed building and was formerly a 19th century coaching house.

With 10 en suite guest bedrooms, this refurbished guest house offers visitors a high level of comfort in tastefully-furnished accommodation. The AA and VisitBritain 4-diamonds/star grading offers an assurance of quality and high standards throughout.

Guests can be assured of a warm, friendly welcome, an enjoyable and comfortable stay, and superb facilities. All guest bedrooms have hospitality trays, teletext TVs and direct-dial phones.

Why not leave your vehicle in the car park and catch a bus into town from just outside the front door? Or enjoy a pleasant 15 minute stroll into the town centre, past the 11th century abbey and River Severn?

Start the day with a tempting, freshly-cooked traditional English breakfast, or choose from continental or vegetarian options.

Make the most of a fine array of shops, attractions and excellent places to eat – both nearby and in town.

Book today for a wonderful break. Ω

Matter of facts

CONTACT
Valerie MacLeod
T +44 (0)1743 364416
E info@abbeycourt.biz
W abbeycourt.biz
Address
Abbey Court Guest House,
134 Abbey Foregate,
Shrewsbury,
Shropshire SY2 6AU

RATINGS
VisitBritain 4 Star Guest House; AA 4 Red Diamonds.

SLEEPING
Three double, four twins, two singles and one family bedroom, all en suite.

FOR THE FAMILY
Children welcome.

FACILITIES
Lounge, TVs and tea and coffee-making facilities in all bedrooms, ample parking.

NEAREST SHOPS, PUBS AND RESTAURANTS
Shrewsbury town centre, a 15-minute walk or short bus ride away.

OUT AND ABOUT
Shrewsbury Abbey, founded 1083; Shrewsbury Castle and Shropshire Regimental Museum; Shrewsbury Museum and Art Gallery. Convenient for Haughmond Abbey and Buildwas Abbey, both founded in 1135; the RAF Museum at Cosford; Wroxeter Roman Vineyard and Roman city; Percy Thrower's Gardening Centre.

PRICES PER NIGHT AND WHAT'S INCLUDED
Single £40.00; double/ twin £30.00 (per person); family room £75.00. Includes breakfast.

Alliblaster House

RUDGWICK, WEST SUSSEX
5 STAR SILVER AWARD B&B

On-site spa, organic food and Fairtrade drinks aid a healthy and happy stay

This beautiful, 18th century Sussex-style country house is set in nine acres of peaceful, lush West Sussex countryside with far-reaching views to the South Downs, endless woodland walks and a host of other indoor and outdoor activities right on the doorstep.

The curiously-named Alliblaster House occupies a site that has been lived on from the time of the Norman invasion and its final name, which is a French term for a crossbowman, seems to have stemmed from William Le Alblaster (1279).

The present house was build in the mid-19th century with two distinctive features: First, it was one of the first houses in the country to have a form of central heating, which was steam powered using water taken from a deep well outside the back door. Second, it had an enclosed squash court with a glass roof which was converted in the 1970s.

Following a lengthy and ongoing restoration project by the new owners, Alliblaster House has seven spacious, tastefully-decorated bedrooms, all of which have marble en suite or private bathrooms. The rooms are equipped with orthopaedic super king-size or twin single beds; comfortable chairs or sofa; writing desks; TVs with DVD players; alarm clock CD players; wireless Internet connection and tea and coffee-making facilities. In addition, the little touches that make a stay at Alliblaster House special include fresh towels and bathrobes; slippers; complimentary mineral water; hairdryers; irons and ironing boards and a range of Spa toiletries.

A fully-organic English or continental breakfast and a

variety of healthy eating options are served in the breakfast room. As a member of the Fairtrade Association and the Soil Association, Alliblaster House uses Fairtrade tea, coffee, hot chocolate, orange juice and sugar along with organic breakfast ingredients wherever possible. These are sourced from local independent farms and suppliers. More specific dietary needs are catered for with prior notice.

Simply Healing is the on-site spa, a holistic rejuvenation centre which offers more than 20 different treatments for the mind, body and soul. The house also features a traditional-style conference room with space for 10 delegates boardroom-style and 25 theatre-style. The grounds have space for a marquee large enough for 200 people, making it ideal for larger functions. Ω

Matter of facts

CONTACT
Dean Barton
T +44 (0)1403 822860
E info@ alliblasterhouse.com
W alliblasterhouse.com
Address Alliblaster House, Hill House Lane, Rudgwick, West Sussex RH12 3BD

RATING
VisitBritain 5 Star Silver Award B&B

SLEEPING
Seven bedrooms, all with en suite or private bathroom.

FOR THE FAMILY
Children over 14 welcome; pets not accepted.

FACILITIES
On-site spa, Simply Healing, with a range of holistic treatments; extensive grounds; conference facilities including audio-visual equipment and Internet connections.

NEAREST SHOPS, PUBS AND RESTAURANTS
Rudgwick village has a Post Office and general store and two traditional pubs serving real ale and home-cooked food. Cranleigh, a five-minute drive away, has a wealth of shops and restaurants.

OUT AND ABOUT
Arundel Castle; Arundel Cathedral; Chichester Cathedral; Hampton Court Palace; Royal Pavilion, Brighton; Petworth House; Cowdray Park; Goodwood.

PRICES PER NIGHT AND WHAT'S INCLUDED
Double/twin room from £95.00. Includes organic English or continental breakfast.

Allt y Golau

FELINGWM UCHAF, CARMARTHENSHIRE
4 STAR FARMHOUSE

Stunning scenery provides great backdrop for rest and meditation

Situated in an uplifting landscape with panoramic views over the Tywi Valley to the dramatic Black Mountains, this renovated 1812 farmhouse claims to serve the best farmhouse breakfast in Wales.

Relying on home baking and local products, including many of its own, Allt y Golau has featured for several years in *The Red Book: Eat Well in Wales* and was awarded Best Farmhouse Breakfast in Wales, 2005.

The three-bedroom property features a visitors' lounge with TV, books and games and a dining room with a splendid old stretcher table.

Outside, the mature and tranquil gardens and orchards extend to almost two acres and in spring are carpeted in snowdrops, daffodils and bluebells. They are also populated by Brecon Buff geese, Welsh Harlequin ducks, free range hens and Norfolk Bronze turkeys.It's a great place to meditate or simply enjoy the stunning views of Grongar Hill and Llyn y Fan Fach, made famous by the Lady of the Lake legend. Ω

Matter of facts

CONTACT
Dr Colin Rouse
T +44 (0)1267 290455
E alltygolau@
btinternet.com
W alltygolau.com
Address Allt-y-Golau,
Felingwm Uchaf,
Carmarthenshire
SA32 7BB

RATING
VisitWales and AA
4 Star Farmhouse

SLEEPING
One ground floor double
with en suite; one ground
floor twin with en suite;
one first floor double with
private bathroom.

FOR THE FAMILY
Secure gardens; cot;
highchair.

FACILITIES
Visitors' lounge with
TV, radio, books, jigsaws
and games.

**NEAREST SHOPS,
PUBS AND
RESTAURANTS**
Short walk to local
inn; other excellent
restaurants within a
five-minute drive.
Market towns of
Carmarthen and Llandeilo
are within nine miles.

OUT AND ABOUT
Ten minutes from
National Botanic Garden
of Wales and Aberglasney
Gardens. The area also
includes excellent
walking, fishing,
horse-riding, golf,
bird-watching, craft
workshops, heritage sites,
Oakwood and Folly Farm
leisure parks, Pembrey
Country Park and the
Millennium Coastal Path.

**PRICES PER NIGHT
AND WHAT'S
INCLUDED**
Double or twin (two
sharing) £60.00 per
room; single room
£40.00. Free entrance to
garden of choice if staying
three or more nights.
Includes breakfast.

25

Alma Mater

LYMINGTON, HAMPSHIRE
4 STAR SILVER AWARD B&B

Savour delights of the Solent after enjoying a hearty breakfast

Alma Mater is a large Georgian-style chalet bungalow in a quiet residential area close to the village of Milford on Sea with its coastal paths, cliffs, sweeping beaches and spectacular views of the Solent and the Isle of Wight.

Start your day in this beautiful part of the world with Alma Mater's superb four-course breakfast, prepared with free-range produce and served in a conservatory which overlooks a lovely quarter-acre garden. Fish, vegetarian and continental breakfasts are also available.

The centrally-heated bedrooms have been thoughtfully decorated and provide a high level of comfort with many practical amenities, such as TV, radio, hairdryer, fresh bed linen, towels, toiletries and tea and coffee-making facilities. All have en suite shower or bathroom and overlook the pretty, well-maintained garden. Outside there is secure, off-road parking for up to six cars available for guests. Ω

Matter of facts

CONTACT
Eileen Haywood
T +44 (0)1590 642811
E bandbalmamater@
aol.com
W newforestalmamater.co.uk
Address Alma Mater,
4 Knowland Drive,
Milford on Sea,
Lymington,
Hampshire SO41 0RH

RATING
Visit Britain 4 Star
Silver Award B&B

SLEEPING
Two double bedrooms and
one twin bedroom, each
with en suite shower or
private bathroom.

FACILITIES
Conservatory; quarter-acre
garden.

**NEAREST SHOPS, PUBS
AND RESTAURANTS**
Seven-minute walk to
Milford on Sea where there
are shops, three pubs and
two restaurants.

OUT AND ABOUT
Close to Beaulieu (top),
New Forest (left), Hurst
Castle and the market
town of Lymington with its
wide variety of shops from
picturesque boutiques on
the cobbled quay to large
supermarkets. There is an
excellent golf course at
Barton on Sea.

**PRICES PER NIGHT AND
WHAT'S INCLUDED**
Single room £40.00-
£42.00; double room
£60.00-£70.00. Includes
breakfast.

The Apartments

SW LONDON
4 & 5 STAR SELF-CATERING

Serviced apartments offer the comforts of home on a trip to the capital

Set in west London's sought-after locations of Chelsea and Knightsbridge, this stylish collection of serviced studios, one- and two-bedroom apartments provides the ideal base for an indulging leisure break.

The Apartments seek to provide visitors with a home-from-home during trips to the West End theatre, the borough's famed museums, Buckingham Palace, Hyde Park or west London's exclusive shops, including Harrods, Harvey Nichols, Sloane Street and the Kings Road.

These elegant apartments are self-contained within red brick Victorian buildings and include fully-equipped kitchens, en suite bathrooms and a full range of modern amenities. Typically, these will include cable TV with DVD and video players, CD players, broadband Internet service, plain paper fax with telephone and answering machine, trouser press, hairdryer and room safe. There is also a personal laundry and dry cleaning service, a daily or weekly maid service and a weekly linen service. Ω

Matter of facts

CONTACT
Maureen Boyle
T +44 (0)20 7589 3271
E sales@
theapartments.co.uk
W theapartments.co.uk
Address
41 Draycott Place,
London SW3 2SH
Booking address
Panorama Property
Services Ltd,
The Garage,
22 Queensgate Place Mews,
London SW7 5BQ

RATING
4 & 5 Star Self-Catering

SLEEPING
42 studio, one and two-bed apartments, each sleeping between two and six people.

FACILITIES
Fully-equipped kitchens, en suite bathrooms and a full range of modern amenities.

NEAREST SHOPS, PUBS AND RESTAURANTS
Many within half a mile.

OUT AND ABOUT
Close to all major London attractions, including West End theatres, museums, Buckingham Palace, St James's and Hyde Parks and shopping at Harrods, Harvey Nichols and the Kings Road, Chelsea.

PRICES PER WEEK AND WHAT'S INCLUDED
From £816.00-£1,880.00.

Apartments in Oxford

OXFORDSHIRE 5 STAR SELF-CATERING

Home-from-home comforts await visitors amid the dreaming spires

A five-minute stroll from the Ashmolean Museum or Christchurch Cathedral in the centre of medieval Oxford will take you to the quiet St Thomas Mews, the setting for 34 luxury, short-stay one, two and four-bedroom apartments.

Ideal as a base for visiting academics, business travellers and pleasure seekers, these spacious apartments provide a sitting/dining room and fully-fitted kitchen with a comprehensive array of appliances. Fine bone china and choice fabrics add a touch of classic style.

For business travellers there is a high-spec personal computer with Internet access, printer, fax and direct-dial telephone with answering machine; for those simply wanting a relaxing break there's satellite TV, radio and CD player.

Add in 24-hour reception, CCTV surveillance, secure off-street parking, Monday-to-Saturday maid service and two wheelchair-accessible apartments and it's easy to see why the Apartments in Oxford takes pride in providing a real home-from-home. Ω

Matter of facts

CONTACT
Mark Illes
T +44 (0)1865 254077
F +44 (0)1865 254099
E resasst@oxstay.co.uk
W oxstay.co.uk
Booking address
Apartments in Oxford, 58 St Thomas Street, Oxford OX1 0JP

RATING
VisitBritain 5 Star Self-Catering

SLEEPING
34 one, two and four-bedroom apartments sleeping two to eight.

FOR THE FAMILY
Introduction to a registered baby-sitting service.

FACILITIES
Fully-equipped kitchen; personal computer with broadband Internet, printer and fax; satellite TV.

NEAREST SHOPS, PUBS AND RESTAURANTS
Westgate and Cornmarket shopping areas and George Street restaurants and bars with a five-minute walk.

OUT AND ABOUT
Said Business School, Christchurch Cathedral, Nuffield and Worcester College, Carfax Tower and The High, Ashmolean Museum, Balliol College, St John's College, The Playhouse, Apollo Theatre and cinema all within a five-minute walk.

PRICES PER NIGHT AND WHAT'S INCLUDED
£130.00-£380.00 per apartment. Concessions for corporates, groups and long-stay.

Armsyde

PADSTOW, CORNWALL
4 STAR SELF-CATERING

Plenty to keep the children occupied in this townhouse full of character

A former sea merchant's home, Armsyde is an 18th century townhouse close to the centre of Padstow. It has been sympathetically renovated and decorated to a high standard in keeping with the character of the building.

The six double bedrooms have all been individually styled and furnished. Four have en suites and all have TVs. The non-smoking, self-catering property is spacious and ideal for families with the added benefit of a separate kids' room – the snug – complete with flatscreen TV, DVD player and Sony PlayStation 2 computer games.

There is a lounge with large sofas and a smaller sitting room, each with flat-screen TV and DVD player. The sitting room has an additional PS2 player plus games and books. Added to this are a separate dining room and a conservatory with slate floor and dining table. Outside there is a barbeque area and secluded patio.

The comprehensively-equipped kitchen and utility room include a dishwasher, microwave, washing machine and fridge-freezer. Ω

Matter of facts

CONTACT
Christine Davis
T +44 (0)1225 837909
or +44 (0)7872 029992
E crismdavis@aol.com
W armsyde.co.uk
Address Padstow, Cornwall
Booking address
Kingham,
Summer Lane,
Combedown,
Bath BA2 7EU

RATING
VisitBritain 4 Star
Self-Catering

SLEEPING
Six double bedrooms of which four are en suite.

FOR THE FAMILY
Separate kids' room – the snug – with TV, DVD and PS2 games.

FACILITIES
Dining room and sitting room, both with TV and DVD; conservatory; PS2, games and books.

NEAREST SHOPS, PUBS AND RESTAURANTS
Two-minute walk to shops. Close to five Rick Stein eateries – the Seafood Restaurant, St Petrocs, Rick Stein's Café plus Stein's Deli and Stein's Fish and Chips, and to Jamie Oliver's Fifteen Cornwall in Watergate Bay. Also there are other excellent restaurants and pubs in the immediate area.

OUT AND ABOUT
Bike the Camel Trail, take a ferry trip to Rock or visit the hushed church of St Enodoc where Sir John Betjeman is buried. Convenient for The Eden Project and the Lost Gardens of Heligan. Sporting activities include walking and cycling, fishing, surfing and sailing and unrivalled golf on nearby seaside links.

PRICES PER WEEK AND WHAT'S INCLUDED
£750.00-£2,000.00, weekends by arrangement. Includes all laundry, sheets, towels, electricity and gas. Bring own beach towel. Small groups can be accommodated at reduced rates in low season.

Artizana Suite

PRESTBURY, CHESHIRE
5 STAR SELF-CATERING

Cosy townhouse apartment for the discerning visitor to Cheshire

An elegantly renovated apartment in a Listed 18th century building, Artizana Suite has been described as the ultimate townhouse accommodation. Lavishly furnished with some of the finest examples of contemporary British crafts and works of art, it's not difficult to see why.

Privacy, convenience, comfort and accommodation of the highest quality best describe this fully-serviced apartment situated in the historic village of Prestbury in Cheshire. It comprises a spacious bedroom with king-size bed, living room, bathroom, study/office and a modern, fully-equipped kitchen with an informal dining area.

Original paintings adorn the living room where a wood-burning fireplace provides a cosy alternative to the apartment's central heating system. Stereo, TV, video and a drinks cabinet are there to help you relax while private telephone and wireless broadband have been installed for the business traveller. Free parking is available in the courtyard and there is a personal laundry service if required. Ω

Matter of facts

CONTACT
Ramez J Ghazoul
T +44 (0)1625 827582
E suite@artizana.co.uk
W artizana.co.uk/suite
Address
Artizana Suite,
The Village,
Prestbury,
Cheshire SK10 4DG

RATING
VisitBritain 5 Star
Self-Catering

SLEEPING
Spacious bedroom with
king-size bed.

FOR THE FAMILY
Cot and highchair
available.

FACILITIES
TV, DVD, CDs, wireless
broadband, board games
and selection of books.

**NEAREST SHOPS, PUBS
AND RESTAURANTS**
Basic shops, two historic
pubs and seven restaurants
within 100 metres;
excellent shopping centres
of Wilmslow, Macclesfield
and Alderley Edge within
a few minutes' drive.

OUT AND ABOUT
Quarry Bank Mill, Silk
Museum, Jodrell Bank
Observatory, Gawsworth
Hall, 13th century St
Peter's Church and 10th
century Norman chapel,
Prestbury Golf Club and
various other sports and
leisure centres.

**PRICES PER NIGHT
AND WHAT'S INCLUDED**
Single occupancy £110.00;
double occupancy £125.00.
Includes all taxes, services,
broadband, and parking.

Ascot House

Four-poster beds and period features abound in Victorian villa

Built by one former Lord Mayor of York almost 140 years ago and now owned by another, Ascot House is a family-run guest house a short walk from the centre of this beautiful and historic city.

This Victorian villa has 14 bedrooms, most with four-poster or canopy beds. There are many fine period features, such as the ornate ceiling in the residents' lounge where you can relax watching TV with a drink from the butler's pantry, and a rare and unusual windowed bay, or oriel, on the half-landing. On sunny days this produces a cascade of colour on the beautiful pitch-pine staircase.

The centrally-heated bedrooms all have TVs, complimentary tea and coffee, hairdryers and radio alarms. Traditional and vegetarian breakfasts are served in the attractive dining room while continental options are available from the buffet with generous portions to start your day. Ω

Matter of facts

CONTACT
June Wood
T +44 (0)1904 426826
E admin@ascothouseyork.com
W ascothouseyork.com
Address Ascot House, 80 East Parade, York, North Yorkshire YO31 7YH

RATING
VisitBritain 4 Star Silver Award Guest House

SLEEPING
14 double, twin and family bedrooms, all en suite or private bathrooms and most with four-poster or canopy beds.

FOR THE FAMILY
Well-behaved pets welcome.

FACILITIES
Sauna, residents' lounge, alcohol licence, tea/coffee served all day.

NEAREST SHOPS, PUBS AND RESTAURANTS
Post Office and shops across the road; two local taverns with good pub food; 15 minutes' walk to a full range of restaurants and shops in the city centre.

OUT AND ABOUT
York Minster, The Castle Museum, National Railway Museum, Jorvik Viking Centre, The Yorkshire Museum and the historic walled city of York a short walk away. Castle Howard, the Herriott Museum, the Yorkshire Dales, the North Yorkshire Moors and the coast all within an hour's drive.

PRICES PER NIGHT AND WHAT'S INCLUDED
£32.00-£38.00 per person with generous reductions for children sharing a room with two adults. Single en suite rooms from £45.00-£70.00 per person. Includes full English, continental or vegetarian breakfast and VAT.

Atlantic House

LIZARD, CORNWALL 5 STAR SILVER AWARD GUEST ACCOMMODATION

Wonderful views of paradise for walkers and those who love wildlife

When Thomas Hardy wrote in *The Woodlanders*, "it was one of those sequestered spots outside the gates of the world where may usually be found more meditation than action," he might have had Atlantic House and its surrounding area in mind.

Set in a tranquil position in an Area of Outstanding Natural Beauty, Atlantic House enjoys glorious sea views on the Lizard Peninsula, a place of special scientific interest which hosts amazing wildlife such as basking sharks, seals, choughs and peregrine falcons.

Open from February to November, this Edwardian house has four double/twin guest rooms, three with en suite facilities and one with a private shower. All are equipped with comfortable, pocket-sprung beds; leather sofa or chairs; TV with DVD; radio/alarm clock, fridge, hairdryer, exclusive handmade toiletries, hospitality tray and Cornish bottled water; handmade chocolates and fresh flowers.

Enjoy your delicious breakfast looking out across open fields to the Atlantic Ocean. Atlantic House has its own green policy, which states that most produce is locally sourced, from handmade sausages and smoked haddock to eggs and yoghurts, thus ensuring the highest quality and tastiest of ingredients. Ω

Matter of facts

CONTACT
Jayne and Philip Hayes
T +44 (0)1326 290399
E jayne@
atlantichouselizard.co.uk
W atlantichouselizard.
co.uk
Address Atlantic House,
Pentreath Lane,
Lizard,
Cornwall TR12 7NY

RATING
VisitBritain 5 Star
Silver Award Guest
Accommodation; Green
Tourism Silver Award.

SLEEPING
Four double/twin bedrooms
(one with a zip-and-link
bed), all en suite or private
shower.

FOR THE FAMILY
Children over 12 welcome;
no pets.

FACILITIES
Packed lunches of freshly-
baked baguettes available;
wireless Internet; open
fires.

**NEAREST SHOPS, PUBS
AND RESTAURANTS**
The Lizard village offers a
friendly pub, restaurants,
cafés, pasty shop, fish and
chip shop, general stores,
Post Office and gift shops.

OUT AND ABOUT
A walkers' paradise;
wildlife at Kynance Cove,
the most southerly point
on mainland Britain,
including rare plants
unique to the area; the
satellite earth station at
Goonhilly; Gweek Seal
Sanctuary; the Flambards
Experience; Royal Naval
Air Station Culdrose;
Trenance chocolate factory;
Bonython Estate Gardens;
Trevano Gardens and
museums; Eden Project;
Lost Gardens of Heligan;
St Ives, Land's End.

**PRICES PER ROOM
PER NIGHT AND
WHAT'S INCLUDED**
Double/twin room £65.00-
£85.00. Includes continental
or full English breakfast.

The Ayrlington

BATH, SOMERSET 5 STAR GOLD AWARD GUEST ACCOMMODATION

English and Asian influences make Georgian house a place to savour

This handsome and imposing Listed Georgian house is a five-minute stroll from the centre of the glorious city of Bath. Built with golden Bath stone, the elegant and tranquil property has an award-winning oriental garden with spectacular views of the city and its medieval abbey and is a multiple winner of the Bath in Bloom competition in the hotel garden category.

The hotel's elegant and tranquil interior is a graceful blend of English and Asian antiques, artwork, fine fabrics and Egyptian cotton bed linen. The Ayrlington has recently been extended and refurbished throughout – all 14 bedrooms have an individual theme and are beautifully furnished, some with four-poster beds and spa baths. Privately owned and managed by Simon and Mee Ling Roper, the emphasis is on creating an atmosphere of peace and tranquillity.

There is a residents' bar and secure private parking. An extensive breakfast menu and buffet, plus same-day guests' laundry help complete The Ayrlington's rather special experience. Ω

Matter of facts

CONTACT
Simon Roper
T +44 (0)1225 425495
E mail@ayrlington.com
W ayrlington.com
Address The Ayrlington, 24/25 Pulteney Road, Bath, Somerset BA2 4EZ

RATING
VisitBritain 5 Star Gold Award Guest Accommodation

SLEEPING
14 en suite bedrooms, all with bath and shower.

FOR THE FAMILY
No children under 14.

FACILITIES
LCD TV, DAB radio and CD hi-fi, free wireless broadband access and laptop available, hospitality trays, direct-dial

telephones, safes and ironing facilities in all rooms, hairdressing in room by appointment.

NEAREST SHOPS, PUBS AND RESTAURANTS
Many quality shops, pubs and restaurants a five-minute level walk away in Bath city centre.

OUT AND ABOUT
Bath's medieval abbey and the Abbey Heritage Vaults;

Roman Baths, 18th century Pump Room; Jane Austen Centre; Sally Lunn's house; The Museum of East Asian Art; Building of Bath Museum.

PRICES AND WHAT'S INCLUDED
Mid-week from £37.50 per person per night; weekend from £50.00; both rates based on two sharing. Includes breakfast and VAT.

Barbican House

YORK, NORTH YORKSHIRE
4 STAR SILVER AWARD B&B

A warm welcome awaits you in B&B overlooking York's medieval city walls

From the moment you enter this very special, family-run guest house you cannot help but appreciate the warmth, comfort and hospitality offered by hosts Adrian and Ann Bradley.

Built in 1888 and formerly named Westbourne Villa, this fine example of a Victorian townhouse of individual charm and character has been restored sympathetically, retaining many of its lovely original features, to provide delightful accommodation.

Each bedroom has been individually decorated to complement the charm and character of the period. All rooms have TVs – some of them widescreen LCD TVs – plus ceiling fans; warm and cosy thermostatically-controlled central heating; radio alarms; hairdryers; tea, coffee and hot chocolate facilities with biscuits, and a complimentary decanter of sherry in your room to welcome you to Barbican House. All the beds have pocket-sprung mattresses for a perfect night's sleep. Barbican Lodge is located directly opposite Barbican House. It contains an English king-size bed and a single bed and has a separate dressing room with sofa and adjoining luxury en suite shower room.

A full English breakfast is served in the attractive dining room. Vegetarian and alternative breakfast menus are readily available and the breakfast table always contains a fresh fruit platter, yoghurt and muffins.

Barbican House is ideally situated, overlooking York's famous medieval city walls and is a mere 10-15 minute stroll away from all the city centre attractions. Those who want to forget about the stresses of motoring while on holiday can leave

their cars safely tucked away in Barbican House's floodlit car park for the whole of their stay. The splendid Barbican Leisure Centre, only 100 metres away, presents many top-rated concerts and functions and Barbican House is close to some of the best and most reasonably-priced restaurants and pubs in town. York University is only 15 minutes' walk away.

Guests are invariably delighted to discover this York luxury B&B guest house, partly because of the convenience of being so close to town, but also because of the charm of this residence and the high standards maintained. It is the ideal base for anyone wanting to explore this wonderful city. Ω

Matter of facts

CONTACT
Adrian and Ann Bradley
T +44 (0)1904 627617
E info@
barbicanhouse.co.uk
W barbicanhouse.co.uk
Address Barbican House,
20 Barbican Road,
York,
North Yorkshire
YO10 5AA

RATING
VisitBritain 4 Star
Silver Award B&B

SLEEPING
Two double rooms with en suite, five superior double rooms with king-size beds and en suite, one twin room with en suite and the Barbican Lodge with king-size and single beds, a separate room with sofa and en suite.

FOR THE FAMILY
Children over 10 welcome; no pets.

FACILITIES
Floodlit car park.

NEAREST SHOPS, PUBS AND RESTAURANTS
York's renowned range of unique, independent shops, pubs and restaurants are all within a 15-minute stroll.

OUT AND ABOUT
York Minster; the Shambles; the Jorvik Viking Centre; Castle Museum; National Railway Museum; medieval city walls. Castle Howard; Richard III Museum; the Merchant Adventurers Hall; York Dungeons; Yorkshire Museum and Gardens.

PRICES PER NIGHT AND WHAT'S INCLUDED
Double rooms £76.00 (two people); superior double and twin rooms £82.00 (two people); Barbican Lodge annex suite £90.00 for two people or £110.00 for three. Single occupancy prices are reduced by £10.00 except in Barbican Lodge.

Barncastle

STROUD, GLOUCESTERSHIRE
5 STAR SELF-CATERING

Old world charm at excellent base for exploration

Built on the site of a medieval castle in the Cotswolds, this converted stone barn nestles in the beautiful Painswick Valley and is the perfect base from which to explore the best of what the English countryside has to offer.

Superbly located for a wide range of outdoor pursuits, which include a plethora of golf courses, equestrian centres and fishing spots, Barncastle is a tranquil haven set in spacious grounds with outstanding views of the countryside.

Oak flooring is a feature of many of the rooms inside this two-storey, five-bedroomed home and the beautiful ground floor dining hall with its Cotswold stone Inglenook fireplace is overlooked by an enchanting oak gallery.

Barncastle's old world charm is supplemented by modern conveniences in the form of a fully-equipped kitchen, Sky TV, DVD/video and broadband Internet, making it perfect for holidays with family and friends, reunions, birthday and anniversary celebrations. Ω

Matter of facts

CONTACT
Valerie King
T +44 (0)1452 812495
M +44 (0)7766514114
E enquiries@
barncastle.co.uk
W barncastle.co.uk
Address Stroud,
Gloucestershire
Booking address
Brook Farm, Stroud Road,
Brookthorpe,
Gloucestershire GL4 0UQ

RATING
VisitBritain 5 Star
Self-Catering

SLEEPING
Five beautifully decorated bedrooms – two have king-size beds, two have double beds and one has twin beds. Four bathrooms.

FOR THE FAMILY
Large gardens in which children can play.

FACILITIES
Sky TV, DVD and video, Internet, ample parking.

NEAREST SHOPS, PUBS AND RESTAURANTS
Several nearby village pubs; restaurants catering for all

tastes in Gloucester, Cheltenham, Stroud, Painswick and Cirencester; basic shopping in Painswick, six supermarkets in Gloucester area and boutique shops along Cheltenham promenade.

OUT AND ABOUT
Convenient for historic Gloucester, Cirencester and the Forest of Dean; the Cotswold villages of Painswick, Stowe-on-the-Wold, Broadway and Bourton-on-the-Water; Slimbridge wildfowl centre; Bibury alms houses and trout farm; Westonbirt Arboretum and Chedworth Roman villa; Cheltenham Racecourse, Badminton and Gatcombe Park horse trials and Castle Coombe motor racing circuit.

PRICES AND WHAT'S INCLUDED
Seven nights £890.00-£2,000.00; three nights (weekends) £590.00-£1,200.00; four nights (mid-week) £490.00-£1,300.00. Includes electricity, heating, bed linen and towels.

Battlesteads Hotel

HEXHAM, NORTHUMBERLAND
4 STAR INN

Former temperance hotel now offers top quality local food – and drink!

Mouth-watering home cooking using top quality, locally-sourced produce ensures many repeat visitors to this converted, stone-built inn and restaurant with its cosy, open fire and sunny, walled beer garden.

This former temperance hotel offers a choice of wines, four cask ales and a wide range of bottle-conditioned beer from local breweries to complement excellent dishes prepared with Northumbria's best farm-assured meat, including prime beef and lamb, and fresh fish and seafood from North Shields fish quay. Menus include a range of game dishes when in season as well as locally-smoked meats, fish and cheeses.

Built in 1747 as a farmstead, Battlesteads is a friendly, family-run hotel where comfort is the watchword. Its carefully-modernised bedrooms all have en suite bathrooms, TVs with Freeview, hairdryers, irons and ironing boards and there are ground floor bedrooms specifically for visitors with disabilities. Broadband Internet is available throughout the hotel. Ω

Matter of facts

CONTACT
Dee Slade
T +44 (0)1434 230209
E info@battlesteads.com
W battlesteads.com
Address Battlesteads Hotel, Wark, Hexham, Northumberland NE48 3LS

RATING
VisitBritain 4 Star Inn

SLEEPING
17 bedrooms with en suite, four with disabled access on ground floor.

FACILITIES
Bar meals and à la carte menus with children's portions available; snacks and sandwiches available all day; beer garden.

NEAREST SHOPS, PUBS AND RESTAURANTS
Short walk away in Wark village.

OUT AND ABOUT
Picturesque walks around Wark village; salmon and trout fishing on the River North Tyne; Hadrian's Wall; Hexham market, theatre and museum; Kielder Forest and Kielder Water with shooting, fishing, riding, boating and windsurfing facilities.

PRICES PER NIGHT AND WHAT'S INCLUDED
£40.00-£45.00 per person including breakfast.

Beacon Hill Farm

MORPETH, NORTHUMBERLAND
4 & 5 STAR SELF-CATERING

Award-winning cottages with woods, games galore and top spa facilities

Fifteen luxury cottages set in 15 acres of gardens within a beautiful 360-acre farm with magnificent all-round views, a superb spa and a comprehensive choice of outdoor activities have helped earn Beacon Hill Farm a virtually unrivalled array of accolades.

Claims that it offers arguably the finest holiday cottage experience in England are supported by the fact that Beacon Hill Farm has reached the final of England's Self Catering Holiday of the Year on three occasions. It is the only business to have won this prestigious award twice, in 1991 and 2000. It has also won the North East of England Self Catering Holiday of the Year on all four occasions that it has entered, including the 2006 honour.

Situated deep in the unspoiled countryside between the Cheviot Hills and the magnificent Northumbrian coastline, Beacon Hill Farm stands on the site of an ancient beacon. Within the estate are 40 acres of ancient beech woods that are home to a wide variety of birds and animals. Ideal for the walker or nature lover and extremely safe and exciting for children, the woods form a marvellous natural playground.

The superb, one, two and three-bedroom, self-catering cottages, set in landscaped gardens, are of an exceptional standard, offering peace and tranquillity, great comfort and warmth. Each is fully equipped with TV, radio, fan-assisted and microwave ovens, dishwasher, washer-dryer and deep freeze. All have central heating, masses of books, quality pictures and prints, comfortable chairs and superb views. Most even have log fires.

All cottages have a CD player and you can access emails by wireless Internet using either your own laptop or Beacon Hill Farm's computer and printer.

With a resident beautician, there is a wide range of treatments available at the fabulous spa which includes a pool heated to 30 degrees, sauna, Jacuzzi, steam room with heated granite benches, Laconium therapy room, gym, orangery and tables at which you can enjoy complimentary tea or coffee. Outdoor leisure facilities include an adventure playground, tennis court, cricket net, football pitch, croquet lawn, trampoline, fly-fishing at the two-acre Meg's Lake and the Harry Potter Trail in the adjoining 20-acre wood with prizes for those resourceful enough to complete it! Ω

Matter of facts

CONTACT
Alun Moore
T +44 (0)1670 780900
E alun@beaconhill.co.uk
W beaconhill.co.uk
Address Beacon Hill,
Longhorsley, Morpeth,
Northumberland NE65 8QW

RATING
Visit Britain 4 &
5 Star Self-Catering

SLEEPING
Fifteen one, two and three-bedroom cottages sleeping two, four and six people respectively.

FOR THE FAMILY
Games room with table tennis, pool, bar football and a lounge area with TV; adventure playground; Harry Potter Trail, football, cricket and tennis.

FACILITIES
Spa with pool, sauna, Jacuzzi, steam room, beauty salon, Laconium therapy room with four heated beds, gym and orangery. Wide range of outdoor activities.

NEAREST SHOPS, PUBS AND RESTAURANTS
Shops in Morpeth, five miles away; Eldon Square, Newcastle and the Metro Centre, Gateshead. Many pubs and restaurants within a five-mile radius.

OUT AND ABOUT
Hadrian's Wall; Lindisfarne (Holy Island); the National Trust's Cragside, first house in the world to be lit by electricity; Wallington Hall; Farne Islands, a sanctuary for many species of sea birds; Alnwick and Bamburgh Castles; Beamish Open Air Museum; Durham Cathedral; Northumberland National Park and Kielder Park and Forest. There are many excellent golf courses in the area, most of which welcome visitors. Riding is available at Redesdale Trekking Centre near Elsdon and from Kimmerston Riding School near Wooler it is possible to go on beach rides on the sands at Lindisfarne.

PRICES PER WEEK AND WHAT'S INCLUDED
From £300.00 to £1,525.00. Fully inclusive of heating, logs, coal, linen, towels and electricity, plus use of spa, sauna, steam room.

Beech Farm Cottages

TETNEY, LINCOLNSHIRE 2/5 STAR SELF-CATERING

Red Room's sensual styling sets the scene for romance

Originally a 19th century Lincolnshire Dairy Farm, Beech Farm consists of seven luxurious and spacious cottages in relaxing and peaceful surroundings.

Included among them is the unique Red Room. It is decorated in luxurious red and black with quality furnishings, including a full-size red leather sofa, glass tables, mirrored doors, solid wooden floors and mood lighting. Paintings, sculptures and artwork reflect the mood of the room. It even has a stainless steel lap-dancing pole with coloured lights and a music system to set the scene for seduction and romance, and a large waterbed on the mezzanine with red silk and velvet covers, wall and ceiling mirrors.

No less charming are Beech Farm's other six, more traditional cottages which sleep between two and six guests. All have a fully-equipped kitchen, including electric cooker, microwave, refrigerator, freezer, coffee maker, toaster, crockery and all cookery utensils. The beautiful living rooms – all furnished to a high standard – have TVs, video recorders and CD/DVD players. Ω

Matter of facts

CONTACT
Norman L Smith
T +44 (0)1472 815935
E norman@
beechfarmcottages.co.uk
W beechfarmcottages.co.uk
Address
Beech Farm Cottages,
Station Road,
Tetney,
Lincolnshire DN36 5HX

RATING
VisitBritain ranging from
2 Star to 5 Star (Red Room).

SLEEPING
The Red Room, Daisy,
Milkmaid and Lavender each
sleep two; Clover and Pastimes
sleep four; Buttermilk sleeps
six.

FOR THE FAMILY
Highchairs and travel cot.

FACILITIES
17 acres of private land with
uninterrupted views; free
parking; pool table; bicycles;
wooded area; barbecue; fish
ponds; covered veranda with
patio heater.

**NEAREST SHOPS, PUBS
AND RESTAURANTS**
Shops half a mile; supermarket
two miles; pub quarter of a
mile. Good restaurants serving
local produce within a
15-minute drive.

OUT AND ABOUT
Cleethorpes; Mablethorpe;
Skegness; Sutton-on-Sea;
Louth; Lincolnshire and
Newmarket Shows; Lincoln
Cathedral; Fishing Heritage
Museum; wildlife reserves;
fishing lakes; miles of
protected coastline; open-air
summer music concerts

**PRICES AND
WHAT'S INCLUDED**
The Red Room – £240.00 per
night; £360.00 for two nights.
Discounts for longer stays.
Includes champagne, flowers
and chocolates, fuel and
heating, towels and bed linen.
Other cottages – £250.00-
£470.00 per week. Includes
welcome tray of milk, tea,
coffee, bread, butter and a
bottle of wine; fuel and
heating; towels and bed linen.

Beech House

KENDAL, CUMBRIA 5 STAR SILVER AWARD GUEST ACCOMMODATION

Top quality B&B and its tranquil setting add up to a relaxing break

Set in a delightful conservation area in Kendal on the edge of the Lake District, this boutique guest house offers top-quality B&B with contemporary touches that ensure each of its six individual, en suite bedrooms provide a relaxing environment.

The deluxe rooms, the Penthouse and Greenside, have superior king-size beds with crisp, high-quality bed linen, cosy sofas, wardrobes and flatscreen plasma TVs. Along with the four classic bedrooms, they also feature hairdryers and refreshment trays. Every room has a TV with a DVD player or video. A fridge stocked with a fine selection of alcoholic and non-alcoholic drinks and snacks is available in reception using an honesty payment system.

The leisurely breakfast, served in the south-facing breakfast room, is prepared using only the best local produce and includes a variety of cooked dishes from traditional full English with premium bacon and delicious thin Cumbrian sausages to pancakes drizzled with lemon and sugar.

Coupled with superb, personalised service delivered by highly professional and friendly staff, Beech House is the perfect base for a romantic few days or simply a relaxing break. Ω

Matter of facts

CONTACT
Hilary and Philip Claxton
T +44 (0)1539 720385
E stay@beechhouse-kendal.co.uk
W beechhouse-kendal.co.uk
Address
Beech House,
40 Greenside, Kendal,
Cumbria LA9 4LD

RATING
VisitBritain 5 Star
Silver Award Guest
Accommodation

SLEEPING
Two deluxe double rooms
and four classic double
rooms, all en suite.

FACILITIES
Guest lounge; breakfast
room; wireless Internet
throughout; DVD and video
library; patio area.

**NEAREST SHOPS, PUBS
AND RESTAURANTS**
All within a five-minute
walk.

OUT AND ABOUT
Lake District; Yorkshire
Dales; Eden Valley;
Brewery Arts Centre,
Kendal; Abbot Hall Gallery,
Kendal; Blackwell country
house.

**PRICES PER NIGHT
AND WHAT'S INCLUDED**
Classic double £35.00-
£40.00 per person; deluxe
double £40.00-£50.00
per person per night;
single occupancy of classic
double £45.00. Includes
breakfast.

The Bentley Kempinski

**KENSINGTON, WEST LONDON
5 STAR HOTEL**

Oasis of timeless elegance and classic luxury combines with a unique spa

One of London's best-kept secrets, the Bentley Kempinski is a hidden gem of a hotel tucked away in residential Kensington and brilliantly located for West End shopping and London's cultural delights.

Six hundred tonnes of marble from Turkey, Italy and Africa, along with inlaid mosaics, crystal chandeliers and Louis XV furniture, have helped create this luxurious refuge for the business and leisure traveller.

Inside is a world of exotic luxury with two award-winning restaurants, a cocktail bar with grand piano and the famed Le Kalon Spa where you can indulge in a range of beauty treatments, work out in the fitness studio with cardiovascular equipment, or relax in the saunas, steam room and the only authentic Turkish bath in a London hotel.

The 64 bedrooms combine timeless elegance and classic luxury. Walk-in showers and Jacuzzis are a feature in all the marble-lined bathrooms. A mere stroll away from Harrods, the Bentley Kempinski offers the best of both worlds – relaxation and indulgence. ΩΩ

Matter of facts

CONTACT
Reservations team
T +44 (0)207 244 5555
E reservations@
thebentley-hotel.com
W thebentley-hotel.com
Address
27-33 Harrington Gardens,
London
SW7 4JX

VISITBRITAIN RATING
VisitBritain 5 Star Hotel

SLEEPING
64 en suite bedrooms,
of which one is a one-
bedroom apartment and
24 are suites.

FOR THE FAMILY
Children's menus and
highchairs.

FACILITIES
Turkish bath and spa with
gym and sauna. Individually

controlled air conditioning;
two-line direct-dial ISDN
phone with voicemail;
high-speed data port; state-
of-the-art TV system with
extensive movie and music
library; whirlpool/Jacuzzi
bathtubs; butler's tray and
private bar. Round-the-clock
room service and overnight
shoeshine.

NEAREST SHOPS
Harrods, Peter Jones,
Kings Road and High
Street, Kensington.

OUT AND ABOUT
Close to London museums,
Olympia, Earls Court,
the Royal Albert Hall,
Kensington Palace and
Hyde Park.

PRICES PER NIGHT
Range from £290 to
£4,000 per night.

Berkeley House

TETBURY, GLOUCESTERSHIRE
5 STAR SELF-CATERING

Magazines always keen to feature hip townhouse escape in the Cotswolds

Berkeley House is a large, much celebrated, eight-bedroom Georgian townhouse. One of the hippest houses you can rent in the UK, it is an exclusive Cotswold escape created by designer and photographer Lena Proudlock and features her original art, furniture and denim fabrics.

Situated in one of the most attractive and historic parts of Tetbury, Berkeley House has been featured by *American Express, Vogue, The Sunday Times, Telegraph Magazine,* Norwegian and Chinese *Elle* and in Judith Wilson's *Private Places*.

The first hip bolthole to have an Xera kitchen, Berkeley has seven bedrooms in the main building comprising four doubles and three twin rooms, plus three bathrooms or shower rooms, two of which are en suite. A 24-foot drawing room and snug provide two entertainment rooms and the dining room seats between 14 and 16.

The contemporary and versatile Orangery overlooks the lower of the gardens designed by two-time Chelsea Flower Show gold medal winner Philip Nixon and can be used for formal dining, informal gatherings or as a cinema room. Ω

Matter of facts

CONTACT
Nigel Stengard-Green
T +44 (0)1666 500051
E e@lenaproudlock.com
W lenaproudlockescapes.com
Address Berkeley House, 16 The Chipping, Tetbury, Gloucestershire GL8 8ET

RATING
VisitBritain 5 Star
Self-Catering

SLEEPING
Eight double/twin bedrooms and four bath/shower rooms, including a concrete wetroom. (Additional nine bedrooms in ancillary accommodation).

FOR THE FAMILY
Garden with croquet and kubb (ancient Viking game) from spring to autumn.

FACILITIES
Orangery which can seat 30 for dinner; main dining room which seats 14-16; garden with state-of-the-art barbeque; Sony PlayStation; wireless Internet; DVD library; flatscreen TVs and DVDs in all bedrooms; LCD TV in master bathroom.

NEAREST SHOPS, PUBS AND RESTAURANTS
Shops are a two-minute walk away; local pubs and eateries include the Cat and Custard Pot, the Trouble House, Woolpack at Slad (Laurie Lee's local pub), Whatley Manor.

OUT AND ABOUT
Westonbirt Arboretum; Golden Valley; Bath (35 minutes); Bristol; Beaufort Polo Club; Highgrove; Dyrham Park; Whatley Manor; Chavenage House; Cotswold Water Park; Castle Combe racing circuit; Bath Races; Cheltenham Racecourse; Cotswold Wildlife Park.

PRICES AND WHAT'S INCLUDED
Weekends from £3,500.00; one week from £5,000.00; Christmas and New Year £7,000.00. Includes all essentials from bathrobes to Molton Brown shampoos and VAT.

Bethany House

TUNBRIDGE WELLS, KENT
4 STAR SILVER AWARD B&B

Visitors get the royal treatment when they arrive at spacious B&B

Bethany House is a very comfortable, spacious Edwardian property in Royal Tunbridge Wells with a classically-designed English interior and well-appointed bedrooms and bathrooms.

Hosts Martin and Corinna Perry offer quality B&B accommodation and their warm welcome provides the basis for a relaxing and enjoyable time for holidaymakers and business travellers.

Three large, individually-designed bedrooms provide a warm and relaxing environment and are all adorned with fresh flowers. They are equipped with high quality feather and down-filled duvets and pillows, TVs, hairdryers and complimentary tea, coffee and quality chocolates. A wide range of beauty treatments is also available in the comfort of your room.

Breakfast is served at individual tables in the elegant dining room and is freshly cooked to order. Choose from home-made fruit compote and muesli and a varied range of fresh fruit and Greek yoghurt. A full English breakfast, which can be prepared with vegetarian bacon and sausages if you prefer, is always available. Ω

Matter of facts

CONTACT
Mrs Corinna Perry
T +44 (0)1892 684363
E info@
bethanyhousetwells.co.uk
W bethanyhousetwells.co.uk
Address Bethany House,
170 St Johns Road,
Tunbridge Wells,
Kent TN4 9UY

RATING
VisitBritain 4 Star
Silver Award B&B

SLEEPING
One double and two twins
which can be made into
doubles, each with en
suite or private bathroom.

FACILITIES
DVD/video player and films
on request; off-street parking.

**NEAREST SHOPS, PUBS
AND RESTAURANTS**
10-15 minutes' walk to
town centre with a good
choice of shops, pubs/bars
and a wide choice of
ethnic restaurants.

OUT AND ABOUT
Convenient for the
Pantiles, Hever Castle,
Scotney Castle Garden,
Penshurst Place, Ightham
Mote, Tonbridge Castle,
Nymans Garden,
Sheffield Park, Bluebell
Railway and Spa
Valley Railway.

**PRICES PER NIGHT AND
WHAT'S INCLUDED**
All rooms £75.00-£85.00
double occupancy; £60.00
single. Includes breakfast.

Bidwell Farm Cottages

NR HONITON, DEVON 5 STAR SELF-CATERING

Award-winning cottages or delicious B&B in an area of natural beauty

Nestling in the Blackdown Hills two minutes from the pretty Domesday village of Upottery, Bidwell Farm Cottages sits in five acres of rolling, unspoiled Devonshire countryside.

Opt for B&B in the 1717-built farm itself or self-catering in one of the two, three-bedroom cottages, the Haybarton or the Cowbyre, and you will enjoy the same superior accommodation and panoramic views of the surrounding hills. Whether a stroll along sun-dappled lanes, golf, horse riding or some fly fishing in Bidwell Farm's own trout pond takes your fancy, this place radiates peace and tranquillity.

Farmhouse guests are pampered at breakfast with a range of fresh produce, including the chance to try the farm's own wonderful duck eggs.

The self-catering Haybarton is a traditional, spacious barn conversion with large beamed lounge, farmhouse kitchen/diner and separate utility room. The Cowbyre is the latest development featuring more contemporary accommodation with open-plan living, kitchen and dining area. Ω

Matter of facts

CONTACT
Patricia Wells
T +44 (0)1404 861122
E pat@bidwellfarm.co.uk
W bidwellfarm.co.uk
Address
Bidwell Farm Cottages,
Upottery nr Honiton,
Devon EX14 9PP

RATING
VisitBritain both cottages
5 Star Self-Catering

SLEEPING
Haybarton and Cowbyre
each have three en suites,
sleeping a total of 12.

FOR THE FAMILY
Five acres in which children
can roam and play.

FACILITIES
Trout pond; full Sky TV.

**NEAREST SHOPS, PUBS
AND RESTAURANTS**
Eight-minute walk to

ancient village inn; four
miles to shops and
restaurants in Honiton.

OUT AND ABOUT
Convenient for Sidmouth,
Lyme Regis, Beer,
Branscombe and Exeter.

**PRICES PER WEEK AND
WHAT'S INCLUDED**
From £399.00-£979.00.
Includes free fly fishing in
trout pond. B&B at £35.00
per person per night.

Black Boys Inn

HURLEY, BERKSHIRE
4 STAR SILVER AWARD INN

Weekly trip to Paris for produce helps 16thC inn earn Michelin status

A weekly run to Paris for foie gras, boudis and other delicacies has helped distinguish this restored, 16th century inn with its outstanding, award-winning cuisine.

Add a delightful country setting and fabulous accommodation, highlighted by polished oak floors, a wood-burning stove and stylish, contemporary bedrooms which retain many period features, and you have some idea of the Black Boys Inn experience.

Old-fashioned French dishes executed in a modern, British way have earned the inn Bib Gourmand status in the *Michelin Guide*. Fine fruit and vegetables direct from New Covent Garden and organic eggs, butter and cream from a local farm go into its culinary creations.

At the end of the day you can gaze at the views of the Chilterns after a relaxing bath in the inn's own well water and you might just be tempted *not* to turn on your in-room TV and DVD... Ω

Matter of facts

CONTACT
Helen Bannister
T +44 (0)1628 824212
E info@blackboysinn.co.uk
W blackboysinn.co.uk
Address Black Boys Inn, Henley Road, Hurley, Berkshire SL6 5NQ

RATING
VisitBritain 4 Star Silver Award Inn

SLEEPING
Six double rooms and one twin, all en suite.

FOR THE FAMILY
Children not permitted under 12.

FACILITIES
In-room TV with DVD player, Internet connection and complimentary tea/coffee; video library.

NEAREST SHOPS, LOCAL PUBS, RESTAURANTS
Short walk away in Hurley and in Henley-on-Thames.

OUT AND ABOUT
Convenient for Cliveden; Stonor Park; the River and Rowing Museum, Henley; Luxters Barn; Grays Court and West Wycombe.

PRICES PER ROOM PER NIGHT AND WHAT'S INCLUDED
From £85.00-£95.00. Includes full English breakfast.

Blaize Cottages

LAVENHAM, SUFFOLK 5 STAR SELF-CATERING

Cottages are just two of 200 Listed buildings in this Suffolk village

These two, luxuriously renovated medieval timber-frame cottages are situated in the stunning village of Lavenham, in the heart of the Suffolk countryside. They are within a two-minute walk of excellent pubs, restaurants and shops in a village which contains 200 Listed buildings, including both Blaize cottages.

The superbly furnished and fitted properties have original oak beams, fully-fitted kitchens, king-size beds and double baths, Sony TVs with Sky channels and DVD players. Both cottages are decorated to a high standard and contain quality furniture and fittings. Blaize Barn comfortably sleeps four but is also popular for two. One if its two double bedrooms, together with the bathroom, is on the ground floor, making it suitable for less-mobile guests. Blaize Barn has vaulted ceilings, Wedgwood china and an attractive, private garden with garden furniture and barbeque.

Wool Cottage sleeps two and is part of a medieval wool merchant's house on Church Street, one of the most prominent streets in Lavenham. It has a small, private, enclosed courtyard, large luxury bedroom, king-size bed, brass bedhead and double bath. Ω

Matter of facts

CONTACT
Carol Keohane
T +44 (0)1787 247402
E info@blaizecottages.com
W blaizecottages.com
Address Blaize House, Church Street, Lavenham, Suffolk CO10 9QT

RATING
VisitBritain 5 Star
Self-Catering

SLEEPING
Blaize Barn has two double bedrooms and sleeps four; Wool Cottage has one double bedroom and sleeps two.

FOR THE FAMILY
Children over 14 or under one welcome in Blaize Barn; under ones only in Wool Cottage; no pets.

FACILITIES
Both cottages have surround-sound entertainment systems with DVD libraries; log fires; private parking; Blaize Barn has a private garden with garden furniture and barbeque; Wool Cottage has an enclosed courtyard.

NEAREST SHOPS, PUBS AND RESTAURANTS
Lavenham village centre, one-to-two minutes' walk away, has a butcher, baker, Post Office, newsagent, grocery store, Co-op, deli, pharmacy, several clothes, gifts, antique and tea shops, plus several pubs and restaurants.

OUT AND ABOUT
Newmarket Racecourse; 200 Listed buildings in Lavenham; countryside walks; coast (one hour).

PRICES PER WEEK AND WHAT'S INCLUDED
Blaize Barn £490.00-£760.00; Wool Cottage £430.00-£660.00. Short breaks available all year from £310.00 (Blaize Barn); from £280.00 (Wool Cottage). Includes linen, towels, logs, power and gas central heating.

Blenheim Lodge

BOWNESS-ON-WINDERMERE, CUMBRIA
4 STAR GUEST HOUSE

Marvellous views and free country club membership in Lake District

Boasting panoramic views of Lake Windermere from an elevated position, Blenheim Lodge nestles quietly against woodlands and enjoys the best of both worlds: it is ideally placed for a quiet retreat from the hustle and bustle of busy Bowness yet is only a five-minute walk to the picturesque village and pier.

Blenheim Lodge has 11 bedrooms, many with antique furniture, including William IV four-posters and Louis XV beds. Breakfast choices range from local handmade sausage and bacon to oven-fresh croissants. For special occasions, we can arrange flowers, champagne and luxury chocolates for your arrival.

Situated beside The Dalesway Walk, Blenheim Lodge is walker, fisherman and golfer-friendly with a drying room and outside taps. It offers country club membership and fishing permits.

After a hard day's enjoyment, why not relax in the comfortable lounge overlooking Lake Windermere, feet up and cuppa in hand? Then enjoy a good night's sleep on deep, pocket-sprung mattresses, snuggled under soft Norwegian duvets, and wake up refreshed to birdsong! Ω

Matter of facts

CONTACT
Robert and Janz Duncan
T +44 (0)15394 43440
E enquiries@blenheim-lodge.com
W blenheim-lodge.com
Address Blenheim Lodge, Brantfell Road, Bowness-on-Windermere, Cumbria LA23 3AE

RATING
AA 4 Star Guest House

SLEEPING
11 single, double, twin and family rooms, 10 en suite, one private bathroom.

FOR THE FAMILY
Children can use country club; extra beds in rooms.

FACILITIES
Free membership to country club and two free fishing permits; all rooms have TV, hot drinks facilities and hairdryers.

NEAREST SHOPS, PUBS AND RESTAURANTS
Good selection of shops five minutes' walk; 20 or more restaurants and pubs two-to-five minutes' walk.

OUT AND ABOUT
World of Beatrix Potter, Windermere Lake cruises, Steamboat Museum. Guided tours and walks with guest house pick-up.

PRICES PER PERSON AND WHAT'S INCLUDED
£38.50-£57.00 per night or £245.00-£330.00 per week; peak rates for bank holidays, long weekends and Valentine's Day/weekend £47.00-£67.00 per night. Special offers and gift vouchers available. Includes breakfast.

Blue Hayes Hotel

ST IVES, CORNWALL 5 STAR GOLD AWARD GUEST ACCOMMODATION

Relax and dine on the terrace while taking in the spectacular views

Set in its own grounds high above Porthminster Beach and overlooking St Ives Bay and harbour, Blue Hayes is a private hotel with its own car park. It is an oasis of calm and tranquillity in this magical part of Cornwall.

It has six, luxurious, individually-bookable suites, all with en suite baths and state-of-the-art showers with body jets. Breakfast is prepared with the finest, mainly local, ingredients and often served on the terrace where guests invariably congregate to enjoy the warm sea breeze, sun, spectacular views of the harbour and the occasional cocktail or two from the imaginatively-stocked bar. Pre-ordered light suppers can also be served on the terrace or in the dining room.

Situated on the South West Coastal Path, Blue Hayes guests can walk from its palm-fringed garden down to the beach below in about five minutes then along to the harbour in about 10 minutes. Ω

Matter of facts

CONTACT
Malcolm Herring
T +44 (0)1736 797129
E info@bluehayes.co.uk
W bluehayes.co.uk
Address Blue Hayes Private Hotel, Trelyon Avenue, St Ives, Cornwall TR26 2AD

RATING
VisitBritain 5 Star Gold Award Guest Accommodation

SLEEPING
Six suites, all with en suite baths and showers, bookable by name.

FOR THE FAMILY
No children under 10 or pets.

FACILITIES
Luxurious pocket-sprung mattresses with goose-down pillows; TV lounge with surround sound; direct dial telephones, tea and coffee, hairdryer in all rooms; broadband Internet access; Molton Brown toiletries.

NEAREST SHOPS, PUBS AND RESTAURANTS
In town, a 15-minute walk along the coastal path.

OUT AND ABOUT
South West Coastal Path, The Tate St Ives, Kidz R Us Youth Theatre Company all within walking distance. Convenient for Godrevy, St Michael's Mount, Penlee House Gallery, Newlyn Art Gallery, Geevor Tin Mine, Museum of Submarine Telegraphy, the Minack Theatre, the Eden Project and Land's End.

PRICES PER NIGHT AND WHAT'S INCLUDED
Double room £140.00-£190.00. Includes breakfast.

The Blue Rooms

YORK, NORTH YORKSHIRE 4 & 5 STAR SELF-CATERING

Top accommodation has close links to restaurant with a colourful past

Situated in a secluded mews in the exclusive Franklins Yard area of York, minutes from York Minster, The Blue Rooms offer luxury, convenience, privacy and comfort of the highest standards.

The Blue Rooms have a cool, minimalist feel and tasteful, contemporary interiors. They are to be found alongside the River Foss and behind the Blue Bicycle Restaurant where award-winning dishes are served above a well-stocked wine cellar, famed for being a house of ill repute at the turn of the last century. In fact, wander downstairs and you will see photographs of some of the girls who possibly plied their trade there.

Today the Blue Bicycle is still a much talked about establishment, but for a very different reason being highly commended for fresh fish dishes, home-made desserts and a seemingly endless selection of fine wines served in a relaxed dining atmosphere. The Blue Bicycle also serves romantic dinners in the private vaulted booths which are situated in the opulent and atmospheric dining area.

Enjoy an aperitif overlooking the River Foss as a prelude to dinner in a dining area that exudes warmth and a busy atmosphere. With an eclectic range of tables and chairs, all beautifully presented, lunch or dinner at the Blue Bicycle is a high quality dining experience in exemplary surroundings set in an intriguingly-historic building, even by York's standards.

The Blues Rooms are equipped to the very highest standards demanded by today's discerning leisure and business traveller. Some guest rooms have king-sized, four-poster beds, luxury fitted Villeroy & Boch bathrooms and individually-fitted kitchen

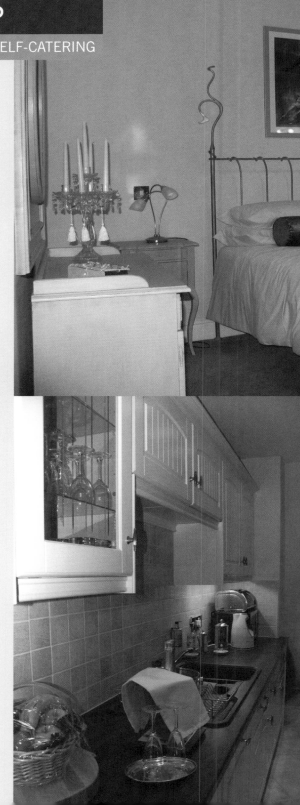

areas with a wide range of built-in appliances. The seating areas are equipped with large, comfortable sofas and chairs to sink into while watching late-night movies or relaxing with a bottle of wine from the honesty bar. And one of the great delights of the Blue Rooms is the unique Foss Room with its 15-foot vaulted ceiling enhanced with exposed, original beams.

With staff committed to their guests' comfort and relaxation and priding themselves on attention to detail, a friendly approach and flexibility of service, The Blue Rooms and the Blue Bicycle is a combination guaranteed to provide a memorable stay. Ω

Matter of facts

CONTACT
Miss K Reid
T +44 (0)1904 673990
E info@
thebluebicycle.com
W thebluebicycle.com
Address Fossgate, York
Booking address
The Blue Bicycle,
34 Fossgate,
York
YO1 9TA

RATING
VisitBritain 4 & 5 Star
Self-Catering

SLEEPING
Four rooms – three of which sleep up to two people; other sleeps up to four.

FACILITIES
Welcome on arrival with bottle of champagne, basket of fresh fruit and full English or continental breakfast; private parking.

NEAREST SHOPS, PUBS AND RESTAURANTS
Many located within a few minutes' walk in York city centre.

OUT AND ABOUT
York Minster, The Castle Museum, National Railway Museum, Jorvik Viking Centre, The Yorkshire Museum and the walled city of York a few minutes' walk away.

PRICES PER ROOM AND WHAT'S INCLUDED
£150.00-£250.00 per night; £700.00-£1,400.00 per week. Includes complimentary bottle of champagne, full breakfast pack, fruit basket and VAT.

Bowling Green Hotel

PLYMOUTH, DEVON
4 STAR SILVER AWARD HOTEL

Top comfort as guests look out on the famous bowling green

Named after the patch of turf opposite where Sir Francis Drake calmly played his last few bowls before defeating the Spanish Armada, this elegant Georgian hotel offers all the modern facilities the traveller requires.

Its prime, city centre location affords superb views over Plymouth Hoe while its 12 beautifully-appointed bedrooms are tastefully decorated and contain details that make each one unique. All have en suites with either bath or shower and comfortable, pocket-sprung beds for a relaxing night plus tea and coffee-making facilities, remote-control TVs, hairdryers and direct-dial telephones.

The hotel serves a hearty breakfast in a light, airy dining room that looks out to an enclosed garden. Afterwards guests can study the morning papers in a comfortable lounge with leather chesterfields and widescreen TV. Add secure parking and a friendly, efficient staff and the Bowling Green Hotel, like Sir Francis himself, promises a memorable experience. Ω

Matter of facts

CONTACT
Tom Roberts
T +44 (0)1752 209090
E info@
bowlinggreenhotel.co.uk
W bowlinggreenhotel.co.uk
Address
Bowling Green Hotel,
9/10 Osborne Place,
Lockyer Street,
The Hoe,
Plymouth,
Devon PL1 2PU

RATING
VisitBritain 4 Star
Silver Award Hotel

SLEEPING
Eight double/twin rooms,
three family rooms and
one single room, all en
suite bath or with shower.

FOR THE FAMILY
Children welcome.

FACILITIES
Guests' lounge with
widescreen TV; gardens
and conservatory.

**NEAREST SHOPS, PUBS
AND RESTAURANTS**
Many fine shops, pubs and
restaurants within a few
minutes' walk in city centre.

OUT AND ABOUT
Perfectly situated for
Plymouth Hoe, Citadel,
National Marine Aquarium,
Historic Barbican,
Mayflower Steps, boat
trips, Plymouth marina,
Dartmoor National Park.

**PRICES PER NIGHT AND
WHAT'S INCLUDED**
Single £46.00; double or
twin £66.00; family room
£76.00. Includes breakfast
and VAT.

Brayscroft House

EASTBOURNE, EAST SUSSEX
4 STAR GOLD AWARD GUEST HOUSE

Artistic influences at house with long tradition of welcoming guests

A guest house for more than 50 years, this smart, Edwardian home by the sea is furnished with antiques and decorated in soft, muted tones. Frequented by local artists, actors and others who enjoy the finer aspects of Eastbourne, the house is adorned with flowers, inside and out, reflecting the owners' interest in art. A short stroll takes you to the prettiest part of the seafront.

The elegantly-furnished single, double and twin guest rooms have en suite facilities, central heating, TVs (mostly flatscreens) with multi-channels, DVD players and a selection of DVDs, fluffy bath towels, a refreshment tray with bone china crockery, hot drinks, biscuits and complimentary mineral water. There is a separate guest lounge furnished with antiques and original paintings and books to borrow. Wireless Internet is available.

An evening meal of the day, tailored to individual tastes and prepared from fresh ingredients, is available on request. Fish is bought from the fish shop on the beach or from Newhaven, eggs are free range and sausages are made by a local butcher. Ω

Matter of facts

CONTACT
Susan Carter
T +44 (0)1323 647005
E brayscroft@hotmail.com
W brayscrofthotel.co.uk
Address Brayscroft House, 13 South Cliff Avenue, Lower Meads, Eastbourne, East Sussex BN20 7AH

RATING
VisitBritain 4 Star Gold Award Guest House

SLEEPING
One single, three double and two twin rooms, all en suite.

FOR THE FAMILY
Children over 10 welcome; pets accommodated occasionally.

FACILITIES
Wireless Internet; book exchange; DVDs to borrow.

NEAREST SHOPS, PUBS AND RESTAURANTS
Nearest shops in Meads; local pubs have good menus and one has a large garden.

OUT AND ABOUT
Seafront is on the doorstep. The start of the South Downs Way is half a mile away. Very near to theatres, restaurants, art centre, Devonshire Park International Tennis Centre. Charleston Farmhouse, home of the Bloomsbury Group of writers, painters and intellectuals, is on the A27 near Eastbourne. Firle and Glynde Manor are also nearby.

PRICES PER PERSON AND WHAT'S INCLUDED
B&B £36.00 per night or £238.00 per week.

Brighton Marina Holiday Apartments

BRIGHTON, EAST SUSSEX 4 STAR SELF-CATERING

Super apartments overlook
tranquil south coast harbour

These three holiday apartments are among the most luxurious the south coast of England has to offer. They are situated in a tranquil waterside setting in the UK's largest yacht harbour, yet are only moments from the vibrant village square and a mile from Brighton town centre.

All feature one double and one twin bedroom and have been furnished to a high standard. Kitchens contain a wide range of modern appliances, including washer/dryer, dishwasher, fridge-freezer, microwave and an electric oven and hob. Master bedrooms have en suite showers and portable TVs with video players while family bathrooms are also fitted with electric showers. Each apartment is equipped with satellite TV, DVD and radio/CD players, payphone and wireless Internet access.

Two apartments, Harbourside and Harbourmaster, which are on the ground floor, each have a large private terrace from which to enjoy their special waterside location. Harbourview, on the top (third) floor, commands superb views of Brighton Marina's inner harbour. Ω

Matter
of facts

CONTACT
Averil Wills
T +44 (0)208 940 6945
E averil.wills@ london.com
W brightonmarina holidayapartments.co.uk
Address Brighton, East Sussex
Booking address
5 Marlborough Road, Richmond, Surrey TW10 6JT

RATING
VisitBritain
4 Star Self-Catering

SLEEPING
Three apartments, each have one double with en suite and one twin room.

FOR THE FAMILY
Children welcome; pets by arrangement.

FACILITIES
All apartments have fully-equipped kitchen, payphone, wireless Internet and designated parking space.

NEAREST SHOPS, PUBS AND RESTAURANTS
Brighton Marina has many harbourside bars, cafés, restaurants, a superstore and a variety of specialist shops a short walk away.

OUT AND ABOUT
Brighton and Brighton Pier; Brighton Marina has a 26-lane bowling alley, eight screen cinema and the Rendezvous Casino; French markets, craft fairs and street theatre during summer; pleasure and fishing boat trips; Undercliff Path walk below the chalk cliffs to Saltdean.

PRICES PER WEEK AND WHAT'S INCLUDED
Each apartment is £425.00-£625.00. Includes electricity, bed linen, towels, unlimited wireless Internet access and one parking space.

Brills Farm

NORTON DISNEY, LINCOLNSHIRE
4 STAR B&B

Hill-top farm has great views outside and much comfort inside

A beautifully-restored, 1720 Georgian farmhouse, Brills Farm occupies a stunning location with outstanding views on top of a Lincolnshire hill. Packed with period features and antique furniture, this working farm has open fireplaces in the dining room, drawing room and individually-decorated bedrooms with their modern, stylish en suites.

Brills Farm is all about comfort in sumptuous surroundings accompanied by fabulous food made from the best local produce, including home-produced eggs and bacon. Breakfast, two-course suppers and four-course dinners are served in the family dining room with its beautiful oak floor, crystal chandelier and big, stone fireplace.

Individually-decorated bedrooms offer style, beauty and comfort and have beautiful views from the vast sash windows. Each has a TV and a range of teas and ground coffee. Bath and shower rooms have also been individually designed with colour and exterior features of the period, but contain ultra-modern power showers and gleaming baths. Ω

Matter of facts

CONTACT
Sophie White
T +44 (0)1636 892311
E admin@brillsfarm-bedandbreakfast.co.uk
W brillsfarm-bedandbreakfast.co.uk
Address
Brills Farm,
Brills Hill,
Norton Disney,
Lincoln,
Lincolnshire LN6 9JN

RATING
Visit Britain 4 Star B&B

SLEEPING
One double/twin with en suite bath and shower; one double room with en suite bath and shower; double room with en suite shower.

FOR THE FAMILY
No children under 12; dogs by arrangement.

FACILITIES
Two-course suppers and four-course dinners available (booking required).

NEAREST SHOPS, PUBS AND RESTAURANTS
Shops at Newark (four miles) and Lincoln (eight miles); many local bars and restaurants ranging from country pubs to smart French restaurants.

OUT AND ABOUT
Several golf courses; easy access to many walks; river boat trips; horse riding and clay pigeon shooting. Close to several National Trust properties, including the Workhouse at Southwell and Belton Path; Belvoir Castle; antique fairs at Newark and Swinnerton; Lincoln Cathedral and Castle; Newark Castle/Museum.

PRICES PER NIGHT AND WHAT'S INCLUDED
£41.00 per person per room; £10.00 supplement for single occupancy. Includes breakfast and VAT. Two-course supper £15.50; four-course dinner £25.00.

Broadoaks
COUNTRY HOUSE

WINDERMERE, CUMBRIA
5 STAR HOTEL

House evokes a bygone era with fine display of period styling

Set in seven acres of grounds two miles from Bowness, Windermere and Ambleside, Broadoaks is a 14-bedroomed Lakeland stone house which was once commissioned by a military officer as a summer residence. As such it exudes the grandeur of a bygone age with its pitch-pine, open-gallery stairs and its rich, oak-panelled entrance hall and music room with barrel-vaulted acoustic ceiling, Bechstein piano and inglenook log fire.

Its bespoke bedrooms feature stunning, hand-carved, period-style four-poster beds, coordinated bed covers and side curtains and large en suite whirlpool or Victorian bathroom, while its traditional rooms are equipped with en suite spa facilities.

Broadoaks serves a feast of a breakfast, morning coffee, luncheon, traditional afternoon teas and dinner using the best local and seasonal produce each day in its multi award-winning restaurant with its period styling. This fine dining, combined with warm, luxurious surroundings, is complemented by service that is second to none. Ω

Matter of facts

CONTACT
Trevor Pavelyn
T +44 (0)1539 445566
E trev@broadoaksf9.co.uk
W broakoakscountryhouse.co.uk
Address Broadoaks Country House, Bridge Lane, Troutbeck, Windermere, Cumbria LA23 1LA

RATING
AA 5 Star Hotel

SLEEPING
14 rooms with four-poster, king-size or luxury double beds, all with en suite facilities ranging from Victorian to Georgian styling, handmade linen and modern Jacuzzi, spa whirlpool and sunken baths.

FACILITIES
In-room hot drinks, fresh fruit and sparkling water, direct-dial telephones, hairdryers, Sky TV and video, luxury bathrobes; free use of facilities at local private health club; conference facilities for up to 12 people; on-site wedding coordinator.

NEAREST SHOPS, PUBS AND RESTAURANTS
Bowness is two miles away.

OUT AND ABOUT
Holehird Garden, Dove Cottage and the Wordsworth Museum, Ullswater and Penrith, Brougham Castle and Long Meg and Her Daughters, Furness Abbey, near Barrow in Furness. Golf at Windermere Golf Club (handicap required), Kendal Golf Club, or pay and play at Beckside Golf Club, Crook near Kendal. Bowling, cycling, fishing and clay pigeon shooting all available locally and bookable at hotel.

PRICES PER NIGHT AND WHAT'S INCLUDED
£55.00-£105.00 per person. Includes breakfast and VAT. Seasonal special offers available (eg £165.00 per person for three nights including dinner and breakfast).

Bruern Stables

CHIPPING NORTON, OXFORDSHIRE
5 STAR SELF-CATERING

Great facilities for young and old in outbuildings of an 18thC abbey

Converted from the mellow stone Victorian stable yard and outbuildings of the 18th century Bruern Abbey, these 12 luxury cottages are complete with four-poster beds, antique furniture, open fires and state-of-the-art bathrooms and kitchens.

Winner of the Excellence in England gold and silver awards in 1998 and 2003, the cottages are individually decorated and can each accommodate between two and 10 guests. They are set in spectacular landscaped gardens in an Area of Outstanding Natural Beauty and each has an enclosed terrace or secluded garden with garden furniture and barbeque.

Guests can relax in the spa with heated indoor pool or work out in a gym that boasts the latest high-tech toning appliance, the Power Plate. Ladies can indulge in a range of beauty treatments, including products from Aromatherapy Associates and CACI. Add the superb facilities for children and it's easy to see why Bruern Stables make the perfect family holiday venue. Ω

Matter of facts

CONTACT
Frances Curtin
T +44 (0)1993 830415
E fran@bruern.co.uk
W bruern-holiday-cottages.co.uk
Booking address
Red Brick House, Bruern, Chipping Norton, Oxfordshire OX7 6PY

RATING
VisitBritain 5 Star Self-Catering

SLEEPING
12 cottages, each sleeping between two and 10 guests.

FOR THE FAMILY
Two-storey wendy house, climbing frame, play cabin, games room, pedal cars, bikes with helmets, children's croquet, baby sitting available. Cots and cot linen, bed guards, stairgates, highchairs and baby alarms provided free. No pets allowed.

FACILITIES
Croquet lawn; tennis court; pool; gym; spa; bicycles. Each cottage has widescreen TV with Sky channels, DVD and video player, books, dishwasher, microwave, washing machine, fridge-freezer, Wastemaster, iron, vacuum cleaner, direct dial telephone, broadband and central heating. Video library available.

NEAREST SHOPS, PUBS AND RESTAURANTS
Nearest shops one mile away in Milton-under-Wychwood. There is a wealth of pubs and restaurants within five miles of Bruern.

OUT AND ABOUT
Sudeley Castle, Hidcote Manor Gardens, Blenheim Palace, Broughton Castle, Kiftsgate Court Gardens, Stowe Landscape Gardens, Buscot Park, Rousham Park, Chastleton House, Sezincote, Lovell Hall, Chedworth Roman villa, the Rollright Stones, various museums and historic buildings in Oxford. Outdoor activities include walking and hiking, fishing, riding, climbing, gliding, ballooning, car rallying and racing and golf.

PRICES PER WEEK AND WHAT'S INCLUDED
£578.00-£5,155.00 per cottage. Includes generous welcome pack and most everything else, but excludes telephone bill, specially ordered food and beauty treatments. Special promotions for Christmas, New Year, Halloween, Valentine's Day and gardeners' weekends.

Bush Nook

Comfortable house with great views owes much to a Roman frontier

Overlooking Birdoswald Roman Fort on Hadrian's Wall, Bush Nook and its recently converted barns are set in some of the most stunning countryside to be found in England.

Built in 1760, the house and its outbuildings were constructed with stones 'borrowed' from the fortifications. Carefully renovated to retain many original features, Bush Nook has a double apartment, two single, two double and two twin guest rooms. All are en suite and are comfortably furnished.

Three rooms in the converted hay loft and hay barn have vaulted ceilings with original open beams. All rooms are en suite, some with baths and power showers and have TV, hairdryer, hot drink-making facilities and a supply of toiletries and a handmade chocolate.

Award-winning dinners are served in the licensed dining room. There is also a cosy, quiet lounge where you will find a good book and a delightful conservatory in which to unwind at the end of the day. Ω

Matter of facts

CONTACT
Paul and Judith Barton
T +44 (0)1697 747194
E info@bushnook.co.uk
W bushnook.co.uk
Address Bush Nook Country Guest House, Upper Denton, Gilsland, Cumbria CA8 7AF

RATING
4 Star Silver Award Guest Accommodation

SLEEPING
Two double, two twin, two singles and deluxe double apartment, all en suite.

FACILITIES
Award-winning evening dinners served in licensed dining room; guest lounge and conservatory.

NEAREST SHOPS, PUBS AND RESTAURANTS
One mile away.

OUT AND ABOUT
Hadrian's Wall and Northumberland National Park; Birdoswald Roman Fort; Roman Army Museum; Vindolanda and North Pennines Area of Outstanding Natural Beauty; historic Carlisle; Gretna Green.

PRICES PER PERSON PER NIGHT AND WHAT'S INCLUDED
£35.00-£50.00. Includes breakfast. Short break discounts on three or more nights. Extra-night -free winter specials available.

Buxton's Victorian Guest House

BUXTON, DERBYSHIRE 5 STAR SILVER AWARD GUEST HOUSE

From the food to the rooms – all at this guest house shows good taste

Built in 1860 for the then Duke of Devonshire, this Grade II Listed guest house has eight beautifully-decorated, en suite bedrooms, tastefully furnished with antiques and period furniture.

Located on the pedestrianised Broad Walk, a stroll away from the town centre, Buxton's Victorian Guest House overlooks the magnificent Pavilion Gardens and Opera House Theatre. On arrival, relax in the tranquillity of the guest drawing room and enjoy a complimentary tray of tea or coffee and biscuits before settling into the luxury of your individually-styled bedroom.

Guest accommodation comprises five double and one twin room plus a four poster room and family suite. All rooms have TVs, hospitality trays and hairdryers and flowers, chocolates and champagne may be ordered to make your stay extra special.

Here the day begins with a choice of cooked breakfasts, including a hearty full English, kippers with wholemeal bread and butter, a full vegetarian breakfast and traditional Derbyshire oatcakes or a cold buffet. Ω

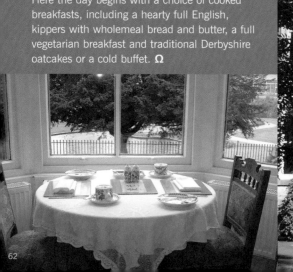

Matter of facts

CONTACT
Barbara and
Alan Baxter
T +44 (0)1298 78759
E buxtonvictorian@
btconnect.com
W buxtonvictorian.
co.uk
Address Buxton's
Victorian Guest House,
3a Broad Walk, Buxton,
Derbyshire SK17 6JE

RATING
VisitBritain 5 Star Silver
Award Guest House

SLEEPING
Five double rooms, one
twin-bedded room, one
family suite and one
four-poster room, all
en suite.

FOR THE FAMILY
Children over four
welcome.

FACILITIES
Guests' drawing room;
fresh milk; ironing
board and iron are
available on request.
Private car park
adjacent to guest house.

NEAREST SHOPS, PUBS AND RESTAURANTS
All within a five-minute
walk of town centre.

OUT AND ABOUT
Pavilion Gardens;
Opera House Theatre;
Peak District National
Park; Chatsworth
House; Haddon Hall;
Eyam Hall, Hope
Valley; Tissington Hall;
Capesthorne Hall;
Gawsworth Hall.

PRICES PER NIGHT AND WHAT'S INCLUDED
Single occupancy
£50.00-£78.00 per
person; double/twin
room £34.00-£46.00
per person; four-poster
room £42.00-£46.00
per person; family
suite £82.00-£170.00
(room price). Includes
full English breakfast
and VAT.

Camelot Lodge Hotel

EASTBOURNE, EAST SUSSEX 4 STAR HOTEL

Camelot Lodge Hotel is a beautiful, large, detached Edwardian house a few minutes' walk from the centre of the seaside town of Eastbourne. With its eight charming bedrooms, this privately-owned and family-run hotel maintains the highest standards of comfort and cleanliness throughout. All rooms are double-glazed, and there is gas central heating throughout with beautiful and tasteful decoration, especially in the stunning bedrooms and en suites.

Owners Dee and Kevin Gillett pride themselves on the hotel's attentive and helpful service and aim to provide a relaxed and happy atmosphere for all their guests. Their efforts at improving the property so far during their ownership have been rewarded by an upgraded rating of four stars and recently received from the **AA a highly commended certificate for 2007-8** which means that they are within the top 10 per cent in the country for their four star rating. They have now have their sights firmly set on the coveted five star award.

All bedrooms have en suite bathrooms with either a bath or shower. All now have teletext TV with integral DVD/CD player coupled with an individual Freeview digibox, clock/radio alarms, hospitality tray and hairdryer. One of the bedrooms is on the

Somewhere special where you are treated as someone special

ground floor for guests who have difficulty with stairs and there is a portable 'T' induction loop for guests who are hard of hearing.

With the hotel being fully licensed, guests can enjoy a drink at the bar in the spacious and attractive guests' lounge where books, games and even a piano are available to keep you entertained. Weather permitting, the garden is also fabulous for a party or for simply relaxing in.

The hotel has its own free car park and can cater for small, private functions such as weddings, anniversaries, christenings, birthdays and family get-togethers.

Breakfast is served in the bright conservatory restaurant which overlooks the family garden and fishpond. Help yourself to a cold buffet of cereal, fruit, yoghurts and juices or start your day with porridge or a delicious and hearty full English breakfast cooked to order.

And if you feel the need to keep in touch with the outside world, Camelot Lodge offers free wireless Internet connection to enable guests to check emails or surf the net with their own laptops. Ω

Matter of facts

CONTACT
Dee and Kevin Gillett
T +44 (0)1323 725207
E info@
camelotlodgehotel.com
W camelotlodgehotel.com
Address
Camelot Lodge Hotel,
35 Lewes Road,
Eastbourne,
East Sussex BN21 2BU

RATING
AA 4 Star 'Highly
Commended 2007-8'
Hotel

SLEEPING
Eight double or family
rooms, all en suite.

FOR THE FAMILY
One mile to seafront,
Treasure Island, boating
lake, miniature railway,
fun go-karts, Rocky's
Adventure Playground.

FACILITIES
Free private car park,
conservatory restaurant,
guests' lounge with bar,
garden, in-room TV with

DVD/CD player,
individual Freeview,
hospitality tray.

**NEAREST SHOPS, PUBS
AND RESTAURANTS**
Many shops, pubs and
restaurants one mile
away in town centre.

OUT AND ABOUT
Pier and harbour,
seafront, Beachy Head,
lighthouse, Eastbourne
Heritage Centre, South
Downs, RNLI Lifeboat
Museum, Military
Museum of Sussex,
bingo, cinemas,
Eastbourne theatres.

**PRICES PER PERSON
PER NIGHT AND
WHAT'S INCLUDED**
£30.00-£40.00 based
on two sharing;
£35.00-£45.00 for
single occupancy of
double/twin room.
Includes breakfast.
Check availability online
with Camelot's best
price guarantee.

Carlyon Bay Hotel

ST AUSTELL, CORNWALL 4 STAR HOTEL

With so much on offer you hardly need to leave the hotel's grounds

Perched majestically atop the cliffs overlooking St Austell Bay, the Carlyon Bay Hotel combines elegance and grandeur with a pleasure seeker's leisure paradise.

A championship golf course; a beautiful, private beach; award-winning, formal dining and 86 bedrooms with every comfort you would expect in a fine hotel make this an exceptional place to stay. Yet the abiding memory many guests take away with them is the breathtaking view from the hotel's stunning location.

While away the day on the magnificent 18-hole golf course or relax with an aromatherapy massage in the health and beauty room. The hotel also has two pools and provides regular entertainment for guests of all ages.

After 7pm it's dress to impress in the restaurant where the menu is a comprehensive table d'hôte with à la carte options on each of the four courses. And with more than 180 wines to choose from, there's something for every budding connoisseur. Ω

Matter of facts

CONTACT
Reservations
T +44 (0)1726 811001
E reservations@
carlyonbay.com
W carlyonbay.com
Address The Carlyon Bay Hotel,
Sea Road, St Austell,
Cornwall PL25 3RD

RATING
AA 4 Star; 1 AA Rosette for
cuisine; RAC Hotel Group of
the Year 2005/2006.

SLEEPING
86 bedrooms ranging from
state rooms to sea view suites
and single rooms.

FOR THE FAMILY
Children's entertainment
programme in school holidays;
unsupervised playroom;
adventure paddock; baby
listening and baby-sitting
facilities.

FACILITIES
Each room has interactive TV,
satellite TV, 24-hour room
service and all the essentials you
would expect from a luxurious
four star hotel. There is also
wireless Internet access
throughout the hotel, 250 acres
of secluded grounds, 18-hole
championship golf course with
10 acres of practice ground, two
putting lawns, 9-hole approach
course, two tennis courts, health
and beauty salon, indoor and
outdoor pools, sauna, spa.

**NEAREST SHOPS, PUBS AND
RESTAURANTS**
Shops in St Austell town
centre two miles away; pubs
and restaurants in Carlyon Bay
(half a mile) and Charlestown
(one mile).

OUT AND ABOUT
Eden Project (two miles); Lost
Gardens of Heligan (five miles);
30 minutes from cathedral city
of Truro and surf capital
Newquay.

**PRICES PER PERSON
PER NIGHT AND
WHAT'S INCLUDED**
Standard accommodation
from £60.00 in winter to
£120.00 in summer. Includes
dinner and breakfast and free
use of golf course.

Carnoustie Golf Hotel

CARNOUSTIE, ANGUS 4 STAR HOTEL

Golfing challenges just don't come much bigger than an Open venue

Adjacent to Carnoustie's famous Championship Course, venue of the 2007 Open, this is one of Scotland's finest golfing, leisure and conference destinations.

The hotel has 75 en suite bedrooms and 10 suites with sensational views of the Championship Course, the sea or the town. Staying at the hotel guarantees you tee times on the Championship Course, Burnside and Buddon links courses.

Its enviable facilities include the Dalhousie Restaurant serving freshly-prepared local Scottish produce, Calder's Bar for informal dining and a complimentary leisure club, including fully-equipped gym and 14-metre swimming pool, at Club Carnoustie Health Spa. Professional instructors help you make the most of your visit while expert beauticians and therapists offer aromatherapy, golfer's tonic, reiki massage and a variety of beauty treatments.

With an outstanding welcome and a commitment to high standards of service, Carnoustie offers ample free parking, excellent road and rail links and a stunning location. Ω

Matter of facts

CONTACT
Amanda Grant
T +44 (0)1241 411999
E reservations.carnoustie@ ohiml.com
W oxfordhotelsandinns.com
Address The Carnoustie Golf Hotel, The Links, Carnoustie, Angus DD7 7JE

RATING
VisitScotland 4 Star Hotel

SLEEPING
75 double/twin bedrooms, 6 Junior Suites, 4 Presidential Suites, all en suite.

FACILITIES
Pool, sauna, steam, whirlpool, gym, beauty treatment rooms.

NEAREST SHOPS, PUBS AND RESTAURANTS
Shop, pubs and restaurants all within walking distance.

OUT AND ABOUT
Carnoustie Championship Course and the Burnside and Buddon links courses adjacent to the hotel. Preferential tee times on these three courses can be arranged. Close to Dundee and Glamis Castle.

PRICES PER NIGHT AND WHAT'S INCLUDED
Twin/double £139.00; single £99.00. Includes dinner, bed and full Scottish breakfast and full use of leisure facilities.

The Cedars

BARROWBY, LINCOLNSHIRE 4 STAR B&B

Italian influences give cosmopolitan atmosphere at Listed farmhouse

This 17th century, Grade II Listed farmhouse in the conservation area of Barrowby village is two miles from the market town of Grantham. Its cosy bedrooms consist of two doubles with private bathrooms and a single with shared bathroom. All rooms have TV, radios and tea and coffee-making facilities.

A five-minute drive from the A1, the Cedars has ample car parking space and a sitting room where guests can relax in front of an open log fire. Italian and French are spoken in addition to English and there are Internet and fax facilities for keeping in touch with the outside world.

Delicious breakfasts can include the Cedars' own free-range eggs, a selection of Lincolnshire sausages, local bacon and home-made preserves. An evening meal of two or more courses can be provided – with Italian cuisine a speciality. The Cedars' own garden provides most of the seasonal vegetables with meat and fish being purchased at local farmers' markets. Ω

Matter of facts

CONTACT
Peter and Kinga Bennett
T +44 (0)1476 563400
E pbcbennett@mac.com
W n/a
Address The Cedars, Low Road, Barrowby, Grantham, Lincolnshire NG32 1DL

RATING
VisitBritain 4 Star B&B

SLEEPING
Two double bedrooms with private bathroom; one single bedroom with shared bathroom.

FACILITIES
Sitting room, private parking, Internet and fax, special diets catered for.

NEAREST SHOPS, PUBS AND RESTAURANTS
Village shop five minutes' walk away in Barrowby; main shopping centre, pubs and restaurants in Grantham town centre two miles away. White Swan pub in Barrowby.

OUT AND ABOUT
Many castles and historic houses close by, including Belton House, Easton Walled Gardens and Woolsthorpe Manor.

PRICES PER NIGHT AND WHAT'S INCLUDED
From £30.00 per person. Includes breakfast. Two-course evening meal from £15.00 per person.

Chequer Cottage

HORSEHEATH, CAMBRIDGESHIRE 4 STAR B&B

Step back into a more leisurely age in this luxurious 15thC cottage

Authentic and special, this 15th century, timber-framed cottage in a picture-book hamlet of thatched dwellings invites you to relax and unwind in a quiet location in gently rolling countryside just 15 minutes from Cambridge.

Lose yourself in the luxurious, private and peaceful accommodation overlooking the pretty cottage garden. Take afternoon tea and home-made cake in the shade of the walnut tree, play croquet, take a stroll or hop on a bike to explore this beautiful area.

Guest accommodation comprises two centrally-heated double rooms, both with views over the garden and surrounding countryside and complete with TV, hairdryer and tea and coffee-making facilities. The en suite Garden Room in the annex has a comfortable king-size bed and is completely private with its own entrance. The Cottage Room in the main house has a separate, spacious, luxury bathroom with shower and large bath. Bathrobes are provided. Gracious, warm and welcoming, this hidden B&B gem exudes huge period appeal and old-fashioned hospitality – and serves up a scrumptious breakfast prepared with seasonal, home-grown and locally-sourced produce. Ω

Matter of facts

CONTACT
Debbie Sills
T +44 (0)1223 891522
E stay@
chequercottage.com
W chequercottage.com
Address Chequer Cottage,
43 Streetly End,
Horseheath,
Cambridgshire CB21 4RP

RATING
VisitBritain 4 Star B&B

SLEEPING
Two double rooms, one
with en suite and one with
separate luxury, private
bathroom.

FOR THE FAMILY
No pets.

FACILITIES
Evening meals by prior

arrangement; off-street
parking; wireless Internet
access; bicycles available.

**NEAREST SHOPS, PUBS
AND RESTAURANTS**
Banks and supermarkets
three miles; market town
of Saffron Walden six miles
and Cambridge 14 miles.

OUT AND ABOUT
Cambridge; Duxford
Imperial War Museum;
Ely; Audley End; Stour
Valley/Constable country.

**PRICES PER ROOM
PER NIGHT AND
WHAT'S INCLUDED**
Double room £65.00 or
£60.00 for two nights or
more; single occupancy
£50.00. Includes
breakfast.

Cheriton House

All that guests expect – and more – at luxury B&B close to the river

This lovely Victorian house, 100 metres from the river in the picturesque village of Houghton, was a highly-commended regional finalist in the Excellence in England Awards.

Its bedrooms have everything you would expect in a luxury B&B – such as en suite bathrooms with power shower and bath, 21-inch teletext TV, radio, trouser-press, hairdryer and hot drinks facilities – plus a few that you wouldn't, like coil-sprung beds, CD/DVD players, safes, exclusive toiletries, chilled fresh milk and wireless Internet. Three bedrooms are situated on the ground floor in a converted barn overlooking the large, landscaped garden.

An extensive, cooked-to-order breakfast menu includes the choice of several herbal teas, mueslis, continental breakfast or an enormous traditional breakfast grill, scrambled eggs and smoked salmon, omelettes and much more. Cheriton House has sourced fresh, local ingredients that are organic or free range where possible and serves its own home-made cakes, breads, jams and marmalades. Ω

Matter of facts

CONTACT
Liz Langley
T +44 (0)1480 464004
E sales@
cheritonhousecambs.co.uk
W cheritonhousecambs.
co.uk
Address Cheriton House,
Mill Street, Houghton,
Huntingdon,
Cambridgeshire PE28 2AZ

RATING
VisitBritain 5 Star Silver
Award Guest Accommodation

SLEEPING
Five double/twin bedrooms
all en suite.

FACILITIES
Private off-road car park;
wireless Internet;
landscaped garden.

**NEAREST SHOPS, PUBS
AND RESTAURANTS**
Houghton is a picturesque
riverside village with two
pub/restaurants, a general
store/off licence, interesting
antique shop and classic

MG garage. Within a
10-minute drive there are
several good restaurants
and riverside pubs and
St Ives and Huntingdon
are both two miles away.

OUT AND ABOUT
150 yards from Houghton
Mill (National Trust) and the
Ouse Valley Way (26 miles
of signposted walks and
cycle tracks) – borrow a
bike from them if you wish!
– or just enjoy a riverside
walk to a pub with a sunny
garden or a warming log fire
in the winter. Cambridge,
the Imperial War Museum
at RAF Duxford, and Ely
Cathedral are all between
20 and 40 minutes' drive
away.

**PRICES PER NIGHT
AND WHAT'S INCLUDED**
£75.00-£90.00 per room.
Reductions for stays of two
nights or more and Sunday
nights. Includes breakfast
and VAT. Ask about special
winter rates.

Cherrygarth Cottages

SLINGSBY, YORK 5 STAR SELF-CATERING

Barn conversions in idyllic setting earn county's best newcomer award

Winner of the White Rose award for the Best Newcomer to Tourism in Yorkshire, these two stunning, new barn conversions share an idyllic setting in the Howardian Hills, an Area of Outstanding Natural Beauty. Each features top-of-the-range luxury fittings and furnishings and unique features created by local craftsmen.

The Hay Barn sleeps eight with its four individually-designed, en suite bedrooms and six-foot beds. It also has a sitting room with log-burning stove, flatscreen TV and Bose sound system, a fully-equipped kitchen and dining room which seats 12 guests. There is underfloor heating throughout.

The Stables also has underfloor heating and sleeps four in its two double bedrooms, again with six-foot beds and en suite bathrooms. The large, open-plan sitting room/dining area also has a log-burning stove and flatscreen TV with Sony Surround Sound.

Both cottages share leisure facilities which include a Jacuzzi, sauna, gym, games room and beauty room. Ω

Matter of facts

CONTACT
Stuart Prest
T +44 (0)1653 628247
E s.prest@btconnect.com
W cherrygarthcottages.co.uk
Address Cherrygarth Cottages, Fryton, Slingsby, York YO62 4AT

RATING
VisitBritain 5 Star Self-Catering

SLEEPING
Hay Barn – four double, en suite bedrooms with six-foot beds, two of which can be converted to singles; The Stables – two double, en suite bedrooms with six-foot beds, both of which can be converted to singles.

FOR THE FAMILY
Games room, table tennis, table football, pool, videos.

FACILITIES
Jacuzzi, sauna, running machine, cross-trainer, rower, bike, weights, beauty room, catering, wireless Internet access.

NEAREST SHOPS, PUBS AND RESTAURANTS
Post Office, general store and public house one mile away in Slingsby; bakery at Hovingham (two miles); award-winning Star Inn at Harome.

OUT AND ABOUT
Castle Howard; York; Flamingoland zoo; North Yorkshire Moors; east coast.

PRICES AND WHAT'S INCLUDED
The Stables – three nights (Friday-Monday) low season £480.00; seven nights high season £940.00. The Hay Barn – three nights (Friday-Monday) low season £790.00; seven nights high season £1,600.00. Changeovers Mondays and Fridays only. Includes welcome hamper and VAT.

Church Farm
COUNTRY COTTAGES

WINSLEY, WILTSHIRE (NR BATH)
4 STAR SELF-CATERING

Beauty surrounds you as you take your leisure on a working farm

These seven, tastefully-converted, old cow byres surround a patio and enclosed landscaped area on a working farm with sheep, free-range hens and horses. Situated in an Area of Outstanding Natural Beauty, the farm has been in the owners' family for 120 years.

Guests can enjoy the superb indoor heated swimming pool with shower and changing facilities and a games room with table tennis, table football, a pool table and a video library.

The all-ground floor accommodation comprises three two-person and four four-person cottages. Named after the various fields surrounding Church Farm, the cottages retain many original features, including natural stone walls, exposed beams, vaulted ceilings and stone pillars. The locally-made, natural wood kitchens include an electric cooker/hob, microwave and fridge with freezer and each cottage has a TV with combined video/DVD player, Freeview, CD player and a selection of games and books. And to welcome you to the West Country, there will be a locally-produced cream tea waiting for you when you arrive. Ω

Matter of facts

CONTACT
Steve and Trish Bowles
T +44 (0)1225 722246
E stay@
churchfarmcottages.com
W churchfarmcottages.com
Address Church Farm
Country Cottages,
Church Farm, Winsley,
Bradford on Avon,
Wiltshire BA15 2JH

RATING
VisitBritain 4 Star
Self Catering; Green
Tourism Silver Award.

SLEEPING
Three one-bedroom
cottages, each sleeping
two people; four two-
bedroom cottages, each
sleeping four people.

FOR THE FAMILY
Children and pets
welcome.

FACILITIES
Indoor pool 12m x 5m
heated to 32 deg C; games
room; two parking places
per cottage; enclosed
garden with patio furniture
and barbeque; laundry
facilities; shared use of deep
freezer; wireless Internet.

NEAREST SHOPS, PUBS AND RESTAURANTS
Village shop and pub, the
Seven Stars, 500 yards
away; amenities of Bath
only five miles distant.

OUT AND ABOUT
Thermae Bath Spa; Kennet
and Avon Canal for
boating, cycling and
walking; Bradford on Avon.
Within an hour's drive are
Lacock, Castle Combe,
Longleat, Stonehenge and
Avebury.

PRICES AND WHAT'S INCLUDED
From £295.00-£875.00
per week. Short breaks of
three nights starting Friday
or four nights from Monday
(excluding school holidays),
both from £265.00-
£495.00. Includes one
bath and hand towel per
person, two tea towels
per cottage, basic
eco-friendly cleaning
materials and all the
bed linen.

Cliff Barns

NARBOROUGH, NORFOLK
5 STAR SELF-CATERING

Named by *The Sunday Times* as one of the world's six most desirable places to spend a weekend, Cliff Barns is an irresistible mix of Mexican hacienda and American hunting lodge. Exquisitely decorated in its own signature style of 'rancho deluxe', Cliff Barns is situated in the peaceful village of Narborough, in the heart of the stunning Norfolk countryside.

This unique and distinctive property sleeps up to 18 people and offers all the luxuries of a first-class hotel with the freedom and exclusivity of a private home. It has seven double bedrooms, a bunk house, four luxurious bathrooms, two wet rooms and a state-of-the-art kitchen, as well as a relaxing hot tub and sauna, which all face on to a formal landscaped courtyard complete with barbeque and Spanish fountain.

With spectacular coastlines and sandy beaches within easy reach, guests even have complimentary use of Cliff Barns' own beach hut a short drive away at Old Hunstanton.

Cliff Barns can provide bespoke catering for parties, reunions, corporate events, hen nights and for a spectacular wedding day with a difference. With its dazzling interior and impressive range of personal services, Cliff Barns can accommodate a wedding reception for up to 120 guests. It has a wedding licence for civil ceremonies, parking for up to 40 cars, three acres of private grounds, a stunning reception room and decadent dining area.

Wherever possible, Cliff Barns sources local produce to create delicious and varied menus, and can even provide house staff from personal chefs to waitresses and barmen. It can cater for up to 30 banquet-style or for up to 50 for a buffet reception. For larger parties, a selection of marquees, tents, tipis and yurts are available.

The large living room features a river rock fireplace, deep, comfy sofas and cartwheel chandeliers. The dining room has an oval dining table seating up to 18 and the adjacent living area has game trophies adorning rough stone walls, stunning chandeliers, sumptuous leather armchairs and another river rock fireplace. With an extensive range of health and beauty therapies and entertainment available, Cliff Barns really is a home-from-home. Ω

Hacienda meets hunting lodge to provide unusual venue in Norfolk

Matter of facts

CONTACT
Edward Robinson
or Russell Hall
T 0870 8505468
E info@cliffbarns.com
W cliffbarns.com
Address Cliff Barns,
Narford Road,
Narborough,
Norfolk, PE32 1HZ
Booking address
PO Box 51393
London N1 7WQ

RATING
VisitBritain 5 Star
Self-Catering; **Voted
one of the top six
'most desirable
places in the world'
to spend a weekend:**
Sunday Times travel
supplement 2005.

SLEEPING
Six double bedrooms
plus a bunk house
which sleeps six.

FOR THE FAMILY
Children welcome.

FACILITIES
Jacuzzi, sauna,
barbeque, table
tennis, board games
and many more
activities available
on request.

**NEAREST SHOPS,
LOCAL PUBS,
RESTAURANTS**
Shops in Swatham
and Downham
Market, Waitrose and
convenience stores.

OUT AND ABOUT
Seal watching; clay
pigeon shooting; go-
karting. Norwich is
40 minutes' drive
away; King's Lynn
20 minutes.

**PRICES AND
WHAT'S INCLUDED**
Weekends (Friday-
Monday) prices range
from £2,960.00
(peak); £2,740.00
off-peak. Rates per
week (Friday-Friday)
£4,390.00 (peak)
and £3,940.00
(off-peak).

Clow Beck House

DARLINGTON, COUNTY DURHAM
5 STAR GOLD AWARD GUEST ACCOMMODATION

Flamboyance and originality typify the approach at double Booker winner

Winner of the Booker Prize for Excellence in the Best Small Hotel category in 2004 and 2005, Clow Beck House is situated in beautiful countryside on the outskirts of Croft-on-Tees, home of author Lewis Carroll for 25 years.

Clow Beck guests have their own private access to 13 separately themed and exquisitely furnished guestrooms, each with views over the garden and surrounding fields to the tree line of the River Tees. The modern, spacious rooms are full of character and, according to *Staying Off The Beaten Track* by Elizabeth and Walter Gundrey, are decorated with some 'flamboyance and individuality'.

The rooms have been carefully put together to provide comfort with a personal touch and are perfect for both leisure and business travellers. All rooms have en suite facilities and are equipped with TVs, direct-dial telephones, modem sockets, CD players, bath pillows, bathrobes and lavishly-prepared hospitality trays. In fact, no detail has been overlooked in this haven of five star luxury.

No one is overlooked at Clow Beck. One of the rooms, Blackthorne, is specially adapted for less mobile guests with a ramped access, extra-wide door, spacious floor area, well-positioned grab and support rails and a direct-dial system so help is at hand at all times. Youngsters are well catered for too with a children's welcome pack, adventure playground, indoor and garden games and special children's meals among the facilities for younger guests.

Dining in the spacious, traditional and stunning dining room is an experience to remember. The

Matter of facts

CONTACT
David and Heather Armstrong
T +44 (0)1325 721075
E david@ clowbeckhouse.co.uk
W clowbeckhouse.co.uk
Address
Clow Beck House,
Croft-on-Tees,
Darlington,
County Durham
DL2 2SW

RATING
VisitBritain 5 Star
Gold Award Guest
Accommodation

SLEEPING
13 rooms, all en suite.

FOR THE FAMILY
Cots; baby monitoring;
baby accessory basket;
children's bath packs;
children's hot water
bottles; highchairs;
toys; play area in
dining room; adventure
playground; garden
trail; indoor and garden
games.

FACILITIES
Two-acre garden
leading to 100 acres
of farmland; evening
meal is available to
residents and their
guests – there is an
extensive wine list and
a good selection of
local bottled beers
and international
lagers.

**NEAREST SHOPS,
PUBS AND
RESTAURANTS**
Half a mile away.

OUT AND ABOUT
Darlington (three miles);
Durham (30 minutes'
drive); York and
Newcastle (one hour).

**PRICES PER NIGHT
AND WHAT'S
INCLUDED**
Single room £85.00;
double/twin room
£130.00. Includes
full English breakfast
and VAT.

extensive menu, complemented by an extensive choice of beers and wine, embraces a wide range of dishes from locally-hung steaks to home-made paté. Guests are encouraged to create their own dishes which they can discuss in the kitchen with the chef. Catch a trout in the beck and he will even cook it for you.

Breakfast is a banquet. Start with home-made muesli, freshly-squeezed orange juice, sliced melon or grapefruit segments and move on to Clow Beck's special porridge, full English with local sausages from Skipton, kippers or mackerel and home-made bread. And, if you can manage it, round off with croissants, toasted home-made fruit bread, preserves and fresh fruit. Ω

Coach House at Crookham

CORNHILL-ON-TWEED, NORTHUMBERLAND
4 STAR SILVER AWARD GUEST ACCOMMODATION

Courtyard exterior and exposed beam interiors at 'your home in the country'

This complex of renovated old farm buildings, including a 1680s cottage and an old smithy, surrounds a sun-trap courtyard. The 17th century, Grade II former dower house has three traditional bedrooms with exposed chestnut beams and vaulted ceilings and seven double, twin and king-size rooms in the courtyard.

The award-winning Coach House at Crookham is the premier guest house for disabled visitors to stay in Northumberland. Several rooms are wheelchair-accessible, while the premier disabled bedroom features a large roll-in shower.

Renowned for its unsurpassed hospitality, the Coach House at Crookham prides itself on being 'your home in the country', offering the chance to relax and escape from it all in an unrivalled position central to all the attractions in north Northumberland and the Scottish Borders.

The beamed barn conversion features a large lounge with a roaring open fire in winter and all-year-round views of the terrace and orchard.

Matter of facts

CONTACT
Leona and Toby Rutter
T +44 (0)1890 820293
E stay@
coachhousecrookham.com
W coachhousecrookham.com
Address
The Coach House
at Crookham,
Cornhill-on-Tweed,
Northumberland TD12 4TD

RATING
VisitBritain 4 Star
Silver Award Guest
Accommodation

SLEEPING
Five spacious rooms and two
double rooms in the courtyard,
all with en suite; two
traditional, double bedrooms
with private bathrooms and
one king-size/twin room with
en suite walk-in shower room.

FOR THE FAMILY
Children welcome; dogs
permitted in some bedrooms
when owners are present (fee
applies).

FACILITIES
Two dining rooms; special
diets catered for; ground-floor
bedrooms.

NEAREST SHOPS, PUBS AND RESTAURANTS
Short walk to local pub
serving real ale and bar meals.

OUT AND ABOUT
Within the Ford and Etal
estate featuring working
watermill, narrow gauge
railway, historic castle, craft
shops and thatched houses
and pubs; numerous walks
locally including the battle site
of Flodden; Berwick-upon-
Tweed; Northumberland
Heritage Coast; Bamburgh and
Dunstanburgh castles; Holy
Island (Lindisfarne); the Farne
Islands and Alnwick.

PRICES PER NIGHT AND WHAT'S INCLUDED
Single room £39.00; single
occupancy of double room
£49.00-£70.00; double room
£35.00-£48.00 per person
(double occupancy). Special
offers available. Includes full
English breakfast.

This is where guests tend to meet
for pre-dinner drinks from the
well-stocked bar and for afternoon
tea or coffee with home-made
cakes and scones (complimentary
on day of arrival).

The two dining rooms are
tastefully decorated and contain
original paintings, period fireplaces
and arched windows. High-quality
meals are prepared using fresh,
local produce. Enjoy a full English
breakfast with locally-produced
sausages and bacon, local free-
range eggs, grilled tomatoes and
butter-fried mushrooms, or try the
kedgeree, kippers and smoked
salmon or haddock as an
alternative. With tables dressed
with crisp linen in the evening, oil
burners are lit and dinner is
served on Wedgwood fine china.
Expect local cheeses, border beef
and lamb and scrumptious home-
made ice creams. If you catch a
Tweed salmon they will even cook
it for you! Ω

Cofton Country Holiday Park

STARCROSS, SOUTH DEVON 4 STAR SELF-CATERING
& 4 STAR HOLIDAY, TOURING AND CAMPING PARK

Environmental awards by the half dozen for this superbly-positioned park

Described by environmentalist David Bellamy as a 'green champion' following six consecutive gold awards for conservation, this fantastic combination of self-catering and holiday park in a glorious corner of South Devon is run by families for families.

Its superb mix of first-class accommodation comprises 13 secluded cottages and six luxury apartments in 18th century Eastdon House along with modern caravan holiday homes, touring and camping pitches. Just a few minutes' drive from Dawlish Warren's Blue Flag beach, Cofton is set in 80 acres with rolling meadows, open parkland, mature woods, five coarse fishing lakes and orchards.

The terraced area for holiday homes was designed around existing trees and bushes, giving a spacious and informal layout. Five charming Cofton Cottages have been tastefully converted from 100-year-old buildings on what was a working farm and the newly-restored Eastdon Stables have been converted into five original two and three-bedroom cottages.

The park's central complex contains two heated swimming pools, the Swan pub, park shop and off-licence, take-away, children's play areas and a games room. Ω

CONTACT

Helen Scott
T +44 (0)800 085 8649
E helen@coftonholidays.co.uk
W coftonholidays.co.uk
Address Cofton Country Holidays, Starcross,
nr Dawlish, South Devon EX6 8RP

RATING

VisitBritain 4 Star Self Catering &
4 Star Holiday, Touring and Camping Park

SLEEPING

13 cottages and six luxury apartments comprising one,
two and three-bedroom units; 60 holiday homes.

FOR THE FAMILY

Children's pool, three outdoor play areas, games
room, family lounge.

FACILITIES

Swimming pool; Swan Pub; park shop and off-
licence; take-away; games room; entertainment
some evenings.

NEAREST SHOPS, PUBS AND RESTAURANTS

Well-stocked shop and off-licence on site; one mile
to nearest local shops; Swan Pub serving bar meals
on site; two excellent local pubs within one mile.

OUT AND ABOUT

Crealy Adventure Park; Woodlands Adventure Park;
River Dart Country Park; Quay West Water Park;
Powderham Castle; seaside resort of Dawlish;
Dawlish Warren nature reserve; Paignton Zoo;
Bicton Botanical Gardens.

PRICES AND WHAT'S INCLUDED

Short breaks £80.00-£260.00; one week £285.00-
£799.00. Prices include accommodation, gas and
electricity, TV and fully-equipped kitchen including
microwave. Promotions: early-bird discount 5%;
over-60s save up to £40.00; two-week holidays get
second week half price (dates apply); two-week
holidays save £25.00; touring and camping save
£2.00 per night in low and mid season.

Coldbeck House

KIRKBY STEPHEN, CUMBRIA
5 STAR GOLD AWARD B&B

Award-winning B&B is easy to get to but very difficult to leave

Built as a farm in 1820 and later converted to a Victorian gentleman's residence, Coldbeck House is a three-bedroom B&B in a tranquil village in Cumbria's Eden Valley, just five minutes from the M6.

Set in two acres of garden with specimen trees, red squirrels, woodpeckers and a now empty mill stream, the house is approached through a fine gateway and drive flanked by old yew trees. Inside there is wonderful, coloured Victorian glass in the hallway and on the landing while the dining room has polished wood floors and a magnificent carved fire surround.

The spacious, en suite bedrooms are all individually designed and equipped with TV and DVD, mini-fridge, hairdryer, tea and coffee-making facilities, a CD player with a small selection of CDs and many other little touches.

A previous winner of numerous awards, including the prestigious Best B&B in England, Belle Hepworth will welcome you on arrival with tea and home-made cakes – either by the log burning stove or overlooking the croquet lawn. Ω

Matter of facts

CONTACT
Belle Hepworth
T +44 (0)1539 623407
E belle@
coldbeckhouse.co.uk
W coldbeckhouse.co.uk
Address Coldbeck House,
Ravenstonedale,
Kirkby Stephen,
Cumbria CA17 4LW

RATING
VisitBritain 5 Star
Gold Award B&B

SLEEPING
One twin room and two
double rooms, all en suite.

FOR THE FAMILY
Children over 12
welcome; pets allowed if
accommodated outside.

FACILITIES
Supper or four-course
dinner by prior arrangement
only for groups of guests;
croquet lawn; drying room.

**NEAREST SHOPS, PUBS
AND RESTAURANTS**
Village store three minutes'
walk away. Nearest shops

in Kirkby Stephen about
10 minutes' drive; two
pubs with good food in
Ravenstonedale village.

OUT AND ABOUT
Lake District and Yorkshire
Dales a short drive away;
Sedbergh 'Book Town'
(15 minute drive); Kirkby
Stephen with its antique
shops and Poet's Walk
(10 minute drive); Rheged
Centre; Dalemain House
and gardens; Ullswater
steamers; Settle-Carlisle
Railway; wonderful walking
in the Howgills; Smardale
Gill (Site of Special Scientific
Interest); Brougham Castle;
good cycling; Bessy Beck
Trout Farm; tennis and golf.

**PRICES PER PERSON
AND WHAT'S INCLUDED**
Double room £45.00 for a
single night, £40.00 per
night for two or more
nights; single occupancy of
double room £50.00 for
single night, £45.00 per
night for two or more
nights. Includes afternoon
tea on arrival and breakfast.

The Colonnade

WEST LONDON 4 STAR HOTEL

Mansion becomes a lavish hotel in fashionable Little Venice area

Chic and unique, this boutique hotel stands near to Regent's Canal in Little Venice, one of London's most fashionable and picturesque neighbourhoods. A converted mansion, the Colonnade has been designed give the feel of a private London residence with the service of a lavish hotel and combines Victorian glamour with sumptuous fabrics, lavish antiques and four-poster beds in many of its 43 rooms.

Here, just a 10-15 minute walk from Paddington Station and the Heathrow Express, you can be pampered with a health spa brought to your room, an array of soothing spiritual treatments, ancient healing practices and traditional massage therapy.

Every room contains a bewildering array of extras, including air-conditioning, tea, coffee, shoeshine, Molton Brown toiletries, hairdryer, safe, bathrobe, slippers, CD player with music library, trouser press, ironing board, minibar, TV, direct-dial telephone and wireless Internet. It's this attention to detail that makes the Colonnade distinctively different. Ω

Matter of facts

CONTACT
Reception
T +44 (0)207 286 1052
E res_colonnade@
theetongroup.com
W theetoncollection.com
Address
The Colonnade,
2 Warrington Crescent,
Little Venice,
London W9 1ER

RATING
VisitBritain
4 Star Hotel

SLEEPING
43 single, club, deluxe double/twin and studio suites.

FOR THE FAMILY
Children welcome, cots provided free, additional charge for extra bed in room.

FACILITIES
Spanish tapas served in the e-bar; licensed bar; wireless Internet access available; al fresco terrace to eat outside in summer.

NEAREST SHOPS, PUBS AND RESTAURANTS
Numerous – all within walking distance. Bakers and newsagent behind hotel.

OUT AND ABOUT
Lord's Cricket Ground; Regent's Park Zoo; Camden market; 15 minutes by Underground to the West End.

PRICES PER NIGHT AND WHAT'S INCLUDED
Prices range from £135.00-£250.00 dependent on room. Includes complimentary newspaper.

Compton Pool Farm

COMPTON, MARLDON, DEVON 5 STAR SELF-CATERING

Ancient farm is right up to date for 21stC pursuits

Set in 14 acres of tranquil valley yet close to all amenities, Compton Pool Farm has something for everyone. With a heated indoor pool and sauna and outstanding landscaped gardens, grounds and lake fishing, this ancient farm, which dates back to the 12th century, has been lovingly converted into nine cottages, each with its own layout and character and with luxurious, contemporary interiors.

The cottages each accommodate between two and eight guests and all have well-equipped kitchens, including dishwasher, microwave and fridge-freezer; well-appointed bathrooms and shower rooms with power showers; hand-crafted contemporary furniture produced in the UK; king-size luxury beds in all double bedrooms and full-size singles in twin rooms; and flatscreen digital TVs, DVD players and Bose hi-fi systems.

Enjoy a dip in the 10-metre pool after a game of tennis on the all-weather court or a work-out in the gym or try your hand at a range of less strenuous pastimes, including table tennis, pool and table football, in the spacious games barn. Ω

Matter of facts

CONTACT
Ann and John Stocks
T +44 (0)1803 872241
E info@comptonpool.co.uk
W comptonpool.co.uk
Address
Compton Pool Farm,
Compton, Marldon,
Devon TQ3 1TA

RATING
VisitBritain 5 Star Self-Catering; Green Tourism Gold Award; South West Self Catering Holiday of the Year finalist 2007.

SLEEPING
Nine cottages sleeping between two and eight.

FOR THE FAMILY
Indoor games barn; extensive children's play area, including trampoline, swings and slides. Cots, highchairs and stairgates available at no extra cost.

FACILITIES
Heated indoor pool; sauna; tennis court; gym; laundry room with washing and

drying facilities; five lakes well stocked with fish; orchard with goats and pot-bellied pigs.

NEAREST SHOPS, PUBS AND RESTAURANTS
Shop in Marldon (one mile); supermarkets in Torquay (six-minute drive); local tea rooms, pubs and restaurants, including Bickley Mills (15-minute walk) and Church House Inn in Marldon.

OUT AND ABOUT
Compton Castle; Paignton Zoo; Buckfast Abbey; Woodlands Leisure Park; Pennywell Farm; Babbacombe Model Village; two steam railways; beaches 10-minute drive; Dartmoor 20-minute drive.

PRICES AND WHAT'S INCLUDED
£240.00 (short break in cottage that sleeps two) to £1,750.00 (peak week in cottage that sleeps eight). Includes all linen, towels (except swimming), electricity and gas.

Cossington Park

COSSINGTON, SOMERSET
5 STAR SELF-CATERING

Centuries of loving care have created a retreat ideal for families and friends

While England and Scotland were contemplating the union that created the Kingdom of Great Britain, two medieval dwellings in picturesque Cossington, Somerset were being acquired by the ancestors of current owner Graham Wason.

Since then, three centuries of stewardship by successive generations of his family have transformed the property, Cossington Park, into a five star retreat in the heart of one of England's finest tourist locations.

Informal and friendly, Cossington Park remains a private home steeped in the history of its custodians, who have included explorers, adventurers, politicians and naval officers. This is reflected in the artefacts, furniture and paintings which adorn the hall, the oak-beamed drawing room, the dining room and six sumptuously-decorated bedrooms, and in the papers and 5,000 books contained in the 100-year-old library. The tranquillity of Cossington Park has long made it a favourite respite for writers and artists.

Set in 25 acres of beautifully-maintained gardens containing many rare species of plants and wildlife, this warm and inviting house can accommodate between eight and 14 people on a self-catering basis for families and friends, reunions and as a retreat. Prepare your own meals in the well-equipped kitchen, take afternoon tea in the pantry overlooking the kitchen garden or, if you prefer, let Cossington Park's external catering specialists serve you a gastronomic feast on the antique oak table, specially imported from Nebraska, in the main dining room.

Matter of facts

CONTACT
Graham Wason or Lesley Pinnell
T +44 (0)800 043 3468
or +44 (0)1278 429852
E ask@cossingtonpark.com
W cossingtonpark.com
Address Cossington, Bridgwater
Booking address 28 Shellthorne
Grove, Bridgwater, TA6 6UJ

RATING
VisitBritain 5 Star Self-Catering

SLEEPING
Full-size beds for up to 12 in six
bedrooms; put-u-ups available,
suitable for use in four of the six;
four bathrooms.

FOR THE FAMILY
Two cots and highchairs available.

FACILITIES
Library of 5,000 books; indoor
and outdoor games.

**NEAREST SHOPS, PUBS
AND RESTAURANTS**
Pub in Cossington Village –
five minute walk; shops and
restaurants in nearby villages.

OUT AND ABOUT
Just 3.5 miles from the M5
so convenient for many of the
West Country's attractions –
Cheddar Gorge and Wookey
Hole Caves; Exmoor, the
Quantocks, Mendips and
Brendon Hills; Bath and Wells;
Glastonbury Priory and Tor;
Dunster Castle and Longleat.

**PRICES AND
WHAT'S INCLUDED**
Three nights £1,225.00-
£1,615.00. Seven nights
£2,055.00-£2,895.00
(Easter £1,895.00-£2,295.00;
Christmas £3,495.00; New
Year £2,625.00-£3,325.00).
Includes heat/ electricity;
linen/toiletries; logs; welcome
hamper and VAT.

When you are not exploring tourist attractions in the area or visiting the many excellent pubs and restaurants in nearby villages then Cossington Park itself has plenty to keep everyone occupied, including a wide range of indoor and outdoor games. Settle into one of the sofas in the library and browse through its fascinating collection of books, some dating from the 17th century, or take a leisurely stroll around the extensive and highly individual gardens, including the intriguingly named Tilting Yard, an orchard and several ponds, one of which, a ha ha, separates the main garden from the paddock.

Cossington Park is indeed somewhere special and all revenues are re-invested in the estate to keep it that way. Ω

The Courthouse Kempinski

CENTRAL LONDON
5 STAR HOTEL

Five star hotel does justice to famous former court building

Scene of many famous legal cases, the former Great Marlborough Street Magistrates' Court is now a Grade II Listed building and a luxurious hotel in a shoppers' paradise. Charles Dickens once plied his trade as a newspaper reporter here while Oscar Wilde, John Lennon, Mick Jagger, Bob Monkhouse and artist Francis Bacon were among those called to answer charges.

Today, instead of cells, the Courthouse has 21 suites among its 116 bedrooms, bedecked with original Robert Adams fireplaces, four-poster beds, fabric walls and marble bathrooms. All rooms have individually-controlled air conditioning, two-line direct-dial telephone with voicemail, high speed data port for laptop connectivity and web mail, state-of-the-art flatscreen LCD satellite TV with foreign language channels, a personal and laptop safe, a writing desk, minibar and an entertainment system.

Chose from five individual eateries serving award-winning cuisine, including the Bar with original prison cells and a 90-seat Roof Terrace for al fresco dining and barbeques, watch a movie in one of the biggest private cinemas in London or relax in a spa which includes a swimming pool, treatment room and gym. Ω

Matter of facts

CONTACT
Reservations
T +44 (0)207 297 5555
E reservations@
courthouse-hotel.com
W courthouse-hotel.com
Address
Courthouse Hotel Kempinski,
19-21 Great Marlborough
Street, London W1F 7HL

RATING
VisitBritain 5 Star Hotel

SLEEPING
116 en suite bedrooms,
including two-bedroom
Penthouse suite and 20
other suites.

FOR THE FAMILY
Children's menus and
highchairs.

FACILITIES
Spa with gym, swimming
pool and treatment room;
94-seater cinema; choice

of five dining areas,
including Roof Terrace;
Laundry, dry cleaning and
ironing service; 24-hour in
room dining; overnight
shoeshine service; 24-hour
concierge (international
service); private butler on
request.

**NEAREST SHOPS, PUBS
AND RESTAURANTS**
Many within walking
distance, including
Liberty's, Selfridges, Bond
Street, Regent Street,
Oxford Street and Carnaby
Street.

OUT AND ABOUT
Royal Opera House,
Palladium, Theatre district,
Regents Park and Trafalgar
Square.

PRICES PER NIGHT
Range from £270.00 to
£2,500.00.

The Cove

PENZANCE, CORNWALL
5 STAR SELF-CATERING

Every amenity on offer in Cornish cove that has long proved popular

These 13 luxury apartments in a beautiful, period property overlook Lamorna Cove which has attracted painters, potters, craftsmen and writers for more than a century. Stunning sea views, a restaurant and terrace bar, heated outdoor swimming pool, gym, sauna, therapy room and children's garden play area are all part of the recipe for a perfect, year-round venue for couples and families in this beautiful part of Cornwall.

Guests have the option of hotel services or choose to cater for themselves. The Cove's contemporary interior features quality furnishings, state-of-the-art kitchens and sublime bathrooms. All apartments are equipped with plasma TVs, DVD and CD players, direct line telephones, broadband, dishwashers and microwaves and most have washing machines. Some have terraces or balconies and one has its own secluded garden.

Enjoy a drink in the terrace bar with its three acres of gardens or in the lounge, complete with wood-burning fire, before dining in the Cove's own restaurant, which serves delicious, locally-sourced meals. Al fresco dining in good weather is also an option. The terrace is open from 10am-10pm. Ω

Matter of facts

CONTACT
Reservations
T +44 (0)1736 731411
E contact@
thecovecornwall.com
W thecovecornwall.com
Address The Cove Cornwall,
Lamorna Cove, Penzance,
Cornwall TR19 6XH

RATING
VisitBritain 5 Star
Self-Catering

SLEEPING
Two studio apartments,
10 one-bedroom
apartments, one two-
bedroom apartment.

FOR THE FAMILY
Children's garden play
area; travel cots, high
chairs, baby listeners and a
child minder are available.

FACILITIES
Outdoor heated pool (April-
October); restaurant;
lounge; terrace bar; five
acres of private gardens;
sauna; gym; wireless
Internet; laundry service;
daily cleaning; free access
to DVD collection.

NEAREST SHOPS, PUBS AND RESTAURANTS
Post Office, Co-op, Tesco
and banks nearby; close to
the Abbey restaurant and
countless other restaurants
and country pubs.

OUT AND ABOUT
The Minack Theatre, the
Eden Project, Land's End
and numerous sandy
beaches.

PRICES PER NIGHT AND WHAT'S INCLUDED
Off-peak £93.00-£248.00;
peak £137.00-£381.00.
Includes breakfast and use
of facilities.

Cressbrook Hall

BUXTON, DERBYSHIRE 4 STAR B&B & SELF-CATERING

Wonderful views overlooking a limestone gorge in Peak District

Built as a private residence by a wealthy cotton mill owner when the stagecoach ruled the highways of England, Cressbrook Hall's imposing facade has changed very little in the 170 or more intervening years. But inside it's a different story with the hall now a spectacular venue for family meetings, reunions and corporate events.

Cressbrook Hall is a blend of self-catering and guest accommodation. It has eight cottages set within its 23 acres of the Derbyshire Peak District plus three B&B guest rooms in the hall itself, which occupies a magnificent location overlooking a natural limestone gorge created by the River Wye. The guest bedrooms all have en suite bathrooms and TVs and most have wonderful views of Water-cum-Jolly and Upper Dale.

Guests have access to a pleasant walled garden suitable for relaxing, picnics and barbecues, and a play area with swings, trampoline and football pitch. The conservatory and orangery adjoining two of the cottages can be hired for private meals. Ω

Matter of facts

CONTACT
Mrs B Hull-Bailey
T +44 (0)1298 871289
E stay@
cressbrookhall.co.uk
W cressbrookhall.co.uk
Address Cressbrook Hall,
Cressbrook, Buxton,
Derbyshire SK17 8SY

RATING
VisitBritain 4 Star
B&B & Self-Catering

SLEEPING
B&B – one double, one twin, one family room, all en suite. Self-catering – eight cottages sleeping between two and nine.

FOR THE FAMILY
Outdoor swings, trampoline and football pitch; indoor table tennis, pool and darts.

FACILITIES
Award-winning orangery; conservatory; laundry with washing machine, tumble dryer and airing facilities; walled garden.

NEAREST SHOPS, LOCAL PUBS, RESTAURANTS
Nearest shops two miles; nearest pubs and restaurants one mile.

OUT AND ABOUT
Chatsworth; Haddon Hall; Castleton caves; Alton Towers. Outdoor pursuits include walking, riding, gliding and fishing.

PRICES PER NIGHT AND WHAT'S INCLUDED
£47.50-£57.50 per person. Includes breakfast. Self catering prices on application.

Crich House

BARNARD CASTLE, COUNTY DURHAM
4 STAR SILVER AWARD GUEST ACCOMMODATION

Little extras mean a lot at this small and friendly B&B in the north-east

Recently renovated and restored, Crich House is small, friendly 1868 family home close to the centre of the town.

Its two luxurious bedrooms are individually styled. One overlooking Galgate has a French feel with cream furniture and a large bed that can be converted into a two singles. Handmade furnishings include cream and gold drapes with a coronet above the bed. The second room overlooks the garden and is more traditional with Victorian wardrobe, large armchairs and red and cream Victorian half-tester drapes over the bed.

Both rooms have en suite showers with toilet, washbasin and mirrored corner unit; TVs with digiboxes and DVD players; tea and coffee trays with freshly-ground coffee, fresh milk and home-made biscuits; and many little extras, including fresh flowers, fluffy towels, bathrobes, toiletries and lots of up-to-date magazines, books and DVDs.

The sumptuous breakfast offers a choice of fresh fruit, porridge, cereals, yoghurt, smoked salmon, scrambled eggs, a vegetarian option, home-made drop scones and toast. Ω

Matter of facts

CONTACT
Alison Morrell
T +44 (0)1833 630357
E info@crich-house.co.uk
W crich-house.co.uk
Address
Crich House,
94 Galgate,
Barnard Castle,
County Durham
DL12 8BJ

RATING
VisitBritain 4 Star
Silver Award Guest
Accommodation

SLEEPING
Two individually-styled
double rooms.

FACILITIES
Sports centre with excellent
facilities a short walk away.

**NEAREST SHOPS, PUBS
AND RESTAURANTS**
Small, individual shops a
five-minute walk away in
town centre; wide variety
of pubs and excellent
restaurants within walking
distance.

OUT AND ABOUT
Bowes Museum; 12th
century Barnard Castle;
Raby Castle; High Force
Waterfall; many river walks.

**PRICES AND
WHAT'S INCLUDED**
£65.00-£75.00 per
double room per night;
£140.00 for two
nights Friday-Saturday or
Saturday-Sunday. Midweek
specials available. Includes
breakfast.

The Crown Inn

Rustic charm and modern facilities combine in a picturesque hamlet

A charming 17th century country inn with an excellent restaurant and luxurious, modern award-winning accommodation, the Crown Inn is set in the picturesque hamlet of Playhatch, nestled between the Thames and the Chilterns Area of Outstanding Natural Beauty.

The Crown Inn has well-appointed bedrooms equipped with luxurious king-size beds and 32in flatscreen TVs. It has built a reputation for excellent food and friendly service with a menu which ranges from the simple and expertly-made Steak and Brakspear ale pie to more adventurous and modern English. Fresh produce is sourced locally wherever possible.

The traditional, oak-beamed main restaurant area leads to three distinct sections, ranging from the rustic atmosphere of the beautifully-restored 18th century barn to the elegance of the conservatory and the stylish ambience and privacy of the newly-refurbished taproom. Following a drink in the charming and well-stocked country bar, the beautiful garden makes an excellent place to while away those long summer evenings. Ω

Matter of facts

CONTACT
Zoe Bailey
T +44 (0)118 947 2872
E hotel@thecrown.co.uk
W thecrown.co.uk
Address The Crown Inn, Playhatch, nr Reading, Berkshire RG4 9QN

RATING
VisitBritain 4 Star Inn

SLEEPING
Ten double or twin rooms.

FOR THE FAMILY
Children eat at half price.

FACILITIES
Restaurant and bar; private patio area with furniture; luxury king-size beds; 32in flatscreen LCD TV; room safe; tea and coffee-making facilities; private residents' garden; room service; iron and hairdryer.

NEAREST SHOPS, PUBS AND RESTAURANTS
Close to Reading's excellent, modern shopping centre. The Crown Inn's own bar and restaurant is just a few steps away from the guest accommodation.

OUT AND ABOUT
Thames Path; Henley Town Centre and River and Rowing Museum; five local golf courses, local walks in the Chilterns.

PRICES PER NIGHT AND WHAT'S INCLUDED
£80.00-£120.00 per room. Includes full breakfast and VAT.

Damerons Farm Holidays

IPSWICH, SUFFOLK 4 STAR SELF-CATERING

Ideal base for families where the dog – and horse – can come too!

If life down on the farm appeals to you, then you'll find Damerons is just the place. This is a quiet countryside retreat where you can feed the chickens and Jacobs sheep or collect eggs. You can take your dog along with you and, with on-site stables and paddocks, you can even bring your horse, if you have one!

Damerons Farm's five individually-styled cottages were previously a milking parlour and old granary and have been tastefully modernised to provide good quality, spacious accommodation. They are based around an old brick-lined courtyard with access to a games and leisure room and each has its own paved patio. One cottage is particularly suitable for mobility-impaired guests. The grass picnic area is an ideal place to relax while the children use up their excess energy on the play equipment or playing football.

A wildlife haven, Damerons Farm guarantees a warm Suffolk welcome away from the hustle and bustle. Ω

Matter of facts

CONTACT
Sue Leggett
T +44 (0)1473 832454
or +44 (0)7881 824083
E info@damerons
farmholidays.co.uk
W damerons
farmholidays.co.uk
Address Damerons Farm
Holidays, Damerons Farm,
Main Road, Henley,
Ipswich, Suffolk IP6 0RU

RATING
VisitBritain 4 Star
Self-Catering

SLEEPING
Five cottages sleeping
two, four or six guests.

FOR THE FAMILY
Grass picnic area/play
area; games room.

FACILITIES
Each cottage has a well-
equipped fitted kitchen
with dishwashers (except
one), DVD players and
flatscreen TVs; on-site

stables and paddocks.

**NEAREST SHOPS, PUBS
AND RESTAURANTS**
Nearest shops two-and-
a-half miles; a wealth of
pubs and restaurants
within two miles.

OUT AND ABOUT
Baylham Rare Breeds
Centre; Easton Farm Park;
Felixstowe Beach Resort;
Helmingham Hall and
Gardens; the Museum of
East Anglia Life; Stoneham
Barn Owls Sanctuary;
Christchurch Mansion and
Museum, Ipswich; sailing
on the rivers Deben and
Orwell; inland watersports
at Alton Water; horse
riding.

**PRICES PER WEEK AND
WHAT'S INCLUDED**
Two-person cottage
£235.00-£335.00; six-
person £365.00-£595.00.
Includes bed linen, towels,
heating and hot water.

Dannah Farm Country House

BELPER, DERBYSHIRE 5 STAR GUEST ACCOMMODATION

Situated on the Chatsworth Estates at Shottle, this working farm with 154 acres to explore, including its own medieval moat, known as the Mottes, dates from the late 1700s. Set in the beautiful Derbyshire Dale, on the southern fringes of The Peak District, Dannah is perfectly located to enjoy the many and varied attractions the area has to offer. The house is seemingly lost in an almost forgotten, stunning rural landscape, yet is close to major road networks and only 20 minutes from the M1.

Guests go to Dannah to escape the noise, crowds, and pressures of everyday life and to relax and unwind in a peaceful and tranquil environment, surrounded by beautiful countryside, with award-winning accommodation, personal service, wonderful food and attention to detail that is second to none.

Dannah has eight stunning, stylish and very individual bedrooms, mixing items and styles from the past with contemporary finishes in furnishings and fabrics. Particular attention has been paid to the feature rooms, some with double spa baths, wet rooms, a private sauna, and one, the Studio Hideaway, with outdoor hot-tub set on a private terrace. All bedrooms

are different in size, colour and finish and all look out on to green fields and rolling countryside.

There are two delightful sitting rooms, exclusively for guests' use, tastefully furnished with open fires and lovely views over the gardens and surrounding farmland. Winner of many local and national awards, Dannah combines classic country with innovation and luxury.

A new feature at Dannah is the Leisure Cabin containing a large, Canadian Spa hot-tub set on a secluded terrace overlooking rolling farmland. The cabin has a superb Finnish sauna, perfect for two but roomy enough for six, a small but perfectly-formed shower room, a beautifully laid-out sitting room with squashy sofas, flatscreen TV, DVD, drinks fridge, and a wealth of films, books and games. The cabin can be booked by the day, along with any of Dannah's rooms.

Dannah aims to serve the very best in farmhouse cooking, using locally-sourced ingredients wherever possible, and its own home-made bread. Originally the lambing shed, the award-winning dining room now has a very different purpose! Ω

Unique luxury accommodation with wow-factor spa facilities

Matter of facts

CONTACT
Joan Slack
T +44 (0)1773 550273
E slack@dannah.co.uk
W dannah.co.uk
Address Dannah Farm Country House, Bowmans Lane, Shottle, Belper, Derbyshire DE56 2DR

RATING
AA 5 Star 'Highly Commended' Guest Accommodation

SLEEPING
Eight individual rooms and suites.

FOR THE FAMILY
Cot, highchair available.

FACILITIES
Sauna, hot-tub, spa baths attached to individual rooms; licensed dining room; two guests' sitting rooms; walled garden, orchard and koi pond.

NEAREST SHOPS, PUBS AND RESTAURANTS
Nearest shops in Belper (three miles), main shopping centres in Derby (20 minutes) and Nottingham (45 minutes). Eight recommended pubs and restaurants within 5-10 minute drive.

OUT AND ABOUT
Alton Towers; the American Adventure; Gulliver's Kingdom; Crich Tramway Village; the Heights of Abraham; Carsington Water; Castleton Caves; Ridgewood Equestrian Centre; Wild Park Leisure; the Yeaveley Estate; Chatsworth House; Haddon Hall; Kedleston Hall; Bolsover Castle; Cromford Mill.

PRICES PER NIGHT AND WHAT'S INCLUDED
Per room – single occupancy £75.00-£85.00; standard double £100.00-£110.00; premier double £130.00-£150.00; feature £170.00-£190.00; suite £195.00-£275.00. Includes breakfast.

De Grey's Town House

LUDLOW, SHROPSHIRE 5 STAR GUEST HOUSE

In look and outlook, De Grey's captures all that visitors to England expect

The black and white façade of De Grey's on a street famously described as 'one of the most memorable in England' is one of Ludlow's most photographed features. Built almost 450 years ago during the reign of Elizabeth I, it has been De Grey's Tearoom, a Ludlow institution, for almost a century.

Quintessentially English, De Grey's has created nine luxury rooms designed to provide guests with a home-from-home. The bedrooms are unique, their design governed by the labyrinth of historic timbers in the Tudor building, and offer plenty of space to sit and enjoy the surroundings. They skilfully combine the newest entertainment technology with period-style furniture and luxurious soft furnishings.

Stunning and superbly equipped bathrooms feature roll-top baths and powerful walk-in showers. And, of course, there is the award-winning tearoom where an army of waitresses in smart black skirts and crisp white aprons provide a friendly and efficient service which is redolent of a bygone age. Ω

Matter of facts

CONTACT
Tracy Turner
T +44 (0)1584 872764
E degreys@
btopenworld.com
W degreys.co.uk
Address De Grey's,
5/6 Broad Street, Ludlow,
Shropshire SY8 1NG

RATING
VisitBritain
5 Star Guest House

SLEEPING
Three twin, three double,
two four-poster rooms and
one suite, all en suite.

FOR THE FAMILY
Highchairs available.

FACILITIES
Ground-floor room suitable

for those with mobility
needs; De Grey's Tearoom,
bakery and shop.

**NEAREST SHOPS, PUBS
AND RESTAURANTS**
De Grey's is in the town
centre and is surrounded
by many shops, pubs and
restaurants.

OUT AND ABOUT
Ludlow Castle; antique
shops; 900 Listed Tudor
buildings; historic churches.

**PRICES AND
WHAT'S INCLUDED**
Per room per night –
single occupancy £60.00-
£120.00; double £80.00-
£180.00; weekend breaks
£220.00-£435.00.
Includes breakfast.

Dolphin Quays

POOLE, DORSET
4 & 5 STAR SELF-CATERING

Now you can sample the life of luxury on the waterfront

A recently completed, top-quality development situated in Poole Quay, Dolphin Quays offers a variety of one, two and three-bedroom luxury apartments.

The three-bedroom, three-bathroom and three-balcony corner apartment on the second floor offers 180 degree-plus harbour views, from the working quay to Brownsea Island and the Purbecks, all from the comfort of the spacious living area.

The comprehensively-equipped apartments have fully-fitted Miele kitchens and lounge/dining areas and many have large balconies and bedrooms with flexible configuration and en suite bathrooms. Many also have widescreen TVs with DVDs and full Sky packages, CD players, dishwashers, electric ovens and gas hobs, fridge-freezers, microwaves, washing machines, tumble dryers and hairdryers.

With 24-hour front desk security, secure on-site parking and with Poole Quay right outside the front door, Dolphin Quays is the ideal base for a range of entertainment, leisure and marine activities. Ω

Matter of facts

CONTACT
Helen Challis
T +44 (0)1202 683333
E stay@
quayholidays.co.uk
W quayholidays.co.uk
Booking address
Quay Holidays,
1 Grand Parade,
High Street, Poole,
Dorset BH15 1AD

RATING
VisitBritain 4 &
5 Star Self-Catering

SLEEPING
One, two and three-bedroom apartments.

FOR THE FAMILY
Cot, highchair, extra linen, games, books and DVDs.

FACILITIES
24-hour front desk security; secure on-site parking; fully-fitted Miele kitchens with dishwashers, microwaves and washing facilities; TV and DVD players; some apartments

have Sky TV and broadband Internet.

NEAREST SHOPS, PUBS AND RESTAURANTS
Shops within two minutes' walk; main supermarket five minutes' walk; a wide choice of eateries ranging from fine dining to pub meals all within walking distance.

OUT AND ABOUT
Poole Quay; Brownsea Island; the Old Town; beaches at Sandbanks and Branksome Chine; fishing trips from Fisherman's Quay; walks in the Purbeck Hills; The New Forest; Beaulieu.

PRICES AND WHAT'S INCLUDED
From £175.00 for two-night stay low season to £1,050.00 for one-week high season. Short breaks and longer stays available. Includes duvets, full linen, cots and highchairs.

Domineys Cottages

DORCHESTER, DORSET 4 STAR SELF-CATERING

Get off the beaten track and discover well-equipped and secluded cottages

These delightful, highly-commended, early 19th century cottages each have two bedrooms and accommodate up to four guests in comfort. They are situated in a peaceful location on the edge of Buckland Newton, between the Dorset Downs and the Blackmore Vale.

Domineys Cottages are tucked away off a no-through road leading to farms and footpaths, making them an ideal base from which to explore Dorset's wonderful countryside with rural landscapes which have retained their tranquil beauty over the centuries.

Furnished, equipped and maintained to a high standard, the cottages combine the cosy comfort of wood-burning fires with modern facilities, including TVs and DVD players and fully-fitted kitchens with microwaves and washer-dryers. They are double-glazed with fitted carpets and central heating throughout. Each cottage has its own furnished patio leading to a pleasant and attractive garden area.

Close by in the acclaimed sheltered garden of the owner's 17th century thatched house is a heated, open-air swimming pool available to cottage guests on summer afternoons. Ω

Matter of facts

CONTACT
Jeanette Gueterbock
T +44 (0)1300 345295
E cottages@domineys.com
W domineys.com
Address Domineys Cottages, Domineys Yard, Buckland Newton, Dorchester, Dorset DT2 7BS

RATING
VisitBritain
4 Star Self-Catering

SLEEPING
Two-bedroom cottages each sleeping up to four.

FOR THE FAMILY
Babies under one and children over five welcome. Cots and highchairs available.

FACILITIES
Heated outdoor summer swimming pool.

NEAREST SHOPS, PUBS AND RESTAURANTS
Shop in village a short walk away; good shops in Dorchester, Sherborne, Weymouth, Poole and Yeovil; village pub which serves meals is 200 metres away; other pubs which serve food in nearby Piddle Valley and Cerne Abbas.

OUT AND ABOUT
World Heritage Jurassic coastline; historic houses; National Trust properties; various museums, gardens, golf courses, wildlife parks and children's attractions.

PRICES PER WEEK AND WHAT'S INCLUDED
£240.00-£530.00 (Friday-Friday). Bed linen included. Electricity charged from meter.

Draycott Hotel

SW LONDON 5 STAR HOTEL

Little touches add up to top service at elegant hotel in shopping mecca

You might not think to head for Chelsea or Knightsbridge in search of a quiet, restful retreat, but that's exactly what you would find at the Draycott Hotel, a small, elegant hotel replete with luxurious finishes and grand interiors overlooking a leafy square between the two popular west London districts.

Complimentary tea in the drawing room at four, champagne at six and hot chocolate at 10 are among the touches that single out the Draycott as a hotel with pedigree. Occupying three Edwardian houses off Sloane Square, the Draycott has 35 beautifully-appointed and individually-decorated rooms. Each bears the name of a theatrical personality with perhaps a tasteful print or a faded photograph in a silver frame.

With splendid high ceilings and fireplaces, the Draycott combines the grandeur of the past with the luxuries and convenience of today. And with attentive staff who take pride in anticipating and attending to the needs of their guests, you get the sense that nothing is too much trouble in this delightful hotel. Ω

Matter of facts

CONTACT
Reservations
T +44 (0)207 730 6466
E reservations@
draycotthotel.com
W draycotthotel.com
Address Draycott Hotel,
26 Cadogan Gardens,
London SW3 2RP

RATING
AA 5 Star Hotel

SLEEPING
35 rooms, including
singles, doubles, deluxe
doubles and suites, all
en suite.

FOR THE FAMILY
Toy box on arrival; Sony
PlayStation.

FACILITIES
All rooms have air
conditioning, complimentary
wireless Internet access,
private bar and CD,
DVD and satellite TV;
24-hour room service;
breakfast room.

**NEAREST SHOPS, PUBS
AND RESTAURANTS**
Knightsbridge, Sloane
Street and King's Road
all in close proximity.

OUT AND ABOUT
Convenient for all London
attractions, particularly
those in west London,
including Buckingham
Palace, The Royal Hospital
Chelsea and Chelsea Physic
Garden.

**PRICES PER ROOM
PER NIGHT AND
WHAT'S INCLUDED**
From £235.00 for double
room; £295.00 for deluxe;
£375.00 for suites. All
plus VAT.

Dunsley Hall

WHITBY, NORTH YORKSHIRE
3 STAR SILVER AWARD HOTEL

A magnet for visitors seeking mix of serenity and sociability

A mellowed stone hideaway set in four acres of landscaped gardens close to the sea, Dunsley Hall Country House Hotel offers traditional comfort and wonderful food against a backdrop of period elegance and modern charm.

Once a dream home built for a shipping magnate, this true Victorian country house is now a haven for visitors from all over the world. Blending the quality of the old with the best of modern hotel tradition without sacrificing its unique character, Dunsley Hall has fast become an open secret among the discerning who appreciate its traditional ambience and refreshing individuality. With 26 en suite rooms, all individually furnished and some with four-poster beds, this independent, family-run hotel offers guests the luxurious freedom of peaceful serenity in their own elegant rooms or sociability in the public areas where a host of historic features include original oak panelling, stained glass windows and other period gems.

For something extra rural, bring your wellingtons and a warm coat and experience Dunsley's working farm at nearby Ramsdale. Ω

Matter of facts

CONTACT
Reception
T +44 (0)1947 893437
E reception@
dunsleyhall.com
W dunsleyhall.com
Address Dunsley Hall
Country House Hotel,
Dunsley, Whitby, North
Yorkshire YO21 3TL

RATING
VisitBritain 3 Star
Silver Award Hotel

SLEEPING
26 bedrooms, all en suite.

FACILITIES
Four acres of landscaped
grounds; the Terrace Suite
for events up to 120
guests; the Oak Room

fine dining restaurant;
Pyman's Bar; Ramsdale
Farm.

**NEAREST SHOPS, PUBS
AND RESTAURANTS**
Shops, pubs and
restaurants in Whitby
town centre, three miles
away.

OUT AND ABOUT
Whitby; Whitby Abbey;
North Yorkshire Moors;
Castle Howard.

**PRICES PER NIGHT AND
WHAT'S INCLUDED**
Dinner, B&B (two nights
minimum) £170.00-
£185.00 per double room.
Room only – £77.50
single; £120.00 double.

Emsworth House

BRADFIELD, ESSEX 4 STAR B&B

Strong artistic influences are all around at this charming B&B

Whether it's a business trip, a holiday or a get-away-from-it-all break, Emsworth House is the perfect place. Convenient for travelling to Europe from Harwich, this 1930s former vicarage on the Essex/Suffolk border is ideally situated for exploring East Anglia and places such as Flatford Mill (pictured below) in Constable Country. Being on the Essex Way, it is also an ideal base for walkers and hikers.

Rooms offer stunning views of the countryside and the River Stour. There are three bedrooms – a double and a twin, both with en suite, and a double with washbasin. Traditional English, vegetarian and continental breakfasts are served in the large dining room which adjoins a lovely drawing room overlooking the garden and river. There is a large parking area away from the road and a locked garage for bicycles.

Proprietor Penny Linton is a local artist and the house and garden feature an extensive collection of her paintings and sculptures. Ω

Matter of facts

CONTACT
Penny Linton
T +44 (0)1255 870860
E emsworthhouse@
hotmail.com
W emsworthhouse.co.uk
Address Emsworth House
Bed and Breakfast, Ship
Hill, Station Road,
Bradfield, Essex CO11 2UP

RATING
VisitBritain 4 Star B&B

SLEEPING
One double room with en suite; one twin room with en suite; one double room with washbasin.

FOR THE FAMILY
Stairgate, cot and toys available.

FACILITIES
All rooms have TVs and tea and coffee-making facilities.

NEAREST SHOPS, LOCAL PUBS, RESTAURANTS
Fifteen-minute walk to shop and Post Office. Close to excellent pubs and restaurants.

OUT AND ABOUT
Constable Country; Dedham; Flatford and East Bergholt; Colchester; specialist gardens including Beth Chatto and The Place for Plants; birdwatching; cycling; walking; golf; tennis; swimming; theatres; cinemas and art galleries; five-minute walk to the shore.

PRICES PER NIGHT AND WHAT'S INCLUDED
£45.00 per single room; £55.00 per double room with washbasin (two occupants); £65.00 per double room with en suite; £95.00 per family room.

Enchanted Manor

NITON, ISLE OF WIGHT 5 STAR GOLD AWARD HOTEL

Some enchanted evening you may discover this unique hideaway

Fancy a magical break? Then a spell at the Enchanted Manor may be right up your street. Inspired by artist Josephine Wall whose work adorns the manor, this boutique retreat with its first class facilities, excellent service, friendly atmosphere and beautiful surroundings is a secluded hideaway for discerning guests fed up with run-of-the-mill accommodation.

Set in stunning woodlands overlooking the dramatic, rugged coastline of the historic St Catherine's point, the Enchanted Manor has handmade mosaic floors, ceiling murals and magnificent suites, all with ornate, hand-carved, four-poster beds and most with separate, sumptuous lounges with private dining areas. Original marble fireplaces add to the ambience. Ornate Venetian glass chandeliers adorn every room along with 26in flatscreen TVs and DVD players and some rooms have sea views. The exquisite bathrooms have deluxe showers with water jets and roll-top baths.

Delicious gourmet breakfasts are served each morning in the Badger Watch garden room. In the evening, badgers, red squirrels, hedgehogs, peacocks and pheasants transform the gardens into a retreat for wildlife. Ω

Matter of facts

CONTACT
Ric and Maggie Hilton
T +44 (0)1983 730215
E info@
enchantedmanor.co.uk
W enchantedmanor.co.uk
Address
St Catherine's Point,
Sandrock Road, Niton,
Isle of Wight PO38 2NG

RATING
VisitBritain 5 Star
Gold Award Hotel

SLEEPING
Seven suites with en suite
showers and baths.

FACILITIES
Outdoor spa and
swimming pool; games
room with billiard table,
a choice of books and
games and a selection of
Josephine Wall's
enchanted jigsaws;
Kirkpatrick drawing room
with oak furniture and
marble fireplace; health
and beauty treatments in
the new Zodiac Salon.

**NEAREST SHOPS, PUBS
AND RESTAURANTS**
Main resorts of Shanklin,
Ventnor and Newport are
all within 10 minutes' drive;
excellent food is available
at The Buddle, one of the
island's most famous and
historic inns, and within a
few minutes' drive there is
a two AA Rosette restaurant
and a choice of good
country pubs.

OUT AND ABOUT
Osborne House (pictured
opposite); Haven Street
Steam Railway; Brading
Experience; Calbourne
Mill; Ventnor Botanic
Gardens.

**PRICES PER NIGHT
AND WHAT'S INCLUDED**
Standard rate for deluxe
four-poster suite £79.00
per person. Reduction of
10% for weekly bookings.
Includes breakfast. Special
rates for three-night
weekend and four-night
mid-week stays.

Eshott Hall

MORPETH, NORTHUMBERLAND
5 STAR SILVER AWARD HOTEL

The essential escape in the heart of a large country estate

An elegant, 17th century country house, Eshott Hall sits in tranquil rolling lawns surrounded by ancient woodland at the heart of a 450-acre secluded estate where red squirrel, deer and other wildlife abound.

Inside, a magnificent stained glass window of the William Morris school dominates the hallway where old family portraits and antiques meet contemporary pieces. Impressive architectural features, exquisite Italianate plasterwork and elegant furnishings blend to create a majestic, yet relaxed, atmosphere. Eshott's luxurious, individually-styled guest rooms have comfortable king-size beds and spacious en suite facilities with large baths and high-pressure showers. Cordon Bleu meals are prepared to order and served in the elegant 17th century dining room.

The Lost Wing includes a large function room where French windows look out over graceful lawns, surrounded by towering sequoia and cedars of Lebanon, while a charming orangery gives access to a beautifully restored and fully-productive walled garden. Also close to the house is a rare Victorian fernery. Ω

Matter of facts

CONTACT
Margaret Sanderson
T +44 (0)1670 787777
E thehall@eshott.co.uk
W eshott.co.uk
Address Eshott Hall, Morpeth, Northumberland NE65 9EN

RATING
VisitBritain 5 Star Silver Award Hotel

SLEEPING
Three double and three twin rooms, all en suite.

FACILITIES
Tennis court; croquet lawn; woodland walks; function room which accommodates up to 150; orangery; licensed for marriage ceremonies; cordon bleu meals prepared with organic produce from private garden.

NEAREST SHOPS, PUBS AND RESTAURANTS
Local shops in the village of Felton and midway between the market towns of Alnwick and Morpeth; comprehensive shopping at Newcastle's Eldon Square and Gateshead's Metro Centre, both within 30 minutes of Eshott; many varied local and stylish urban pubs and restaurants locally and at Newcastle Quayside.

OUT AND ABOUT
Eshott is ideally located to visit a wealth of attractions, including Northumberland's unspoilt coastline; Druridge Bay; the castles of Bamburgh, Warkworth, Dunstanborough; architecture and gardens at Alnwick, Howick, Wallington and Seaton Delaval; the Cheviot Hills; Hadrian's Wall; Baltic Art Gallery; the Sage Gateshead.

PRICES PER NIGHT AND WHAT'S INCLUDED
Rooms £128.00. Includes breakfast. Dinner £33.00.

Fairfield Garden
GUEST HOUSE

BOWNESS-ON-WINDERMERE, CUMBRIA
4 STAR GUEST HOUSE

Just the spot to have a relaxing and comfortable break from it all

Once owned by Annie Garnett, the famous water colourist, gardener, designer and manufacturer of fabrics and textiles, the Fairfield is one of Lakeland's original country houses, built more than 200 years ago.

Situated just above Bowness village and Lake Windermere, the Fairfield has a half acre of secluded garden. Inside there are single, twin, double, four-poster, deluxe and family rooms, all with en suite or private bath/shower rooms and equipped with TVs, tea and coffee-making facilities, assorted toiletries, hairdryers and radio alarms. Some four-poster rooms have deluxe bathrooms, including an en suite wet room with heated floor, massage pebbles and a two-person power shower with body jets. Available extras in the room include champagne on ice, chocolates, flowers or having the bed showered with rose petals.

The residents' lounge has a unique fireplace with a roaring log fire on chilly evenings and there is a licensed bar. Fairfield breakfasts are a real feast with full English or alternatives chosen at the table. Vegetarian and special diets are also catered for. Ω

Matter of facts

CONTACT
Tony and Liz Blaney
T +44 (0)1539 446565
E relax@the-fairfield.co.uk
W the-fairfield.co.uk
Address Fairfield Garden Guest House, Brantfell Road, Bowness-on-Windermere, Cumbria LA23 3AE

RATING
VisitBritain 4 Star Guest House

SLEEPING
Ten double rooms, including a two-room suite, all en suite and two with full bathrooms.

FOR THE FAMILY
Children over seven welcome; family room sleeps up to five; dogs permitted with prior notice.

FACILITIES
Facilities for the disabled including ground-floor rooms; free Internet access via public terminal or wireless hot-spot; private car park.

NEAREST SHOPS, PUBS AND RESTAURANTS
Many within 200 yards.

OUT AND ABOUT
Bowness village and lake shore are a few minutes walk and nearby footpaths give access to the open countryside and the fine local viewpoint at the top of Brantfell; Windermere lake cruises; Blackwell arts and crafts house; Wordsworth House; gardens and walks, including the Dales Way from Ilkley to Windermere.

PRICES PER PERSON PER NIGHT AND WHAT'S INCLUDED
£30.00 (double room low season) to £49.00 (deluxe room high season) based on two sharing. Discounts of 5% for three days midweek. Includes full breakfast and VAT.

Faweather Grange

A Scandinavian lodge to yourselves is just the place for a romantic break

These nine luxurious, award-winning, romantic Scandinavian round-log lodges are set in nine acres overlooking an ancient wooded valley on the edge of Ilkley Moor. Each has space and privacy and is individually furnished to an exceptionally high standard with a blend of co-ordinated designer fabrics, leather suites, antiques and artifacts.

With in-lodge spa therapy now available, all have hot tubs, log fires and top-of-the-range TVs and hi-fi systems while many have four-poster beds and en suite saunas and Jacuzzis. All guests receive complimentary membership of an exclusive health club which offers a full range of spa and beauty treatments.

Why not celebrate with a fabulous Bentley Bollinger Break? You will be greeted at your lodge with Bollinger Champagne, Molton Brown gifts and hand-tied flowers. Faweather's own chauffeur will take you by Bentley to one of the excellent local restaurants. Return and relax in your private hot tub ... what better way to spend that special time together! Ω

Matter of facts

CONTACT
Debbie Skinn
T +44 (0)1943 878777
E skinn@attglobal.net
W faweathergrange.com
Address The Grange, Sconce Lane, High Eldwick, Yorkshire BD16 3BL

RATING
VisitBritain 4 and 5 Star Self-Catering

SLEEPING
Six lodges with four-poster double rooms; two lodges each with one double and one twin bedroom; one three-bedroom lodge with one double, one twin and two bunk beds.

FOR THE FAMILY
Cots and highchairs available to rent.

FACILITIES
Outdoor hot tub; digital flatscreen TV with DVD/CD/video and home theatre cinema system; kitchen including microwave and dishwasher; Jacuzzi bath and sauna; parking; front garden; sheltered rear garden with patio and furniture; fishing lake; all non-smoking accommodation.

NEAREST SHOPS, PUBS AND RESTAURANTS
Shops three miles, fine pubs and restaurants within two miles. Ilkley (five miles) has a great range of quality shops and restaurants and is a gateway to The Dales National Park.

OUT AND ABOUT
The surrounding area offers numerous places of interest including Saltaire; a preserved Victorian village and World Heritage site; the Brontë parsonage at Haworth; and the Keighley and Worth Valley Railway. Ilkley, with famous Betty's Tea Room, is five miles away as are the many amenities of Bradford; Harrogate and Leeds both 12 miles; York 30 miles. Excellent golf, walking and riding locally; fishing 400 metres.

PRICES PER WEEK AND WHAT'S INCLUDED
Lodges £410.00-£1,000.00. Includes bed linen and duvets (beds made up for arrival), gas and electricity.

Fern Cottage

PUCKLECHURCH, SOUTH GLOUCESTERSHIRE
4 STAR SILVER AWARD FARMHOUSE

Passionate about good food using home-grown and local produce

Set in two acres of gardens adjoining conservation land, Fern Cottage is a registered smallholding just 15 minutes' drive from Bath and Bristol, producing its own vegetables and fruit without the use of chemicals or pesticides.

Owners Sue and Pete are passionate about good food and serve a delicious West Country breakfast using only locally-produced or home-made/home-grown fare. Such is the quality that Fern Cottage won the South West B&B of the Year in the Taste of the West Food & Drinks Awards in October 2006.

If you are planning a weekend's sightseeing, Fern Cottage is ideally situated in a greenbelt/conservation area close to Bath and Bristol.

Three guest rooms are in the converted stable block and the fourth is separate in the annex at the rear of the cottage. All are en suite doubles with fantastic views. There is seating in the wildlife field, garden and outside the rooms.

Whatever the weather, guests can relax in the hot tub in the comfort of the summerhouse. Enjoy the calming experience of stepping into a warm bubbling tub while enjoying the views. Ω

Matter of facts

CONTACT
Sue James
T +44 (0)117 9374966
E sueandpete@ferncottage
bedandbreakfast.co.uk
W ferncottagebedand
breakfast.co.uk
Address Fern Cottage,
188 Shortwood Hill,
Pucklechurch,
South Gloucestershire
BS16 9PG

RATING
VisitBritain 4 Star Silver
Award Farmhouse; Green
Tourism Gold Award.

SLEEPING
Four double rooms, all
en suite.

FOR THE FAMILY
No children or pets.

FACILITIES
Hot tub (small charge);
Digital TVs and wireless
Internet; tea/coffee
hospitality tray; hairdryers;
iron/ironing board available;
Ecover toiletries; bathrobes;
bath sheets; free videos;
radio/alarm clocks.

**NEAREST SHOPS, PUBS
AND RESTAURANTS**
Supermarket, pharmacy
and other shops one mile
away; recommended local
restaurants and pubs in
guest information pack.

OUT AND ABOUT
Cities of Bath and Bristol 15
minutes' drive; The Thermae
Spa, Bath; Maritime Bristol
with the *SS Great Britain;*
Westonbirt; Arboretum;
Dyrham Park; Cotswold
villages; Stonehenge; Lacock;
Castle Combe; Cheddar;
Wells; Tyntesfield House.

**PRICES PER NIGHT
AND WHAT'S INCLUDED**
£65.00-£68.00 for two
in an en suite double.
Includes award-winning
West Country breakfast.

The Firs

BATH, SOMERSET 4 STAR B&B

Leave the car behind and explore this beautiful city

Within a 20-minute stroll from the centre of one of England's most beautiful cities, the Firs is a Victorian house which has been recently renovated to a high standard. Its three guest rooms are all en suite and well equipped with a range of modern amenities, including TVs and radios, Internet access, tea and coffee, hairdryers and ironing facilities.

The property also features open log and coal fires, a separate lounge for the exclusive use of guests and large gardens with a patio that visitors are welcome to use.

Close to shops, parks, pubs and restaurants, the Firs has the benefit of being on a bus route that operates a 10-minute service to the centre of Bath, just under a mile away. You don't need a better excuse to leave the car parked safely at the Firs and set off to explore this wonderful city. Ω

Matter of facts

CONTACT
Dawn Osborne
T +44 (0)1225 334575
E dawnsandora@
gmail.com
Address The Firs,
2 Newbridge Hill,
Bath BA1 3PU

RATING
VisitBritain 4 Star B&B

SLEEPING
Three double rooms,
all en suite.

FOR THE FAMILY
Children's menus.

FACILITIES
Dining room; guests'
lounge; large gardens;
parking.

NEAREST SHOPS, PUBS AND RESTAURANTS
Many in the immediate vicinity including those in Bath city centre, just under a mile away.

OUT AND ABOUT
Bath's medieval abbey and the Abbey Heritage Vaults; Roman Baths, 18th century Pump Room; Jane Austen Centre; Sally Lunn's house; The Museum of East Asian Art; The Building of Bath Museum; Holbourne Museum of Art and Victoria Gallery.

PRICES PER NIGHT AND WHAT'S INCLUDED
Double room £55.00-£65.00; single occupancy £45.00. Includes breakfast.

Foxes Reach

NR TINTERN, MONMOUTHSHIRE
5 STAR SELF-CATERING

Traditional stone cottage in idyllic Wye Valley hamlet

This immaculate, whitewashed stone cottage with its charming, sheltered cottage garden is situated in a rural hamlet in the idyllic Wye Valley.

Foxes Reach is just 15 minutes from the Severn Bridge at Chepstow and a mile from the spectacular ruins of Tintern Abbey, which inspired JMW Turner and William Wordsworth. The well-equipped cottage is perfect for reunions with easy access to the M4 and M5/M50.

Fully renovated and modernised, it retains many original features and contains two double bedrooms – one with a king-size bed and one with a standard double – and two single bedrooms. Other features include a very comfortable sitting room with wood-burning stove, fully-fitted kitchen, two newly-refurbished luxury bathrooms, hot tub, full central heating and double glazing and a comprehensive entertainment system with three TVs, three DVD players and a VCR.

There is exposed stone walling, flagged flooring, slate window ledges, old-style iron bedsteads and private parking. The well-stocked garden with barbeque and quality furniture is sheltered and makes a lovely place to unwind. Ω

Matter of facts

CONTACT
Fiona Wilton
T +44 (0)1600 860341
E fionawilton@
btopenworld.com
W foxesreach.com
Address Catbrook, nr Tintern, Monmouthshire
Booking Address
Ty Gwyn, Catbrook, Chepstow, Monmouthshire NP16 6ND

RATING
VisitWales 5 Star
Self-Catering

SLEEPING
Two double and two single bedrooms.

FOR THE FAMILY
Travel cot for babes in arms; children able to use normal bed and ungated stairs welcome (no toddlers). Well-behaved pets welcome.

FACILITIES
Sky TV; books; games; collection of DVDs and videos; garden draughts and darts; hot tub; safe; Internet access. Guests receive special discount at

health and beauty spa 30 minutes' drive away.

NEAREST SHOPS, PUBS AND RESTAURANTS
Village shop and Post Office about 1.5 miles; full town shopping facilities eight miles; numerous local pubs and restaurants including Real Ale, AA and Michelin Pubs/Restaurants of the Year.

OUT AND ABOUT
Tintern Abbey, castles, canoeing, horse racing, Offas Dyke long distance footpath, the Wye Valley Walk and the Tintern Trail close by; 2010 Ryder Cup venue of Celtic Manor and 20 other golf courses within easy reach; salmon fishing on the Wye and trout fishing on the Usk.

PRICES PER WEEK AND WHAT'S INCLUDED
£360.00-£749.00.
Includes bed linen, towels, oil central heating and electricity. Indulgent short breaks available in spring, autumn and Advent.

Foxgloves

WIGTON, CUMBRIA 4 STAR SELF-CATERING

Comfortable farm cottage is super base for exploring the Lake District

This spacious, well-equipped and comfortable cottage is situated in a wonderful, rural setting on Greenrigg Farm, a 275-acre working farm just 1.5 miles from the small Cumbrian market town of Wigton.

Foxgloves is a lovely, three-bedroom house with a large garden complete with plentiful garden furniture and a barbeque. The stone-built cottage adjoins the farmhouse and has been fully modernised while retaining its original character, including a spacious, well-equipped farmhouse kitchen with dining area and an Aga. Sleeping up to eight, the cottage has one family room with a double bed and two adult-sized bunk beds, one double room and one twin room. Other amenities include a bathroom with shower, an additional shower room, sitting room and utility room with a second toilet.

Foxgloves is an ideal base to explore the Lake District, Solway, Northumberland and southern Scotland, or simply the perfect place to sit back in front of an open fire or soak up the sun in the garden while enjoying the glorious views. Ω

Matter of facts

CONTACT
Edward and Jan Kerr
T +44 (0)16973 42676
E kerr_greenrigg@
hotmail.com
W foxglovescottagewigton.
co.uk
Address
Foxgloves,
Greenrigg Farm,
Westward,
Wigton,
Cumbria CA7 8AH

RATING
VisitBritain 4 Star Self-Catering; *Warwickshire Times* Award of Excellence for Quality and Service.

SLEEPING
Sleeps eight – one family room, one double room, one twin room.

FOR THE FAMILY
Children and pets welcome.

FACILITIES
Night storage heaters; Aga plus electric cooker; microwave, fridge-freezer; dishwasher, washing machine and tumble dryer, TV with Freeview, video and DVD player.

NEAREST SHOPS, PUBS AND RESTAURANTS
All within 1.5 miles. Weekly Tuesday and large Friday market in Wigton.

OUT AND ABOUT
The Lake District; Carlisle (10 miles); Penrith (18 miles); west Cumbrian coast; Hadrian's Wall (25 miles); Gretna Green and southern Scotland.

PRICES PER WEEK AND WHAT'S INCLUDED
From £225.00-£455.00. Includes linen, towels, electricity, logs and coal.

Friary Close

CHICHESTER, WEST SUSSEX
4 STAR SILVER AWARD B&B

House next to the city wall is perfect for those who enjoy a nice stroll

Sitting astride the ancient city wall in the centre of Chichester, this early 19th century Grade II Listed Georgian house is sheltered from the bustle of the city by it own large grounds and walled garden. Nevertheless, all Chichester's main attractions, such as the cathedral, theatre and Roman palace, are within easy reach.

The three twin rooms are located on the second floor with good stair access. All rooms are tastefully furnished and fully equipped with en suite baths or showers. The extensive gardens are a restful oasis and provide access to the city wall. The house has one car parking space available per room.

Breakfasts are cold buffet-style, providing an ideal foundation for a day spent exploring this fascinating corner of the south coast. Chichester Harbour, Arundel Castle and glorious Goodwood are all within easy reach and both bus and mainline stations within walking distance of Friary Close. Ω

Matter of facts

CONTACT
Brian and Majella Taylor
T +44 (0)1243 527294
E bb@friaryclose.co.uk
W friaryclose.co.uk
Address Friary Close, Friary Lane, Chichester, West Sussex PO19 1UF

RATING
VisitBritain 4 Star Silver Award B&B

SLEEPING
Three twin rooms, all with en suite bath or shower.

FACILITIES
Cold buffet breakfast.

NEAREST SHOPS, PUBS AND RESTAURANTS
Town centre shops, pubs and restaurants all within easy walking distance.

OUT AND ABOUT
Chichester Cathedral; local museums; Pallant House Gallery; Festival Theatre and Walls Walk all within walking distance. Goodwood House; Goodwood racecourse, aerodrome and motor circuit; Fishbourne Roman palace; canal walk; Weald and Downland Museum and West Dean college and gardens all within five miles. Uppark; Parham House; Petworth House; Arundel Castle and wildfowl reserve and Sussex Downs all within 15 miles.

PRICES PER NIGHT AND WHAT'S INCLUDED
£60.00-£75.00 per twin room per night; one night only £65.00 (not available weekends or bank holidays). Includes breakfast.

Gallon House

KNARESBOROUGH, NORTH YORKSHIRE
4 STAR GOLD AWARD B&B

Beautiful views of gorge greet guests as they dine on local produce

A small hotel with a touch of architectural eccentricity, Gallon House offers breathtaking views, charming accommodation and delicious food from its lofty perch above Yorkshire's beautiful Nidd Gorge (seen below).

Winner of *Yorkshire Life* magazine's 'Small but Special' accommodation award and the Yorkshire Tourist Board's White Rose for 'Best Guest Accommodation 2006', Gallon House has three stylish, individually-decorated and beautifully-furnished en suite rooms to provide guests with a home-from-home level of comfort.

Well-known Yorkshire chef Rick Hodgson places his culinary emphasis on great quality, locally-sourced food to create an eclectic combination of English classics, like beef casserole made with Black Sheep ale from the brewery at Masham, or brasserie favourites like crepe alfredo or chicken livers in a signature pastry box.

Meals are served in the charming dining room overlooking the gorge while guests can also enjoy stunning views from a pretty terrace or relax in a delightful panelled sitting room and conservatory. The hotel is tastefully decorated to complement the building's architectural style. Ω

Matter of facts

CONTACT
Rick and Sue Hodgson
T +44 (0)1423 862102
E gallon-house@
ntlworld.com
W gallon-house.co.uk
Address Gallon House Hotel,
47 Kirkgate,
Knaresborough,
North Yorkshire HG5 8BZ

RATING
VisitBritain 4 Star
Gold Award B&B

SLEEPING
Three double/twin rooms,
all en suite and with
charming views.

FOR THE FAMILY
Children welcome
(z-bed available for use
in parents' room); well-
behaved dogs welcome.

FACILITIES
All rooms have soft robes,
tea/coffee, home-made
biscuits, Harrogate spa
water, Black Sheep ale,
CD, TV and video, basket
of books, magazines,
videos and CDs; licensed
bar; private dining available
for parties of 8-14.

**NEAREST SHOPS, PUBS
AND RESTAURANTS**
All plentiful and within
a two-minute walk.

OUT AND ABOUT
Historic Knaresborough,
Harrogate, York, Leeds,
and the Yorkshire Dales.

**PRICES PER ROOM
PER NIGHT AND
WHAT'S INCLUDED**
Double/twin/single
£110.00. Includes
breakfast.

Garden Lodge

FOLKESTONE, KENT
4 STAR GUEST ACCOMMODATION

Here's one of Kent's best-kept secrets ... with guaranteed private parking

This award-winning, family-run guest house with a beautiful pool and guaranteed private parking is one of the Garden of England's best-kept secrets. With its motto 'Arrive as strangers – leave as friends', the motorcycle-friendly Garden Lodge has a comfortable lounge, beautiful dining room and extensive gardens.

An outdoor, solar-heated swimming pool is available during summer months. Guest rooms all have en suite or private shower and include a ground-floor single and a ground-floor four-poster room with an extra single bed. Tastefully-decorated, they all have TVs, DVDs, alarm clock radios, central heating, smoke detectors, electric shaver points, electric trouser presses, hairdryers, toiletries and complimentary hospitality trays. All family and double rooms have refrigerators.

A full restaurant service is available. Dishes feature fresh vegetables and fruit from Garden Lodge's own garden. Cakes, pastries, chutneys and preserves are home-made and during summer months delicious Kentish cream teas are served. Extensive gardens feature aviaries and have storage for bicycles. Alternative therapy treatments are also available. Ω

Matter of facts

CONTACT
Ron and Sue Cooper MCFA (CG)
T +44 (0)1303 893147
or +44 (0)7885 933683
E stay@garden-lodge.com
W garden-lodge.com
Address Garden Lodge, 324 Canterbury Road, Densole, Folkestone, Kent CT18 7BB

RATING
VisitBritain 4 Star Guest Accommodation

SLEEPING
One ground-floor single with en suite; one single with private shower; one five-bed family room with en suite; one twin with en suite; one en suite ground floor four-poster room with extra single bed.

FOR THE FAMILY
Well-behaved children welcome; cot and highchair available.

FACILITIES
Solar-heated pool (summer only); full restaurant service; extensive grounds with aviary; laundry service; fax, and wireless Internet for your laptop.

NEAREST SHOPS, PUBS AND RESTAURANTS
Local shops in Densole village and large selection of stores, pubs and restaurants in Folkestone and Canterbury.

OUT AND ABOUT
Romney, Hythe & Dymchurch Light Railway; Dover Castle, cruise terminal and cross-Channel services; Eurotunnel terminal; Leeds Castle; Ashford's designer outlet shopping centre; Canterbury; wildlife parks and gardens.

PRICES PER NIGHT AND WHAT'S INCLUDED
Single room from £45.00; double room from £78.00; family room from £78.00 plus £16.00 per child under 10; four poster room from £85.00 (extra single bed £20.00); cot £6.00. Includes full English breakfast.

Glebe House

CHIPPENHAM, WILTSHIRE 4 STAR B&B

Owners' philosophy is bound to make your stay a truly memorable one

The philosophy at Glebe House is simply that travelling for pleasure or business should be an exploring experience. Your hosts leave no stone unturned to make your stay enjoyable, comfortable, relaxing and memorable.

Success is evident to anyone who has stayed at this peaceful house nestling on a hillside yet within easy distance of the World Heritage sites of Avebury, Bath and Stonehenge.

Set in the tiny hamlet of Chittoe on the edge of Spye Park, Glebe House has three elegant and comfortable bedrooms, two with en suite and one with private bathroom. Dinner is delicious local food produced with care and to the highest standard using home-grown fruit and herbs from the garden. The owners are passionate believers in sustainable tourism and source local produce wherever possible. At Glebe House they make their own bread, marmalade and jams.

Whether your visit is for business or for pleasure, you can be sure Glebe House will do everything to make it memorable. Ω

Matter of facts

CONTACT
Ginny Scrope
T +44 (0)1380 850864
E gscrope@aol.com
W glebehouse-chittoe.co.uk
Address Glebe House, Chittoe, Chippenham, Wiltshire SN15 2EL

RATING
VisitBritain 4 star B&B

SLEEPING
Three rooms comprising one double with en suite, one twin with en suite and one twin with private bathroom.

FOR THE FAMILY
Children welcome; well-behaved dogs welcome.

FACILITIES
Dining room; gardens; wireless broadband Internet.

NEAREST SHOPS, PUBS AND RESTAURANTS
Many within three-six miles of Glebe House.

OUT AND ABOUT
Avebury, Silbury Hill and West Kennet in the World Heritage site; Bath; Castle Coombe; the White Horse at Cherhill; Corsham; Devizes; Kennet and Avon Canal; Lacock Abbey and National Trust village; Marlborough; Glastonbury, Salisbury; Stonehenge and Wells; an extensive network of walks and cycle ways; some of the most impressive public gardens in the UK.

PRICES PER PERSON PER NIGHT AND WHAT'S INCLUDED
£35.00-£45.00. Includes breakfast. Dinner £20.00-£25.00 per person.

Godshill Park Farmhouse

Farm has all the organic produce, walks and views visitors expect

Situated near the picturesque village of Godshill on the Isle of Wight, this working organic farm in an Area of Outstanding Natural Beauty is perfectly located for touring the island's many towns and villages.

There are lovely walks on the farm which is home to Aberdeen Angus cattle, North Country mule sheep, rare pedigree Castlemilk Moorit sheep, llamas, chickens, dogs, ponies and horses. There are just two beautifully-appointed, en suite guest rooms, one with a four-poster bed, and both with bath, shower, TV, telephone, Internet access and countryside views.

Breakfast is prepared from local and organic produce and includes free-range bacon and sausages produced on a neighbouring farm, free-range eggs, organic milk and butter and home-made preserves using the farm's own fruit and locally-pressed apple juice together with a selection of other pure fruit juices. The farm's baronial hall with its open log fireplace is available exclusively to guests. Ω

Matter of facts

CONTACT
Kathy Domaille
T +44 (0)1983 840781
E info@
godshillparkfarm.uk.com
W godshillparkfarm.uk.com
Address Godshill Park
Farm, Godshill,
Isle of Wight PO38 3JF

RATING
AA 5 Star Self-Catering;
AA Breakfast Award.

SLEEPING
Two doubles, both en suite.

FACILITIES
Wildlife haven with woodlands containing ancient woodland plants, red squirrels, badgers, foxes, owls and buzzards. Ponds are home to swans, kingfishers, various geese, ducks, moorhens and herons. Organic food; baronial hall.

NEAREST SHOPS, PUBS AND RESTAURANTS
Organic shop, Post Office and gift shops in village;
comprehensive shopping in county town of Newport, 15 minutes' drive away. The Essex, a two AA Rosette restaurant, is 10 minutes' walk, as are two village pubs.

OUT AND ABOUT
Godshill is renowned for its pretty thatched cottages, 14th century church and tea gardens, model village, old smithy and a small natural history museum. Sandy beaches of Shanklin and Ventnor are a seven minute drive away; Osborne House 25 minutes' drive.

PRICES PER NIGHT AND WHAT'S INCLUDED
Low season (November-Easter) £80.00 for two people; high season (Easter-October) £99.00 for two. Includes breakfast. Winter promotion – two nights' B&B for two plus dinner at the Essex Wednesday, Thursday or Friday evening, £200.00.

Grand Hotel

KENILWORTH, WARWICKSHIRE
HOTEL AWAITING GRADING

Nice touches in the decor and cuisine at ideal spot to entertain

The Grand Hotel is a luxurious, boutique townhouse hotel with outstanding bedrooms and fabulous food. The Coliseum Restaurant offers an excellent European menu with local produce and the finest ingredients. It is ideal for functions, events, weddings and conferences for up to 100.

Guest accommodation ranges from club bedrooms with opulent décor and design through to the more modern, executive rooms, all with large and extravagant en suite bathrooms. In-room facilities also include plasma TV with Sky; complimentary fruit, tea, coffee and shoeshine; luxury toiletries; DVD/CD player and music library; bathrobe and slippers; trouser press; ironing board; hairdryer and Internet access.

The Grand's landscaped garden and fountain is perfect for weddings and summer parties and, while staying at the hotel, you can enjoy the full range of holistic and beauty treatments at Aromatics. Afterwards, relax with a drink in the hugely impressive, first floor residents' conservatory, or entertain guests at the hotel's Coliseum Restaurant or its nearby sister restaurants, Raffles and Coconut Lagoon. Ω

Matter of facts

CONTACT
Selva Muthalagappan
T +44 (0)1926 863100
E reservations@
grandhotelkenilworth.com
W grandhotelkenilworth.
com
Address Grand Hotel,
95 Warwick Road,
Kenilworth,
Warwickshire CV8 1HP

RATING
Awaiting grading

SLEEPING
Club bedrooms with king-size beds; executive bedrooms with double or twin beds.

FOR THE FAMILY
Family rooms; cots provided; children's pack with DVD.

FACILITIES
Cromwell's Bar; Coliseum Restaurant; lounge menu; 24-hour room service; wedding coordinator.

NEAREST SHOPS, PUBS AND RESTAURANTS
Located in town centre, the Grand is a few minutes' walk from supermarkets and high street shops. There is a large selection of pubs and restaurants on the same road, including the Grand's sister restaurants, Raffles and Coconut Lagoon.

OUT AND ABOUT
Warwick and Kenilworth castles; Shakespeare houses at Stratford-upon-Avon; Cadbury World; Heritage Motor Museum.

PRICES PER ROOM PER NIGHT AND WHAT'S INCLUDED
Executive bedrooms £59.00-£80.00; club bedrooms £79.00-£110.00. Weekend leisure offer, three nights for the price of two. Includes full English breakfast, service and VAT.

The Grange

SHANKLIN, ISLE OF WIGHT
4 STAR GUEST ACCOMMODATION

Invigorate the body and the mind at this holistic haven

This beautiful, Georgian house, situated in Shanklin's charming Old Village, is the perfect retreat. An offshoot of Skyros, the pioneering holistic holiday company, the Grange's original features, such as the ornate, carved fireplace in the lounge, are complemented by a collection of paintings and sculptures.

The high-ceilinged dining room leads into the bar area with access to an outdoor terrace. The stunning garden includes a log cabin housing a sauna and a treatment room for a variety of health and beauty therapies. In addition, you can book one-to-one tuition in various subjects, including personal fitness training, yoga, T'ai Chi, Alexander Technique, Creative Writing and Life Coaching.

Most of the 17 recently-refurbished double and twin bedrooms have views of the sea or downs. All have newly-installed power showers and luxury toiletries.

The Grange's buffet-style meals are prepared with the freshest ingredients – organic where possible – with fruits and vegetables, natural yoghurts and cheese, fresh fish and meat with vegetarian options. Ω

Matter of facts

CONTACT
Jenni Canakis
T +44 (0)1983 867644
E jenni@
thegrangebythesea.com
W thegrangebythesea.com
Address The Grange,
9 Eastcliff Road, Shanklin,
Isle of Wight PO37 6AA

RATING
AA 4 Star Guest
Accommodation

SLEEPING
17 double/twin rooms,
including 13 with en suite
and three with adjoining
private bathrooms.

FOR THE FAMILY
Cots available; child-
minding can be arranged.

FACILITIES
Sauna, health and beauty
treatments, including
aromatherapy, shiatsu
massage and holistic
facials; dining room; lounge;
licensed bar; picturesque
grounds; wireless Internet.

**NEAREST SHOPS, LOCAL
PUBS, RESTAURANTS**
Two-minute walk to shops
in the Old Village and in
Shanklin High Street where
there are also many varied
pubs and restaurants.

OUT AND ABOUT
Shanklin Chine; Brading
Roman villa; Sandown
Tiger Sanctuary. Long,
sandy beaches offer a great
variety of water sports, and
five hundred miles of
footpaths make the island
a walker's paradise. For
cyclists, there are a myriad
of designated routes,
bridleways and spectacular
coastal tracks.

**PRICES AND
WHAT'S INCLUDED**
Low season £80.00 per
person for two nights with
breakfast based on two
sharing. High £96.00 per
person for two nights' half
board based on two sharing.
£25.00 supplement for
single occupancy of
double/twin room. Weekend
courses £60.00; one-week
courses £140.00.

The Grange Hotel

NEWARK, NOTTINGHAMSHIRE
3 STAR SILVER AWARD HOTEL

Secret garden and much more to delight at elegant and homely hotel

Elegant furnishings, fine dining and an idyllic secret garden set apart this vibrant hotel with its original Victorian façade and interior features.

Located in a quiet conservation area a short walk from the centre of this historic market town, it contains an absorbing collection of pictures, silverware and pottery which create a homely atmosphere.

Nineteen en suite bedrooms, all with their own unique character, are equipped for both leisure and business travellers. Cutlers, the elegant, high-ceilinged, 40-seater restaurant, named after the antique cutlery that adorns the walls, has an impressive, frequently-changing à la carte menu. Similarly, Potters, the hotel bar, takes its name from the framed illustrations of antique breakfast, dinner and bathroom potters' sets which decorate its walls.

Tucked away at the back of the three-storey property is a tranquil, Victorian landscaped garden with immaculate lawns, pathways, ornaments and a fountain. A floodlit, alfresco dining area is located next to the bar. Ω

Matter of facts

CONTACT
Sandra Carr
T +44 (0)1636 703399
E info@
grangenewark.co.uk
W grangenewark.co.uk
Address The Grange Hotel,
73 London Road, Newark,
Nottinghamshire
NG24 1RZ

RATING
VisitBritain 3 Star
Silver Award Hotel

SLEEPING
19 en suite bedrooms,
including executive and
four-poster rooms.

FACILITIES
Cutler's Restaurant; all
rooms have TV, radio/
alarm, direct-dial telephone,
hairdryer, iron and ironing
board, trouser press, tea
and coffee-making facilities,
in-room safe and wireless
Internet access.

NEAREST SHOPS, PUBS AND RESTAURANTS
Many unique shops in the centre of this market town a 10-minute walk away; local restaurants and pubs offer a wide choice of international cuisine.

OUT AND ABOUT
Palace Theatre; Newark Castle; museum; marina; riverside walks; Sherwood Forest; antique fairs (Europe's largest antiques and collectors' fair is held every other month).

PRICES PER NIGHT AND WHAT'S INCLUDED
Single room £75.00-£100.00; double/twin room £100.00-£150.00. Includes breakfast and VAT. Special promotion – two nights Friday, Saturday and Sunday, dinner, B&B £140.00 per person based on two sharing.

Green Hotel

KINROSS, PERTHSHIRE 4 STAR HOTEL

If a mixture of sport, comfort and good food appeals, look no further

One of Scotland's independently-owned country hotels, the Green began life as an 18th century coaching inn on the main route north from Edinburgh.

An ideal touring base for family holidays or short breaks, the Green's extensive leisure facilities include two 18-hole golf courses, two all-weather tennis courts, a swimming pool and sauna, a well-equipped fitness area, squash court, petanque, croquet, putting lawns, trout fishing on Loch Leven and even a curling rink which can be used from September to April.

Dine in style in the award-winning Basil's Restaurant, sample the more traditional fare served in Jock's Bar, enjoy a pre-dinner drink in the cocktail bar or relax with afternoon tea in the Kinross Lounge. Whatever your preference, you will discover just why the Green has earned a reputation for warm hospitality and excellent service.

Its 46 spacious, en suite bedrooms have been designed with comfort in mind and include TV with some Sky channels, hospitality tray, trouser press, direct-dial telephone, hairdryer and Internet access. Ω

Matter of facts

CONTACT
Reservations
T +44 (0)1577 863467
E reservations@
green-hotel.com
W green-hotel.com
Address The Green Hotel,
2 The Muirs, Kinross,
Perthshire KY13 8AS

RATING
VisitScotland
4 Star Hotel

SLEEPING
46 bedrooms including
double,twin and family
accommodation.

FOR THE FAMILY
Family rooms available;
children's menus in both
restaurants.

FACILITIES
Fine dining at Basil's
Restaurant (one AA rosette),
Scottish and international
cuisine using local produce;
Jock's Bar serving meals
and snacks all day in
traditional pub atmosphere;
two 18-hole golf courses;
leisure club with pool,
sauna, solarium, fitness
area; curling rink.

**NEAREST SHOPS, PUBS
AND RESTAURANTS**
Shop at the Green –
on-premises retail outlet
selling designer fashion,
gifts and cards

OUT AND ABOUT
Loch Leven Castle; Kinross
House Gardens; Scottish
Gliding Centre; Scone
Palace; Glamis Castle.
St Andrews, Edinburgh and
Perth within easy reach.

**PRICES PER PERSON
PER NIGHT AND
WHAT'S INCLUDED**
B&B £95.00; dinner, B&B
£125.00; seasonal offers
from £75.00 for dinner,
bed and full Scottish
breakfast (minimum stay
two nights).

Green Lawns Hotel

Seven Britain in Bloom prizes plus award-winning restaurant

Set in award-winning, sub-tropical gardens, the privately-owned Green Lawns Hotel has been a Britain in Bloom winner for seven years running and offers equally elegant accommodation and a comprehensive range of facilities.

The hotel's pride in its cultural and historical heritage is reflected in its elegant range of luxury guest rooms, classic cuisine and leisure amenities. Located between the main beaches and Falmouth town centre, the chateau-style hotel is an ideal base for touring Cornwall and blends both traditional and modern values in a warm, friendly and cosy atmosphere, catering for individual guests, large parties, weddings and conferences with equal emphasis.

Unwind at the end of the day in the indoor pool, Jacuzzi, sauna and solarium, or work up an appetite in the gym before dining in the award-winning Garras Restaurant, which uses the finest local produce. And for those special occasions, why not treat yourself to the luxury of a four-poster and double Jacuzzi overlooking Falmouth Bay? Ω

Matter of facts

CONTACT
Sanchia Gale
T +44 (0)1326 312734
E info@
greenlawnshotel.com
W greenlawnshotel.com
Address Green Lawns Hotel,
Western Terrace, Falmouth,
Cornwall TR11 4QJ

RATING
VisitBritain 3 Star
Silver Award Hotel

SLEEPING
39 bedrooms, all
en suite.

FOR THE FAMILY
Paddling pool; cots;
children's teatime menu.

FACILITIES
Award-winning Garras
Restaurant; indoor
swimming pool; Jacuzzi;
sauna; solarium; mini-
gym; tennis and squash.

**NEAREST SHOPS, PUBS
AND RESTAURANTS**
Falmouth's main shopping
centre is a 10-minute walk.

OUT AND ABOUT
Falmouth Maritime Museum;
Eden Project; Pendennis
Castle; Trebah Gardens;
Trelissick Gardens; Helford
River; Falmouth Docks.

**PRICES PER NIGHT AND
WHAT'S INCLUDED**
B&B £60.00-£115.00
single; £110.00-£180.00
double. Dinner, B&B
£60.00-£140.00 per
person. Autumn/winter
two-day breaks from
£35.00 per person with
breakfast, or from £50.00
per person with breakfast
and dinner. Spring two-day
breaks from £45.00 per
person with breakfast, or
from £60.00 per person
with breakfast and dinner.

Grendon
GUEST HOUSE

BUXTON, DERBYSHIRE
5 STAR GOLD AWARD GUEST HOUSE

Town's highest graded B&B knows how to make its guests welcome

Buxton's highest graded guest accommodation, this five star B&B offers the very best of those elements that make for a memorable visit, including fine, spacious, en suite double bed/sitting rooms with an abundance of homely touches and AA award-winning breakfasts and dinners.

Grendon is a detached house built in 1913 for a wealthy cotton mill entrepreneur and is set in one acre overlooking the Cavendish golf course with distant views to the Peak District hills.

The lovely en suite double bedrooms are very spacious, have comfortable armchairs or a settee, antique furnishings and large, uncluttered windows through which to enjoy natural light and rural views and are lavishly equipped with white fluffy bath sheets and Gilchrist & Soames toiletries. All rooms have tea and coffee-making facilities, TVs and hairdryers and some have DVDs.

The comprehensive breakfast choice embraces home-produced muesli, home-made fruit compotes, full English using local best back bacon and sausages, scrambled eggs and smoked salmon, omelets, pancakes and home-baked bread. Ω

Matter of facts

CONTACT
Hilary Parker
T +44 (0)1298 78831
E grendonguesthouse@ hotmail.com
W grendonguesthouse.co.uk
Address
Grendon Guest House, Bishops Lane, Buxton, Derbyshire SK17 6UN

RATING
VisitBritain 5 Star Gold Award Guest House

SLEEPING
Five single and double en suite rooms, including the Duchess four-poster suite.

FOR THE FAMILY
No children or pets.

FACILITIES
Guest lounge; garden; laundry service; wireless broadband Internet.

NEAREST SHOPS, PUBS AND RESTAURANTS
Shops plus 25 or more pubs and restaurants within one mile.

OUT AND ABOUT
Buxton Opera House; Pavilion Gardens; Go Ape high wire forest adventure at Poole's Cavern; Chatsworth House; Haddon, Eyam, Hardwick Hall and Kedleston halls; Derby University Dome and Spa.

PRICES PER NIGHT AND WHAT'S INCLUDED
Double rooms from £65.00; four-poster suite from £78.00, or as a triple with an additional single room from £100.00; single en suite room from £35.00. Includes breakfast.

Grimblethorpe Hall
COUNTRY COTTAGES

NR LOUTH, LINCOLNSHIRE 5 STAR SELF-CATERING

Rural links with a modern touch add to the charm of these cottages

These three country cottages in the grounds of 16th century Grimblethorpe Hall in the beautiful Lincolnshire Wolds are all converted, Listed buildings with oak beams, stonework and oak and flagstone flooring.

The spacious, four-person Anvil Cottage once contained the anvil and forge which the blacksmith used when shoeing the working horses on the farm. The cottage has quality furnishings and decor with all up-to-date appliances. It consists of two spacious bedrooms – one king-size double and one with two single beds – lounge, kitchen/dining area, bathroom and shower room, private garden, patio and gazebo.

The lovely 16th century, two-person Shepherd's cottage was for centuries the cottage in which the farm's shepherd stayed during lambing time. It has a very spacious king-size double bedroom, lounge, kitchen/dining area and en suite bathroom.

The newly-refurbished, four-person Barn consists of a galley area, lounge, kitchen, dining area and two en suite double/twin bedrooms. Guests can enjoy strolling around the surrounding grounds, which include a tranquil lake and summerhouse. Ω

Matter of facts

CONTACT
Annie Codling
T +44 (0)1507 313671
E enquiries@
grimblethorpehall.co.uk
W grimblethorpehall.co.uk
Address
Grimblethorpe Hall
Country Cottages,
nr Louth,
Lincolnshire
LN11 0RB

RATING
VisitBritain 5 Star
Self-Catering

SLEEPING
Anvil and Barn each
sleep four; Shepherd's
sleeps two.

FOR THE FAMILY
Large grounds in which
children can play. Pets by
prior arrangement.

FACILITIES
All have cooker, microwave,
fridge-freezer, washing
machine and dryer,
dishwasher, central heating,
TV, DVD and garaging.

**NEAREST SHOPS, LOCAL
PUBS, RESTAURANTS**
Two shops 2.5 miles away;
pubs and restaurants in
nearby Louth, Tealby and
Wragby.

OUT AND ABOUT
Market Rasen Racecourse;
walking; biking; horse
riding; fishing.

**PRICES PER WEEK
AND WHAT'S INCLUDED**
Shepherd's £160.00-
£380.00; Anvil £210.00-
£490.00; Barn £220.00-
£514.00. Includes all bed
linen, towels and electricity.

Groomes
COUNTRY HOUSE

Listed house in big grounds is just the place for that family function

Groomes is an exclusive, 16th century, Grade II Listed country house set in 185 acres of glorious countryside on the Surrey/Hampshire border. Renovated and refurbished in 2006 to the highest standards throughout, Groomes provides accommodation and family-focused functions such as wedding receptions, reunions, parties, breakfasts, lunches, dinners and romantic weekend breaks.

Accommodation exudes comfort and quality creating, as far as possible, an anti-allergenic environment featuring huge, luxurious rooms furnished to a high standard with en suite bathrooms, big comfy beds, the latest high-definition LCD TVs, huge fluffy towels and Molton Brown toiletries. Fantastic views come as standard in all rooms.

The Aga-equipped kitchen uses the finest locally-produced and, where possible, organic ingredients. Evening meals are unlike you will find on any menu but if you find the choice too challenging tell chef what you don't like and try a suitably seasonal surprise. Fantastic! Ω

Matter of facts

CONTACT
Peter Dale
T +44 (0)1420 489858
or +44 (0)7970 054767
E pete.groomes@
hotmail.co.uk
W groomes.co.uk
Address
Groomes Country House,
Frith End,
Bordon,
Hampshire GU35 0QR

RATING
VisitBritain 5 Star
Gold Award Guest
Accommodation

SLEEPING
Six rooms, all with en suite bathrooms and most large enough to sleep a family of four comfortably. One ground-floor disabled room with no steps from car park.

FACILITIES
Licensed restaurant; CD library and games room;

LCD TVs with DVD/CD players; hot drinks facilities in room.

NEAREST SHOPS, PUBS AND RESTAURANTS
Shopping centres nearby in Farnham, Petersfield, Haslemere, Aldershot, Camberley and Guildford; many good local pubs and restaurants to suit all tastes.

OUT AND ABOUT
Birdworld; Watercress railway line; Butser Farm; Ascot Racecourse; Cowdray Park; Goodwood; hot-air ballooning; many good walks.

PRICES PER NIGHT AND WHAT'S INCLUDED
From £75.00 single occupancy Monday-Thursday to £150.00 double occupancy in a suite at weekends. Includes breakfast and VAT.

Halfway Bridge Inn

LODSWORTH, NR PETWORTH, WEST SUSSEX
5 STAR GOLD AWARD INN

Contemporary but classic, this inn harks back to its 17thC roots

This 17th century, brick and flint coaching inn has been converted to a classic yet contemporary country retreat, successfully blending the traditional with the modern in five star luxury.

Situated in beautiful countryside, the inn features six guest bedrooms in recently-converted, beamed Sussex barns which retain a rustic feel within their contemporary styling. Bathrooms are fitted with power showers, baths and a selection of luxurious toiletries while all bedrooms have large, flatscreen TVs, DVD and CD players and even Sony PlayStations.

The restaurant and bar areas have a modern ambiance, but open fireplaces remind diners of the inn's 17th century roots. Numerous, split-level dining areas create an intimate and casual atmosphere in which local produce is served wherever possible, along with fresh fish, meat and vegetables from the London markets. There is a comprehensive wine list to suit even the most discerning of palates and a range of Sussex ales to slake the fiercest of thirsts. Ω

Matter of facts

CONTACT
Paul Carter
T +44 (0)1798 861281
E enquiries@
halfwaybridge.co.uk
W halfwaybridge.co.uk
Address
Halfway Bridge Inn,
Halfway Bridge,
Lodsworth,
nr Petworth,
West Sussex GU28 9BP

RATING
VisitBritain 5 Star
Gold Award Inn

SLEEPING
Six rooms comprising two
doubles and four suites.

FOR THE FAMILY
Highchairs available; Sony
PlayStations.

FACILITIES
Garden and patio
areas; private car park;
complimentary DVD
library.

**NEAREST SHOPS, PUBS
AND RESTAURANTS**
Comprehensive facilities in
Petworth (including
antiques), Midhurst and
Chichester, all about a
20-minute drive.

OUT AND ABOUT
Petworth House and Park;
Cowdray Park Polo and
Golf Club; Goodwood;
countryside walks.

**PRICES PER NIGHT AND
WHAT'S INCLUDED**
Double rooms £110.00-
£120.00; suites £130.00-
£160.00. Includes full
English breakfast,
complimentary newspaper
and VAT. Special offers –
from end October to end
February, two nights for the
price of one midweek,
three nights for the price of
two at weekends (excluding
Christmas/New Year); must
dine in the restaurant on at
least one offer night.

Halsteads Barn

NR SETTLE, NORTH YORKSHIRE 4 STAR SILVER AWARD B&B

An oasis of luxury and tranquillity in spectacular surroundings

Situated within the Forest of Bowland, three miles from the Yorkshire Dales National Park and 30 minutes from the Lake District, Halsteads Barn offers a relaxing and peaceful retreat in some of England's most spectacular countryside.

Relax in the outdoor hot tub with uninterrupted views of the Three Peaks with only the sound of the nearby stream and multitude of birds that reside upon the moor on which the house nestles.

This is a barn conversion with character and style. While retaining a lot of the original features, the house provides all the modern facilities expected in three individually-designed rooms.

Guest facilities include a large lounge with log-burning stove, dining room, snug and minstrels' gallery. Fine food prepared on the Aga and wherever possible using produce from the local farms, along with an impressive wine list, means you can spend the maximum amount of time relaxing in the peace and tranquillity of this country residence. Ω

Matter of facts

CONTACT
Jon Brook
T +44 (0)1524 262641
E info@ halsteadsbarn.co.uk
W halsteadsbarn.co.uk
Address Halsteads Barn, Mewith, High Bentham, nr Lancaster, North Yorkshire LA2 7AR

RATING
VisitBritain 4 Star Silver Award B&B

SLEEPING
Three double bedrooms, all en suite.

FACILITIES
In-room DVD player, tea tray, bathrobes, hairdryer and radio/alarm; outdoor hot tub; spectacular walks from the property.

NEAREST SHOPS, PUBS AND RESTAURANTS
Limited number of shops, pubs and restaurants three miles away.

OUT AND ABOUT
Yorkshire Dales; Lake District; caves and waterfalls.

PRICES PER NIGHT AND WHAT'S INCLUDED
B&B £35.00-£38.00 per person; four or more nights £30.00-£33.00. Evening meal £16.00-£20.00 per person. Christmas Day/New Year's Eve £95.00 per person including four-course evening meal with one bottle of champagne per couple.

The Hampshire Court

Tennis courts are just part of wide range of leisure facilities on offer

If you are seeking leisure facilities that are second to none coupled with luxury accommodation, then The Hampshire Court is the hotel for you! Its magnificent leisure facilities include five indoor and four outdoor French soft-clay tennis courts, an adults-only pool, a 'fun' pool for all ages, exercise studios offering a wide range of classes and a fully equipped state-of-the-art gymnasium. There are also fabulous spa rooms for massage, body and holistic treatments.

Imaginative, fresh food is served in the Restaurant and Terrace Brasserie, along with a good selection of wines. Combined with friendly, efficient service in an intimate atmosphere, the hotel provides the perfect recipe for a relaxing meal. The stylish brasserie also serves a good selection of refreshments and food throughout the day.

Comfort and style run throughout from the bedrooms to the lounge areas. Many of the 90 bedrooms have private balconies and all have private bathrooms and are equipped with TV with selected Sky channels, radio, direct-dial telephone, broadband Internet, trouser press hospitality tray and hairdryer. Ω

Matter of facts

CONTACT
Reception
T +44 (0)1256 319700
E hampshirereservations@qhotels.co.uk
W qhotels.co.uk
Address The Hampshire Court, Centre Drive, Great Binfields Road, Chineham, Basingstoke, Hampshire RG24 8FY

RATING
VisitBritain 4 Star Silver Award Hotel

SLEEPING
57 double rooms, 29 twin rooms, one family room and three suites, all en suite.

FOR THE FAMILY
Baby-sitting service available; children aged 16 and under sharing parents' accommodation are charged only for meals taken and those sharing with one adult or in separate rooms are charged at 50% of the adult rate.

FACILITIES
AA rosette-awarded restaurant; extensive spa and leisure facilities with treatment rooms; two swimming pools; five indoor and four outdoor tennis courts.

NEAREST SHOPS, PUBS AND RESTAURANTS
Chineham Shopping Centre and Festival Place.

OUT AND ABOUT
Legoland, Windsor; Jane Austen's House, Alton; The Vyne, Basingstoke; Marwell Zoo, Winchester; The Watercress Line steam railway, Alresford; Beaulieu; Winchester Cathedral; Milestones, Hampshire's living history museum in Basingstoke.

PRICES PER NIGHT AND WHAT'S INCLUDED
B&B – single £69.50-£144.50; double £90.00-£221.00.

Harbour Heights

DARTMOUTH, DEVON 4 STAR SELF-CATERING

Views from this upside-down house are just spectacular

An upside-down house high above the River Dart with a 'wow' factor, Harbour Heights has five bedrooms with breathtaking 180-degree views along the river to the sea and one bedroom looking out on to woodland.

Just a five-minute walk from its idyllic location to the waterfront and town centre, Harbour Heights is a luxurious and spacious house with superb and flexible accommodation for up to 14-16 people or extreme luxury for just two. This warm and welcoming home has three contemporary-style floors which include a large, open-plan living space with kitchen and dining areas and two bedrooms on the top level and a magnificent, luxury suite with a conservatory leading into the garden and two bedrooms on the lower or middle floor. The lower ground floor has a bedroom which leads onto a patio.

Outside there is a large, mature, terraced garden and patio with sunbeds and dining furniture and two parking places on the front forecourt along with street parking. Ω

Matter of facts

CONTACT
Reservations
T +44 (0)7815 824821
or +44 (0)1392 428154
E harbourheights@aol.com
W dartmouthholiday.co.uk

RATING
VisitBritain 4 Star Self-Catering.

SLEEPING
Six bedrooms (five separate and one inter-connected) sleep up to 16.

FOR THE FAMILY
People with disabilities welcome; cot; highchair; toys; dog-friendly.

FACILITIES
Main dining table seats 10; breakfast bar and balcony for al fresco dining; two TVs/DVD players.

NEAREST SHOPS, PUBS AND RESTAURANTS
Dartmouth, a five-minute walk away, is renowned for its unique quality shops, stylish galleries, old inns and a fantastic choice of restaurants, bistros and cafes, many serving local organic produce.

OUT AND ABOUT
Dartmouth's first class harbour and river make it an excellent sailing, boating and fishing centre; award-winning Blackpool Sands, a centre for wind surfing and swimming; Dartmouth Golf and Country Club; Dart Marina's health spas; Dartmouth Leisure Centre; the Flavel arts and entertainment centre; Woodlands Leisure Park; Paignton Railway; Shapham Vineyard and Creamery; Dartington Cider Press; Dartmoor National Park.

PRICES PER WEEK AND WHAT'S INCLUDED
£695.00-£2,995.00. Weekend and short breaks available plus reductions for two people, especially in low- and mid-season. Includes gas, electricity, bedding and tea towels. Personal towels are not provided.

Hayden's

RYE, EAST SUSSEX 5 STAR B&B

Owners put great store in running luxury B&B on eco-friendly lines

Situated in the centre of the ancient Cinque Port of Rye, Hayden's is a small, luxurious B&B ideally placed for visitors to stroll to pubs, restaurants, the Ypres Tower, Lamb House and the many other attractions in this fascinating town.

Formerly known as Cheyne House, Hayden's is a three-storey, 18th century building with a south-facing terrace garden. It is run by Richard and Kate Hayden through applying a set of eco-friendly principles in order to reduce the impact the business has on the environment. Richard and Kate use Fairtrade products because they believe Fairtrade gives farmers in the developing world a better deal, and organic foods wherever possible because, in their words, they are healthier and better for the environment.

There are two suites available for guests. The Chocolate Room, named after the leather furniture it contains, has a king-size bed; small lounge area; TV; Fairtrade or organic teas, freshly-ground coffee and hot chocolate; fresh milk; a hairdryer and bathrobes. The spacious, en suite shower room contains complimentary shampoos, conditioners

and moisturisers made by Aveda, a company that sources plant-based ingredients from environmentally-conscious suppliers.

The slightly smaller Red Room at the rear of the house has superb views over Romney Marsh and contains a double bed, flatscreen LCD TV, an en suite bath and shower plus the same range of drinks and toiletries found in the Chocolate Room.

Hayden's modern dining room and coffee shop on the ground floor serves a traditional English breakfast menu, light snacks and lunches, plus evening meals on Fridays and Saturdays, prepared from mostly organic and locally-sourced food, including its meat, bread, eggs, fruit juices and milk. There are 11 tables inside the restaurant and five on the rear terrace overlooking Romney Marsh.

Hayden's also uses Ecover plant-based ecological detergents and cleansing agents when cleaning rooms and in the home laundry. Ecover also supply the hand soap and shower gel provided in the rooms. All glass and plastic bottles generated in the coffee shop and all cardboard used by the business are recycled. Ω

Matter of facts

CONTACT
Richard Hayden
T +44 (0)1797 224501
or 223813
E haydens_in_rye@mac.com
W haydensinrye.co.uk
Address Hayden's,
108 High Street,
Rye, East Sussex TN31 7JE

RATING
VisitBritain 5 Star B&B

SLEEPING
One king-size and one double suite, both en suite.

FACILITIES
Coffee shop; street parking and private parking five minutes' walk away; ironing facilities on request.

NEAREST SHOPS, PUBS AND RESTAURANTS
All high street amenities in the immediate area.

OUT AND ABOUT
Rye and its attractions, including Ypres Tower and Lamb House; nearby Camber Sands and Romney Marsh; walking; cycling; steam engines across Romney Marsh.

PRICES PER ROOM PER NIGHT AND WHAT'S INCLUDED
£100.00, including two breakfasts, on Fridays and Saturdays, on Sundays before bank holidays and from 24 December to 2 January; £80.00, including two breakfasts, Sundays to Thursdays.

Heatherly Cottage

NR CORSHAM, WILTSHIRE 4 STAR B&B

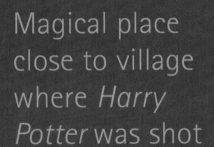

Magical place close to village where *Harry Potter* was shot

Built in the 17th century, Heatherly Cottage is situated in a quiet country lane about nine miles from Bath and close to the National Trust village of Lacock where several films, including scenes from *Harry Potter*, have been shot.

The cottage has two acres of garden with beautiful views and plenty of parking space. Guests' accommodation is in a separate wing of the house with its own front door and staircase.

The spacious, twin-bedded, ground-floor Penguin room has a beamed ceiling and fireplace and can be made up as a king-size double. There are two first-floor doubles -- the Gate room with queen-size bed and a separate sitting area, and the Lemon room with a standard double bed. All have en suite facilities.

Full English breakfast, prepared with local produce where possible and free-range eggs from the cottage's own hens, is served along with home-made jams and preserves in an attractive, dual-aspect dining room, overlooking the garden. Continental breakfasts with hot croissants and vegetarian breakfasts are also available. Ω

Matter of facts

CONTACT
Jenny Daniel
T +44 (0)1249 701402
E pandj@
heatherly.plus.com
W heatherlycottage.co.uk
Address Heatherly Cottage,
Ladbrook Lane, Gastard,
nr Corsham, Wiltshire
SN13 9PE

RATING
VisitBritain 4 Star
Gold Award B&B

SLEEPING
One ground-floor room
with twin/king-size bed;
two first-floor rooms, one
with queen-size and one
with standard double bed.
All rooms en suite.

FOR THE FAMILY
No children under the age
of 10.

FACILITIES
All rooms have TV,
clock/radio, tea/coffee,
mini-fridge, hairdryer, iron
and ironing board, central
heating and fans during
hot weather.

**NEAREST SHOPS, PUBS
AND RESTAURANTS**
Shops in Corsham (one
mile), Chippenham (four)
and Bath (nine). Many
pubs and restaurants
nearby, including one
within walking distance.

OUT AND ABOUT
National Trust's Lacock
Village; Stonehenge;
Avebury Rings; Longleat
House and Safari Park;
Bath; Castle Combe; Fleet
Air Arm Museum; Bowood
House and gardens; many
National Trust properties.

**PRICES PER NIGHT
AND WHAT'S INCLUDED**
Double/twin room from
£66.00; for single rate
please contact the B&B.
Includes breakfast.

Hell Bay

ISLES OF SCILLY
3 STAR GOLD AWARD HOTEL

Visit the island where you can go to Hell and enjoy a heavenly time

The ultimate escape on an island with almost no roads and even fewer cars, Hell Bay enjoys a private and secluded, yet far from remote, location overlooking the crystal clear waters of the Atlantic which are ideal for swimming and snorkelling.

Stylish but not too precious, the hotel has 25 suites, all beautifully furnished in Lloyd Loom with Designers' Guild fabrics. Most have dazzling sea views and private balconies or patios and each has a bedroom with sitting room and en suite. Leisure facilities include an outdoor heated pool, sauna and spa bath, gym, games room, par-three golf, boules and croquet.

Classical but up-to-date dishes are prepared using dawn-fresh crab, lobster and fish hand-picked from the local boats. Fine meats, fruit and vegetables are brought in daily. In the evening you can dine al fresco warmed by a patio heater, or indoors with a backdrop of breathtaking, uninterrupted views across the Great Pool. There is a daily changing table d'hôte menu and a selection of carefully chosen wines. Ω

Matter of facts

CONTACT
Reception
T +44 (0)1720 422947
E contactus@hellbay.co.uk
W hellbay.co.uk
Address Hell Bay,
Bryher, Isles of Scilly,
Cornwall TR23 0PR

RATING
VisitBritain 3 Star
Gold Award Hotel

SLEEPING
25 suites, all en suite.

FOR THE FAMILY
Outdoor play area; games
room; children's high teas.

FACILITIES
Bar and Restaurant menu;
outdoor heated pool;
sauna and spa bath, gym,
games room, par-three
golf, boules and croquet.

**NEAREST SHOPS, PUBS
AND RESTAURANTS**
On-site gift shop; Fraggle
Rock, Bryher or the New
Inn, Tresco.

OUT AND ABOUT
There are a variety of boat
trips with excursions
round the islands, fishing
and diving expeditions,
inter-island hops and
evening gig races. Tresco
Abbey Garden is only a
stone's throw away. The
hotel can organise
watersports and jet boat
rides to explore the myriad
of rocky coves and
uninhabited islets.

**PRICES PER NIGHT
AND WHAT'S INCLUDED**
£130.00-£275.00 per
person. Includes dinner,
breakfast and transfers.

Spectacular scenery at the Valley of Rocks near Lynton in Devon.

Highcliffe House

Commanding views of hills and the coast make this a house to savour

Built as a gentleman's des res in the 1870s, Highcliffe House is now a beautifully restored guest house standing in one acre of land 500 feet above sea level and commanding stunning views of the Exmoor Hills and coastline, Lynmouth Bay and across the Bristol Channel to South Wales.

All seven guest rooms are en suite and enjoy uninterrupted seascapes and dramatic views across the steeply wooded hills and valleys of Exmoor. Each room is individually decorated with attention to comfort and detail in William Morris and Laura Ashley styles and features original or antique-style beds and furniture and a modern bath or shower room.

Cuisine leans towards modern European with a creative twist. Fish arrives fresh from the Brixham day boats, raspberries are collected from a local market gardener, herbs are picked from Highcliffe's own gardens while ice creams, sorbets, scones and bread are home-made. With fine dining available on Fridays, Saturdays and Sundays, the light-filled conservatory-style restaurant offers spectacular sea views from your candlelit table. Ω

Matter of facts

CONTACT
Karen and Michael Orchard
T +44 (0)1598 752235
E info@
highcliffehouse.com
W highcliffehouse.com
Address Highcliffe House,
Sinai Hill,
Lynton,
Devon EX35 6AR

RATING
VisitBritain 5 Star
Silver Award Guest
Accommodation

SLEEPING
Seven individually-designed
and themed double
bedrooms, all with en suite
baths or showers and one
with a four-poster bed.

FOR THE FAMILY
Unsuitable for children or
pets.

FACILITIES
Licensed conservatory
dining room (fine dining
Friday-Sunday, breakfast
only Monday-Thursday);
beauty treatments from
visiting therapist; TV/DVD
player and tea and coffee-
making facilities in all
rooms; ironing facilities
available; private parking.

**NEAREST SHOPS, PUBS
AND RESTAURANTS**
Lynton shopping centre is
three minutes away; there
are numerous pubs and
restaurants in the
immediate area.

OUT AND ABOUT
South West Coastal Path;
Exmoor National Park.

**PRICES PER PERSON
PER NIGHT AND
WHAT'S INCLUDED**
Deluxe four poster £50.00;
superior rooms £55.00;
premier rooms £60.00.
Includes breakfast and
VAT. Single occupancy
75% of room rate.
Discounts available for
stays of four or more
nights. See website for
special offers.

Higher Wiscombe

COLYTON, DEVON 5 STAR SELF-CATERING

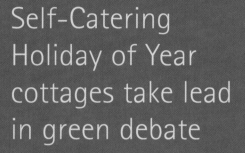

Self-Catering Holiday of Year cottages take lead in green debate

Gold medal winner in the 2007 Enjoy England Self-Catering Holiday of the Year competition, Higher Wiscombe comprises three luxurious holiday cottages, recently converted from old stone barns, at the head of the peaceful Southleigh Valley. Formerly owned by Hank Marvin of the Shadows, the farm dates from the early 1800s and recently became the first holiday venue of its kind to offset guests' carbon emissions within the price of the holiday.

The cottages can accommodate parties from six to 32 and are perfect for traditional seaside, bird watching and walking holidays. The oak dining table in the largest barn can be extended to dine up to 32 guests, making this ideal for family reunions, anniversaries and house parties.

The cottages combine exposed beams and brickwork with high-standard new oak kitchens, bathrooms, furniture and decoration. All have modern en suite shower rooms and sumptuous roll-top baths. Guests can explore 52 acres of grounds, which include woodlands, orchards, pasture and streams with abundant wildlife. Ω

Matter of facts

CONTACT
Alistair and Lorna Handyside
T +44 (0)1404 871360
E alistair@higherwiscombe.com
W higherwiscombe.com
Address Higher Wiscombe, Southleigh, Colyton, Devon, EX24 6JF

RATING
VisitBritain
5 Star Self Catering

SLEEPING
Sixteen bedrooms in three cottages:
Thatched Barn (sleeps 6);
Old Winery (sleeps 20);
Flint Barn (sleeps 6).

FOR THE FAMILY
Stairgates, cots and highchairs available; enclosed gardens.

FACILITIES
Quality catering available; games room; heated pool in summer.

NEAREST SHOPS, PUBS AND RESTAURANTS
Shopping in Honiton, Beer, Ottery St Mary and Sidmouth all about five miles away. Many local pubs and restaurants.

OUT AND ABOUT
Pecorama; Bicton; Escot Gardens; Crealy Adventure Park; World Heritage Jurassic Coast; Beer, Sidmouth and Lyme Regis.

PRICES AND WHAT'S INCLUDED
Minimum weekend break at Old Winery £1,995.00; maximum week-long holiday (Christmas) £4,550.00. Includes bed linen, towels, logs for wood-burners, electricity, heating and eco-friendly cleaning products.

Highgate House

A SUNDIAL GROUP VENUE

CREATON, NORTHAMPTON
4 STAR GUEST ACCOMMODATION

Country mansion moves with times while retaining a family atmosphere

Originally a 17th century coaching inn in the picturesque village of Creaton, Highgate House is a striking country mansion which is moving with the times while retaining its original character and charm.

Although offering modern leisure facilities, such as a swimming pool, sauna, fitness suite and all-weather tennis court, the historic, family atmosphere remains prevalent in and around the main house and throughout the grounds.

The 98 spacious rooms, housed throughout the estate, have a good mixture of single, double and family bedrooms with en suite baths, showers or both. They are individually decorated, comfortable and beautifully appointed. All contain TV, iron and ironing board, hot drinks-making facilities, bottled mineral water, direct-dial telephone and Internet access. Guests are also supplied with toiletries from The White Company. The beds are handmade by an English supplier.

Additions to the main house mean Highgate House can also offer more than 30 well-appointed meeting rooms and five elegant function rooms. Ω

Matter of facts

CONTACT
Mia Butler
T +44 (0)1604 505505
E highgate@
sundialgroup.com
W sundialgroup.com
Address Highgate House,
Sundial Group, Creaton,
Northampton NN6 8NN

RATING
VisitBritain 4 Star
Guest Accommodation

SLEEPING
98 single, double and family
bedrooms, all en suite.

FOR THE FAMILY
Family rooms available.

FACILITIES
Private dining and
restaurant; conference
facilities; swimming pool;
fitness suite; sauna; tennis
courts.

**NEAREST SHOPS, PUBS
AND RESTAURANTS**
Village shops in Creaton;
shopping in Kingsthorpe
nine miles away;
restaurants and pubs in
nearby villages.

OUT AND ABOUT
Althorp; Kelmarsh Hall;
Rockingham Castle;
Silverstone.

**PRICES PER NIGHT
AND WHAT'S INCLUDED**
Single room £45.00-
£123.37; double £58.00-
£149.80. Includes breakfast.
Valentine's Day and Easter
packages available.

Hob Green Hotel

HARROGATE, NORTH YORKSHIRE
3 STAR SILVER AWARD COUNTRY HOUSE HOTEL

Here you can enjoy one of the best hotel gardens in England

Hob Green dates back to the late 18th century. Set in 800 acres of glorious, rolling countryside, the house has been carefully altered and restored to form a charming and elegant hotel. The main rooms retain many original features, including their antique furniture, and enjoy a stunning view of the valley below.

All 12 bedrooms are individually decorated and have en suite facilities. One room has a four-poster bed and another has a separate sitting room attached. Each room contains a TV, radio, electric blanket, hairdryer, tea and coffee-making facilities, a well-stocked minibar and luxury consumables in the bathroom.

Hob Green enjoys an excellent reputation for good quality, home-cooked food and a vast selection of fine wines from all around the world. Dishes are created using local ingredients from small, family suppliers and are complemented with Hob Green's own home-grown fruits and vegetables from the Victorian kitchen garden. Its 2.5-acre garden has previously been voted one of the top 20 hotel gardens in England. Ω

Matter of facts

CONTACT
Reception
T +44 (0)1423 770031
E info@hobgreen.com
W hobgreen.com
Address Hob Green Hotel,
Markington,
Harrogate,
North Yorkshire HG3 3PJ

RATING
VisitBritain 3 Star
Silver Award Country
House Hotel

SLEEPING
12 bedrooms, including
single, standard double/
twin, superior double/twin,
a four-poster room and a
junior suite, all en suite.

FOR THE FAMILY
Large garden.

FACILITIES
Drawing room; sunroom
and terrace with disabled
access; dining room with
tables for two-six and
adjoining butler's pantry
for larger parties; 2.5-acre
gardens, including
Victorian kitchen garden.

**NEAREST SHOPS, PUBS
AND RESTAURANTS**
Post office and pubs within
walking distance.

OUT AND ABOUT
World Heritage Site of
Fountains Abbey and
Studley Royal Water
Garden; Newby Hall;
Harewood House; Castle
Howard; historic city of
York; Yorkshire Dales and
North Yorkshire Moors;
Rippon; Harrogate.

**PRICES PER ROOM
PER NIGHT AND
WHAT'S INCLUDED**
B&B from £115.00 for
a standard double/twin;
£140.00 for a suite.
Dinner, B&B from
£160.00 for a standard
double/twin; £190.00 for
a suite. Single occupancy
of double/twin £95.00 for
B&B; £120.00 for dinner,
B&B. Discounts available
for stays of two nights
or more.

Holiday Inn
ASHFORD NORTH

ASHFORD, KENT
3 STAR SILVER AWARD HOTEL

Great for exploring Kent's delights or as a launch pad to the continent

Enjoying a deceptively rural outlook, the Holiday Inn Ashford North is conveniently located for travel to the continent via the Eurostar terminal at Ashford and the Channel port of Dover. Its exceptional facilities include eight air-conditioned meeting rooms and a romantic terrace and gazebo which provide the ideal backdrop for a civil wedding ceremony or a drinks reception.

Following a lavish refurbishment, the hotel offers a host of outstanding modern facilities. Its 92 air-conditioned, beautifully-designed and furnished en suite bedrooms provide guests with the space and facilities to relax – for the business traveller, a convenient desk area with modem and email connection and for families, spacious family suites with both a double and twin single beds. Luxuriously fitted bathrooms, including branded toiletries, enhance the atmosphere of quality and comfort.

The stylish, comfortable bar and lounge provide the perfect setting for a drink or bite to eat. The hotel offers a full menu in the lounge or a more extensive à la carte menu in the restaurant. There is a secondary restaurant on site, The Hop Pickers. Ω

Matter of facts

CONTACT
Samantha Foster
T +44 (0)1233 713333
E enquiries@
hiashford.com
W hiashford.com
Address
Holiday Inn Ashford North,
A20 Maidstone Road,
Hothfield, Ashford,
Kent TN26 1AR

RATING
VisitBritain 3 Star
Silver Award Hotel

SLEEPING
92 fully air-conditioned
bedrooms, all en suite.

FOR THE FAMILY
Superb family rooms;
children's menu in the
lounge.

FACILITIES
Stylish, welcoming bar,
restaurant and lounge

areas; 24-hour menu; mini
gym; extensive business
services; excellent
conference and banqueting
facilities; extensive free
on-site parking.

**NEAREST SHOPS, PUBS
AND RESTAURANTS**
Ashford town centre and
McArthur Glen Designer
Outlet nearby.

OUT AND ABOUT
Leeds Castle; historic
Canterbury; Eurostar
terminal; within an hour's
drive of many of Kent's
coastal resorts.

**PRICES PER NIGHT
AND WHAT'S INCLUDED**
From £65.00 room only;
B&B from £75.00 per
room. Supplement of
£10.00 per room for
rooms that sleep more
than two people.

Holme House

Those looking to explore Pennines will find this a perfect base

This charming Georgian house is situated in the centre of Hebden Bridge, a unique, lovely and unspoilt market town. Superbly furnished, all three spacious bedrooms have en suite bathrooms, hairdryers, shaver points, TV, DVD, chocolates, fresh flowers, books, magazines and tea and coffee-making facilities.

The magnificent dining room has a table seating eight and is furnished with original Georgian and early Victorian furniture. Breakfast at Holme House provides a good start to the day with a wide selection of home-cooked and locally-sourced produce on offer. Packed lunches are also provided for those who wish to spend the day walking in the surrounding countryside. The comfortable guest lounge provides elegant surroundings with views over parkland.

Add in its excellent location, ample off-road parking and friendly and efficient service and it's easy to see why Holme House is a great choice for bed and breakfast accommodation in the heart of the Yorkshire Pennines. Ω

Matter of facts

CONTACT
Sarah and Charles Eggleston
T +44 (0)1422 847588
E mail@holmehouse
hebdenbridge.co.uk
W holmehouse
hebdenbridge.co.uk
Address Holme House,
New Road,
Hebden Bridge, West
Yorkshire HX7 8AD

RATING
VisitBritain 5 Star
Silver Award B&B

SLEEPING
Three en suite bedrooms,
one with king-size bed, one
with double bed and one
with twin beds.

FOR THE FAMILY
Cot, highchair and put-up
bed available.

FACILITIES
Luxury wedding packages
available; semi self-
contained apartment in
converted cellars.

**NEAREST SHOPS, PUBS
AND RESTAURANTS**
In town centre two minutes'
walk away.

OUT AND ABOUT
Haworth and Brontë country;
Heptonstall; Hardcastle Crags;
Shibden Hall; Halifax Piece
Hall; South Pennines; Skipton;
Harrogate; Ilkley and
Heptonstall.

**PRICES PER NIGHT AND
WHAT'S INCLUDED**
£35.00 per person Sunday-
Thursday; £42.50 per person
Friday-Saturday; £55.00 single
occupancy. Includes breakfast.

Hope Farm House

ALSTONEFIELD, DERBYSHIRE 5 STAR SELF-CATERING

Farmhouse and barn offer all the ingredients for a fun get-together

This fully-restored, early 18th century farmhouse and barn with all the original features lovingly preserved are the perfect venue for family reunions and get-togethers with friends. The farmhouse sleeps eight and is let on its own or with the barn, which extends the sleeping capacity to 10. Equipped with antiques and country furniture, the property features various pieces and textiles from around the world, such as Persian rugs and Afghan kelims.

Hope Farm House comprises a cosy sitting room with log stove; a stunning dining room; fully-quipped kitchen with a Lacanche double-oven cooker; a scullery and a sunny conservatory. There are three double bedrooms, one of which is en suite, two single attic bedrooms, and two additional bathrooms.

The Barn makes a spacious and unusual place for two to stay with a comfortable sitting room with log stove; a separate dining room; a kitchen; and a cosy double bedroom with an en suite shower room. The upstairs recreation room houses a snooker table, piano and library. Ω

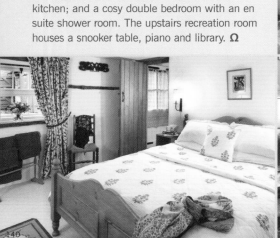

Matter of facts

CONTACT
Su Hanson
T +44 (0)1298 687418
E su.hanson@virgin.net
W hopefarmhouse.co.uk
Address Alstonefield,
Derbyshire
Booking address
Su Hanson,
Laundry House,
Warslow Hall, Warslow
Buxton SK17 0HD

RATING
VisitBritain 5 Star
Self-Catering

SLEEPING
Three double, one small
double, two singles.

FOR THE FAMILY
No children under eight.

FACILITIES
Ground-floor barn
accommodation ideal for
elderly relatives; pretty,
formal garden with lovely
views, a wild-flower
meadow and orchard,
drystone walls, and an old
spring-fed pond full of newts.

**NEAREST SHOPS, PUBS,
AND RESTAURANTS**
Village shops in Hartington
five miles away; high street
shops in Ashbourne eight
miles away; two pubs with
food within easy walking
distance and many others
in the area.

OUT AND ABOUT
The Dales; moors; Haddon
Hall; Chatsworth and many
other historic houses; the
ancient custom of well
dressing in the Peak
District; Buxton Festival and
Opera House; cycle tracks.

**PRICES PER WEEK FOR
HOUSE WITH BARN AND
WHAT'S INCLUDED**
£1,250.00–£1,750.00.
Includes electricity, central
heating, bed linen, towels
and welcome basket. Barn
also available as separate
let when house not in use.

Hornby Hall

PENRITH, CUMBRIA 4 STAR HOTEL

Open fires and candles add to the atmosphere at manor house

An attractive, Tudor manor house built around 1540, Hornby Hall is a Grade II Listed building set in peaceful, idyllic countryside next to a working farm on the fringe of the Lake District.

The imposing 450-year-old dining hall features the original sandstone floor, a Victorian cooking range and a large, open fireplace. When the fire is burning and the candles are lit, the house has a very special, homely atmosphere. As well as a generous English breakfast, two-course and four-course evening meals, using traditional country recipes and locally-grown produce, are available on request.

The five main bedrooms all face south and overlook the garden. They all have en suite or private bathroom and are individually furnished. Up a stone spiral staircase there are two children's bedrooms which share a shower room. They date from 1564 – the year Shakespeare was born – and one used to be the chapel.

Dry fly trout fishing is available on a two-mile stretch of the River Eamont for which day tickets can be purchased. Ω

Matter of facts

CONTACT
Ros Sanders
T +44 (0)1768 891114
E enquire@
hornbyhall.co.uk
W hornbyhall.co.uk
Address Hornby Hall Country House, Brougham, Penrith, Cumbria CA10 2AR

RATING
VisitBritain 4 Star Hotel

SLEEPING
Two doubles with en suite; one twin with en suite; two twins with private bathroom; two children's rooms with shared shower.

FOR THE FAMILY
Cot, highchair and baby-sitting service available.

FACILITIES
Two-mile stretch of river for guests to fish; all rooms have TV and tea and coffee-making facilities.

NEAREST SHOPS, LOCAL PUBS, RESTAURANTS
Four miles away in the market town of Penrith.

OUT AND ABOUT
Lake District (Ullswater nearby); Carlisle to Settle steam railway; Hadrian's Wall and the Yorkshire Dales.

PRICES PER NIGHT AND WHAT'S INCLUDED
From £25.00 per person for a child's room to £44.00 per person for a double room with en suite; 5% discount for two or more nights; 10% discount in low season. Includes breakfast.

The Island Hotel

TRESCO, ISLES OF SCILLY
3 STAR GOLD AWARD HOTEL

Hotel with its own beach, sailing school and views is a must stay

This delightful, swish, colonial-style hotel has a spectacular waterside location fringed by white, sandy beaches and ringed by uninhabited islands and the dramatic Golden Ball reef.

Set in its own manicured gardens and private beach with a seasonal sailing school, the Island Hotel overlooks Old Grimsby Sound and the Cromwellian fort known as the Blockhouse. All its 48 spacious, en suite bedrooms are brightly-furnished and many have lounge areas, balconies and terraces. The superior rooms and suites have bespoke Designer Guild interiors and unparalleled sea views.

Decking leads from the terrace bar and lounge to the extensive lawns, furnished with loungers in secluded corners of the two-acre garden. Activities and facilities include a tennis court, croquet, outdoor heated swimming pool, kite flying, shrimping and fishing.

Lunches are served in the terrace bar and evening meals in the hotel's two restaurants. Well prepared, imaginative cuisine makes an excellent showcase for locally-caught fish, island vegetables and Tresco-reared beef. Ω

Matter of facts

CONTACT
Reception
T +44 (0)1720 422883
E islandhotel@tresco.co.uk
W tresco.co.uk
Address Island Hotel,
Tresco,
Isles of Scilly,
Cornwall TR24 0PU

RATING
VisitBritain 3 Star
Gold Award Hotel

SLEEPING
45 bedrooms, three suites
all en suite.

FOR THE FAMILY
Children's games room
with pool, table football,
table tennis; Sony
PlayStation; high teas
and family dining.

FACILITIES
Outdoor heated swimming
pool; cycling; seasonal
sailing school; tennis
court; two-acre gardens;
wireless Internet; terrace
bar and lounge; reference
library.

**NEAREST SHOPS, PUBS
AND RESTAURANTS**
On-site gift shop; Tresco
stores; the New Inn,
Tresco has the vibrant
Driftwood Bar and award-
winning bar meals.

OUT AND ABOUT
Tresco Abbey Garden; boat
trips; diving, snorkelling
and swimming with seals.

**PRICES PER PERSON
PER NIGHT AND
WHAT'S INCLUDED**
Single room £130.00-
£170.00; double/twin
room £135.00-£250.00;
suites £175.00-£325.00.
Includes dinner and
breakfast.

Isle of Eriska Hotel

ISLE OF ERISKA, ARGYLL 5 STAR HOTEL

Private island has just about every leisure activity you can imagine

The Isle of Eriska Hotel, Spa and Island is a unique combination of a 300-acre, privately-owned island, a five star, 25-bedroom hotel with world-renowned three AA Rosette restaurant and a stunning combination of outdoor activities and indoor sporting facilities with a full-service Espa Spa.

The 1884-built baronial house contains 16 bedrooms while in the surrounding gardens lie the spa suites and two-bedroom cottage suites with their own hot tubs.

Public rooms include a piano room, drawing room, library and hall where the open fire burns constantly every day of the year. The dining room comprises the morning room, the business room, the butler's pantry and the conservatory.

The stables, beside the old formal garden, house a 17-metre swimming pool, sauna, steam room, spa, treatment rooms, gymnasium and a lounge and balcony with views over the six-hole, par 22 golf course, complete with putting green, teaching academy and driving range. Other outdoor activities on the island include clay pigeon shooting, watersports, fishing, tennis, croquet, mountain biking and nature walks. Ω

Matter of facts

CONTACT
Reception
T +44 (0)1631 720371
F +44 (0)1631 720531
E office@eriska-hotel.co.uk
W eriska-hotel.co.uk
Address
Isle of Eriska Hotel,
Benderloch, by Oban,
Argyll PA37 1SD

RATING
AA 5 Star Hotel

SLEEPING
16 bedrooms in the main house; two two-bedroom suites and five one-bedroom suites in the surrounding grounds.

FACILITIES
Indoor pool; sauna; steam room; spa; hot tubs in private gardens; golf course; tennis; nature trails.

NEAREST SHOPS, PUBS AND RESTAURANTS
Shops on the island.

OUT AND ABOUT
Glencoe; Mull; Iona; Oban; Inveraray Castle and Jail.

PRICES AND WHAT'S INCLUDED
Double/twin room with breakfast £300.00-£420.00 for two people per night.

Jeakes House

RYE, EAST SUSSEX
5 STAR GUEST ACCOMMODATION

From the moment visitors arrive the pleasant surprises just keep coming

Open any door in Jeakes House and you will open a door to yet another delight – a further sign that this hotel prides itself on old-fashioned, friendly and efficient hospitality and service. Each bedroom has been individually restored to combine traditional elegance and luxury with modern amenities. There are brass or mahogany bedsteads, antique four-poster beds and roll-top baths. On chilly mornings a roaring fire greets guests in the oak-beamed parlour.

Jeakes House stands on Mermaid Street, one of the most beautiful and ancient cobbled streets in Rye. Delicious breakfasts, including devilled kidneys, vegetarian and fish dishes, are served in the elegant galleried hall of what was a Quaker meeting house. Pre-dinner drinks are sipped in the comfort of the book-lined bar, while guests peruse the menus of the restaurants they are about to visit. All this amid the beauty and fascination of the ancient Cinque Port, an ideal base from which to explore this historic part of the south east. There is a private car park nearby – a great bonus in Rye. Ω

Matter of facts

CONTACT
Jenny Hadfield
T +44 (0)1797 222828
E stay@jeakeshouse.com
W jeakeshouse.com
Address Jeakes House, Mermaid Street, Rye, East Sussex TN31 7ET

RATING
VisitBritain 5 Star Guest Accommodation

SLEEPING
Ten bedrooms with en suite; one bedroom with private bathroom; four four-poster suites.

FOR THE FAMILY
Not recommended for children under eight. Dogs charged at £5.00 per night.

FACILITIES
Book-lined bar; oak-beamed parlour; dining room (breakfast only); private car park.

NEAREST SHOPS, PUBS AND RESTAURANTS
Rye has a wide selection of shops within walking distance. There are many pubs and restaurants in the vicinity and Jeakes House has sample menus in the bar.

OUT AND ABOUT
Museum; castle; beach; Rye; Hastings. Also within striking distance of a number of interesting places, including Battle and the city of Canterbury.

PRICES PER NIGHT AND WHAT'S INCLUDED
£90.00-£124.00 per room. Includes breakfast and VAT. Special offer: November-March, Sunday-Thursday, 20% discount for two nights or more. March-November 10% discount for seven nights or more.

Jinlye

CHURCH STRETTON, SHROPSHIRE
5 STAR GOLD AWARD GUEST HOUSE

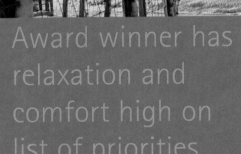

Award winner has relaxation and comfort high on list of priorities

A stroll from this 200-year old former crofter's cottage takes you through some of England's most stunning countryside. Adjoining the Long-Mynd and 6,000 acres of National Trust land in an Area of Outstanding Natural Beauty, Jinlye is an award-winning B&B in 15 acres of private grounds with lush, landscaped gardens, rare birds and wild ponies.

There is comfort too – the raftered Reading Lounge with its huge open fire, comfortable, deep sofas and easy chairs; a cosy TV room, large Victorian conservatory and, of course, the swish dining room for breakfasts. Enjoy the special taste of Jinlye's own supply of spring water and fabulous home-made biscuits and cakes. The spacious en suite bedrooms are bright and elegantly furnished with antiques and fine fabrics. There are deep-pile carpets, new mattresses and sumptuous touches – floral sinks, Tiffany-style lamps and boudoir chairs.

Remote and beautiful, yet within easy reach of Ludlow, Shrewsbury and Ironbridge, Jinlye is an ideal base for exploring Shropshire and a wonderful place to return to. Ω

Matter of facts

CONTACT
Kate Tory
T +44 (0)1694 723243
E info@jinlye.co.uk
W jinlye.co.uk
Address
Jinlye,
Castle Hill,
All Stretton,
Church Stretton,
Shropshire SY6 6JP

RATING
VisitBritain 5 Star Gold Award Guest House; Heart of England Tourist Board B&B of the Year 2004.

SLEEPING
Six bedrooms, all en suite.

FACILITIES
Ground-floor rooms; wedding room furnished around a 17th century French wedding bed; 1940s Italian boudoir suite; Reading Lounge;

TV room; Victorian conservatory; 15 acres of grounds.

NEAREST SHOPS, PUBS AND RESTAURANTS
Within three miles of Jinlye there are shops and a wealth of good places to eat, many providing award-winning food and service.

OUT AND ABOUT
Powis Castle and gardens; Ironbridge Gorge museums; Stokesay Castle; Dingle Garden and Nursery; the Severn Valley Railway; Burford House Garden.

PRICES PER PERSON PER NIGHT AND WHAT'S INCLUDED
£34.00-£45.00. Includes breakfast. Special breaks February-March and November, stay two nights and get third half-price.

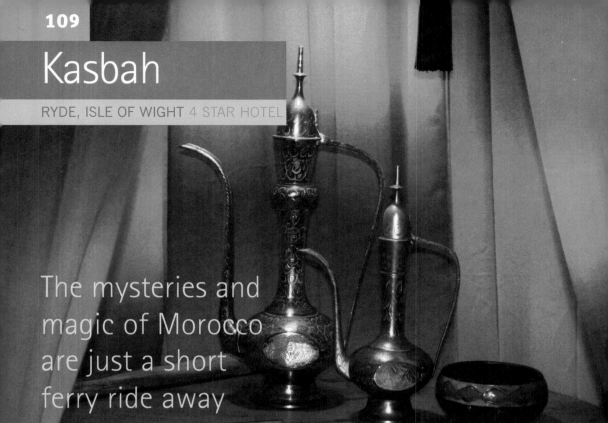

Kasbah

RYDE, ISLE OF WIGHT 4 STAR HOTEL

The mysteries and magic of Morocco are just a short ferry ride away

Kasbah is a hidden treasure offering intimate, boutique-style accommodation a stone's throw from Ryde seafront.

The café-bar has captured the magic of Morocco. Beautifully furnished with ornaments from North Africa, it is a sanctuary from the hustle and bustle of everyday life.

Relax and unwind, enjoy a mint tea or a mouth-watering meal – a full tapas menu, accompanied by daily specials, is available all day. Listen to New World music, surf the net with free wireless Internet access, watch a movie or simply have a game of chess. There is also a garden and patio for guests to use.

Kasbah's newly-refurbished en suite bedrooms are individually themed. All have TVs and tea and coffee-making facilities while some have DVDs, radios, minibars and four-poster or king-size beds.

Here you can even indulge in the luxury of a range of massage, yoga therapy, stress and relaxation therapy, hypnosis and beauty treatments in the comfort of your own room. Ω

Matter of facts

CONTACT
Matthew Parker
T +44 (0)1983 810088
E newkasbah@
btconnect.com
W kas-bah.co.uk
Address Kasbah,
76 Union Street,
Ryde,
Isle of Wight PO33 2LN

RATING
VisitBritain 4 Star Hotel

SLEEPING
Nine bedrooms, all en suite.

FOR THE FAMILY
Children welcome; pets by arrangement.

FACILITIES
Café-bar (special diets catered for); garden and patio; wireless Internet access; conference facilities; fax and photocopying.

NEAREST SHOPS, LOCAL PUBS, RESTAURANTS
All in the immediate vicinity.

OUT AND ABOUT
The Isle of Wight is home to some of the most diverse countryside in the UK. Discover historic farms, pretty lanes, thatched villages, coastal trails and woodlands and there are more than 500 miles of carefully-maintained footpaths and signposts to follow. Walking, cycling and bird watching are popular all year round.

PRICES PER NIGHT AND WHAT'S INCLUDED
From £25.00 per person. Includes breakfast.

Kildonan Lodge Hotel

EDINBURGH 4 STAR SMALL HOTEL

Well situated to explore the Scottish capital's sights and delights

Kildonan Lodge Hotel is a friendly country-style, four star small hotel located close to the city centre (1.5 miles), easily accessible to Edinburgh Castle, Roslyn Chapel and the Scottish capital's major attractions. The hotel has been magnificently restored to retain its Victorian grandeur. Its charming, warm and friendly atmosphere provides the perfect retreat for a weekend away or the business guest.

All rooms have been beautifully furnished to capture the country-style ambience of the hotel. Designed with romance in mind, its Superior Four-poster Rooms feature elegant canopied beds and Jacuzzi spa baths, perfect to complement any special occasion.

Delicious full Scottish breakfasts are served in the elegant dining-room, and for tantalising evening meals Mathew's Fine-dining Restaurant provides a romantic atmosphere to sample sumptuous delights. The splendid lounge and bar provide a tranquil setting in which guests can relax by an open fire and enjoy a dram from the honesty bar. Free wireless broadband Internet access is available throughout the hotel and guests have ample space to leave their cars while they explore Edinburgh on foot or by utilising the frequent bus services opposite the hotel. A warm welcome awaits you. Ω

Matter of facts

CONTACT
Maggie Urquhart
T +44 (0)131 667 2793
E sales@
kildonanlodgehotel.co.uk
W kildonanlodgehotel.co.uk
Address Kildonan Lodge
Hotel, 27 Craigmillar Park,
Edinburgh EH16 5PE

RATING
VisitScotland 4 Star
Small Hotel

SLEEPING
Superior rooms with four-poster double beds; Executive Rooms with king-size/twin beds; Classic Rooms with double/twin beds. All en suite, Jacuzzi in some rooms.

FOR THE FAMILY
Children welcome; family rooms available.

FACILITIES
Residents' lounge with honesty bar; Mathew's Fine-dining Restaurant; Internet access; small wedding parties and other small functions a speciality.

NEAREST SHOPS, LOCAL PUBS, RESTAURANTS
Five-minute walk to shops at Cameron Toll; 1.5 miles to shops at Princes Street; pubs and restaurants within 10 minutes' walk.

OUT AND ABOUT
Edinburgh Castle; Rosslyn Chapel.

PRICES PER ROOM PER NIGHT AND WHAT'S INCLUDED
Superior four-poster £98.00-£149.00; executive king-size/twin £89.00-£125.00; classic double/twin £78.00-£98.00. Includes full Scottish breakfast.

Kingfisher Barn

ABINGDON, OXFORDSHIRE 4 STAR SELF-CATERING

Great customer service awaits in the ancient town of Abingdon

These stunning holiday cottages and fabulous barn conversions are set a few minutes from the River Thames in the glorious Abingdon countryside.

All self-catering accommodation is personally prepared to a refreshingly high standard and Kingfisher Barn prides itself on attention to detail that makes the difference. Kyte and Kestrel lodges and Hazel and Stable cottages have been fully adapted to accommodate wheelchair users.

All cottages and lodges have their own garden and patio area with barbeque. Guests of each one are entitled to private and exclusive use of the heated indoor pool for one hour a day.

Kingfisher Barn is ideal for a romantic weekend, a family get-together or a relaxing break, and with its staff having achieved the Investors in People Standard during 2006, you can be sure of great customer service. Kingfisher Barn offers 15 years' experience of making people feel right at home. Ω

Matter of facts

CONTACT
Sarah Jefferies
T +44 (0)1235 537538
E info@kingfisherbarn.com
W kingfisherbarn.com
Address Kingfisher Barn, Rye Farm, Abingdon, Oxfordshire OX14 3NN

RATING
VisitBritain 4 Star
Self-Catering

SLEEPING
Granary sleeps 2-4; The Nest Two sleeps 2-4; Hazel sleeps 4; Stable sleeps 6; Kyte sleeps 8-10; Kestrel sleeps 8-10.

FOR THE FAMILY
Wendy house; private gardens; toy box and children's videos; highchairs and travel cots; pets welcome.

FACILITIES
Heated indoor pool; all units have fully-equipped kitchens and TVs, CD players and radios; large off-road car park; Wispa ceiling track, hoists, cot sides, shower chairs and commode available free on request.

NEAREST SHOPS, PUBS AND RESTAURANTS
Abingdon town centre, a 10-minute walk away; Oxford is eight miles away.

OUT AND ABOUT
Blenheim Palace; Oxford with its university and museums.

PRICES PER WEEK AND WHAT'S INCLUDED
From £332.00 for one-bedroom cottage to £1,266.00 for four-bedroom lodge. Includes bed linen, bath and hand towels and welcome basket on arrival.

Kingston Estate

TOTNES, DEVON 5 STAR SELF-CATERING

Modern leisure facilities enhance beautifully-restored period cottages

Surrounding the cobbled north courtyard of 18th century Kingston House lie these nine beautiful, period cottages, created from the restored outbuildings but packed with 21st century amenities.

The cottages range from the thatched Bass Court (circa 1650) with its Canadian hot tub to Bull Cottage, Little Shippen, Doves, Jackdaws and Owls (circa 1830). All have been sympathetically converted to provide the highest standard of self-catering accommodation and can sleep between two and six people. Each cottage has a modern, fully-equipped kitchen; sitting room; beautiful bedrooms and high-quality bathrooms and four-poster beds in master bedrooms with beautiful linen and thick towels. Some cottages have wood-burning stoves and fenced gardens.

Communal facilities include a leisure suite with indoor exercise pool, sauna, gym, spa and billiards room, paddocks and pleasure grounds. Moveable Feasts consist of meals cooked by Kingston Estate's own chef and delivered to the cottages while dinners for adults can be served in the historic house by prior arrangement. Ω

Matter of facts

CONTACT
Elizabeth Corfield
T +44 (0) 1803 762235
E info@kingston-estate.co.uk
W kingston-estate.co.uk
Address The Kingston Estate, Kingston
House, Staverton, Totnes, Devon TQ9 6AR

RATING
VisitBritain 5 Star Self-Catering

SLEEPING
Nine cottages sleeping between
two and six people each.

FOR THE FAMILY
Cots and highchairs provided (plus linen
if required); pets charged at £20.00 each
(includes free doggie pack).

FACILITIES
Indoor exercise pool; spa; mini gym;
sauna; snooker table; table tennis (bring
your own bats). All cottages have
telephone, TV/DVD, dishwasher,
washer/dryer, microwave, double ovens
and a full range of small appliances.

**NEAREST SHOPS, PUBS
AND RESTAURANTS**
Shops 1-3.5 miles away; home-cooked
meals and fine ales at the Old Church
House Inn, Torbryan; the Sea Trout Inn,
Staverton plus other pubs and restaurants
in Totnes and surrounding villages.

OUT AND ABOUT
Numerous historic houses, castles and
gardens, including Dartington Hall,
Buckland Abbey, Castle Drogo, RHS
Rosemoor Gardens, Saltram House; steam
trains including the Primrose Line, Totnes
to Buckfastleigh via Staverton and Paignton
to Kingswear lines; golf (Kingston offers
half-price green fees at a range of courses
within easy reach); coarse and sea fishing;
horse riding; sailing; clay pigeon shooting;
carriage driving.

**PRICES PER WEEK
AND WHAT'S INCLUDED**
From £355.00 for a two-person cottage
low season to £1,445.00 for a six-person
cottage high season. Includes all bed
linen, towels, heating, logs, toiletries plus
welcome cream tea and wine for those
on a week's stay. Short breaks and some
offers available out of high season.

Kingston House

Blue, red or green – whichever room you choose it will be a colourful stay

As one of the finest examples of early 18th century architecture in Britain today, Kingston House and its grounds are packed with history. Included in *England's Thousand Best Houses* by Simon Jenkins, Kingston provides outstanding accommodation in three period suites on the first floor, known in 18th century architecture as the 'piano nobile'.

The bedrooms have all been sympathetically restored to reflect the style and luxury of the age in which the house was built. The re-creation of an original 1735 Angel tester bed forms the centrepiece of the Blue Suite, a room steeped in history and featuring a beautiful panelled bathroom with 15th-to-17th century carving and the original china closet.

The Red Suite exudes warmth from the moment you step into the room. The wallpaper design is from 1740, as are the Austrian blinds echoing the tastes of the time to perfection. The bed canopies, which have been in the house since the 19th century, have been restored and hung with red and gold silk. The Red Suite is also available as a twin room and has an elegant en suite bathroom.

The Green Room is dominated by its magnificent bed, which was made for the room in 1830. The wallpapers, fabrics and furniture are all true to the period with the colours of the room being taken from a Wedgwood tureen, part of a service in daily use at that time.

Guests enjoy the exclusive use of the grandest bathroom in the house. The Blue Bathroom is

Matter of facts

CONTACT
Elizabeth Corfield
T +44 (0)1803 762235
E info@kingston-estate.co.uk
W kingston-estate.co.uk
Address Kingston House, Staverton, Totnes, Devon TQ9 6AR

RATING
VisitBritain 5 Star Gold Award Guest Accommodation

SLEEPING
Three suites.

FOR THE FAMILY
Adults only. Children and dogs welcome in Kingston Estate Cottages (see previous spread).

FACILITIES
Access to formal gardens and leisure suite consisting of indoor exercise pool, spa, mini gym, sauna, snooker table and table tennis.

NEAREST SHOPS, PUBS AND RESTAURANTS
Shops one mile to 3.5 miles away; home-cooked meals and fine ales at the Old Church House Inn, Torbryan; the Sea Trout Inn, Staverton plus other pubs and restaurants in Totnes and surrounding villages.

OUT AND ABOUT
Numerous historic houses, castles and gardens, including Dartington Hall, Buckland Abbey, Castle Drogo, RHS Rosemoor Gardens, Saltram House; steam trains including the Primrose Line, Totnes to Buckfastleigh via Staverton and Paignton to Kingswear lines; golf (Kingston offers half-price green fees at a range of courses within easy reach); coarse and sea fishing; horse riding; sailing; clay pigeon shooting; carriage driving.

PRICES PER NIGHT AND WHAT'S INCLUDED
Suites £170.00-£190.00 for two people. Includes full English breakfast. Dinner £35.00 and £40.00.

renowned for the faux marble wall painting, its huge, original bath and wonderful views over the surrounding countryside.

The gardens are continually evolving or being re-created in keeping with the 18th century style. They consist of a series of areas culminating in a formal rose garden and magnificent Listed walled garden. The elegant dining room, which overlooks the walled garden, serves delicious dinners prepared from fresh, local produce, including vegetables and fruit from the gardens in season.

With candlelight, fresh flowers, crackling fires in colder weather and wines from the cellar for every palate, the scene is set for a perfect evening. Ω

Lakelovers

BOWNESS-ON-WINDERMERE, CUMBRIA
FROM 3-5 STARS SELF-CATERING

Wide choice of properties awaits those who wish to explore the Lakes

Spoilt for choice – that's the obvious thing to say about the huge selection of sumptuous, quality self-catering accommodation facing guests of Lakelovers Holiday Homes.

There are hundreds of places to stay – from traditional Lakeland farmhouses set in the heart of the Langdale Valley and sleeping up to 14, to luxury modern romantic retreats, sleeping two and complete with 21st century indulgences.

All holidays include free leisure club membership with every booking. All Lakelovers properties throughout central and southern Lakeland are three, four or five star rated and inspected and graded by VisitBritain.

Prices vary according to the kind of property and are available on request. The full range of accommodation appears in the Lakelovers' brochure. Ω

Matter of facts

CONTACT
The Lakelovers Team
T +44 (0)15394 88855
E bookings@
lakelovers.co.uk
W lakelovers.co.uk
Address Lakelovers,
Belmont House, Lake Road,
Bowness-on-Windermere,
Cumbria LA23 3BJ

RATING
VisitBritain from 3-5 Stars
Self-Catering

SLEEPING
More than 300 houses,
bungalows, cottages,
lodges and apartments
across the Lake District
sleeping 2-14 guests.

FOR THE FAMILY
Facilities vary from
property to property.

FACILITIES
Free membership of one of
seven private leisure clubs.

**NEAREST SHOPS, PUBS
AND RESTAURANTS**
Varies from property to
property.

OUT AND ABOUT
Aquarium of the Lakes;
Barrow-in-Furness;
Cartmel Priory and village;
Conishead Priory; Coniston
Launch; Dalton-in-Furness;
the Dock Museum; Fell
Foot Park; Furness Abbey;
Grange-over-Sands;
Gleaston Watermill;
Graythwaite Hall Gardens;
Holker Hall and Gardens;
Lakeland Motor Museum;
Lakeside & Haverthwaite
Railway; Laurel & Hardy
Museum; South Lakes
Wild Animal Park;
Ulverston; Windermere
Lake Cruises.

PRICES PER WEEK
Low season £250.00-
£800.00; high season
£350.00-£2,000.00.

Langdale Hotel

NR AMBLESIDE, CUMBRIA
3 STAR SILVER AWARD HOTEL

Village-style estate has leisure facilities to appeal to all family members

Set in a 35-acre estate in the centre of the Lake District, the Langdale Hotel offers an unusual blend of luxury with a more relaxed, casual atmosphere than the region's traditional hotels. It is the focal point of an estate that includes a Leisure Club, health and beauty facilities, the Terrace Café-bar and Restaurant, Purdey's Restaurant and Wainwright's Inn.

The Langdale's 57 en suite, village-style bedrooms are in historic buildings and all have satellite TV, phone, trouser press, radio/alarm clock, hairdryer and tea and coffee-making facilities. All have air baths.

The Leisure Club features a 21-metre pool, spa, sanarium, steam room, tropical and deluge showers, exercise studio, gym, tennis and children's play area.

With these superb facilities, central location and wide choice of dining available on an estate which has been recognised internationally for its commitment to the sustainability of the countryside, Langdale is the ideal venue for a Lake District holiday. Ω

Matter of facts

CONTACT
Sales office
T +44 (0)15394 38014
E sales@langdale.co.uk
W langdale.co.uk
Address The Langdale Hotel, The Langdale Estate, Great Langdale, nr Ambleside, Cumbria LA22 9JD

RATING
VisitBritain 3 Star Silver Award Hotel

SLEEPING
57 bedrooms, all en suite.

FOR THE FAMILY
Children's play area; no pets.

FACILITIES
Leisure club with 21m pool; health and beauty facilities; three restaurants, including traditional pub; conference facilities.

NEAREST SHOPS, PUBS AND RESTAURANTS
Store 400 metres; shops, pubs and restaurants in Ambleside (four miles); two restaurants and pub on-site serving food.

OUT AND ABOUT
Windermere; Rheged Centre; Aquarium of the Lakes; The World of Beatrix Potter; Lake District Visitor Centre; The Armitt Museum; Sizergh Castle; Kendal Museum; Ullswater Steamers.

PRICES PER NIGHT AND WHAT'S INCLUDED
From £100.00 per room. Includes breakfast.

Langley Castle Hotel

HEXHAM, NORTHUMBERLAND 4 STAR SILVER AWARD HOTEL

Enjoy 14thC splendour today in the heart of Northumberland

Built in 1350 during the reign of Edward III, Langley Castle has been restored to a magnificent and comfortable hotel set in a 12-acre woodland estate with brush-mown lawns.

Just 30 minutes from the centre of Newcastle, Langley Castle has nine guest bedrooms, all with private facilities, some with window seats set into seven-foot thick walls, and four-poster beds and some with sauna and spa bath. Castle View and Castle View Lodge, converted Grade I Listed buildings within the grounds, provide 10 additional guest rooms, all of which have draped canopies over the bed, satellite TV and stunning views of the main castle.

The magnificent drawing room, with open fire, traceries and stained glass, and the oak-panelled cocktail bar, complement the intimate Josephine Restaurant where meals of the highest order make the most of local produce with fish and game a speciality.

Gold winner in the North East of England Tourism Awards 2006, the castle went through to win Silver in the national Enjoy England Awards for Excellence 2007. Ω

Matter of facts

CONTACT
Anton Phillips
T +44 (0)1434 688888
E manager@
langleycastle.com
W langleycastle.com
Address Langley Castle
Hotel, Langley on Tyne,
Hexham, Northumberland
NE47 5LU

RATING
VisitBritain 4 Star
Silver Award Hotel

SLEEPING
Nine individually-designed bedrooms in the main castle, some with features including saunas, semi-sunken baths and real-flame fires.

FACILITIES
Fine-dining, candle-lit restaurant using local produce to create variety of cuisines with a modern English twist; Stuart Banqueting Suite for up to

120 guests; five conference rooms for up to 130 delegates; civil weddings.

NEAREST SHOPS, PUBS AND RESTAURANTS
Shops in market town of Hexham 10 minutes' drive; MetroCentre shops, Gateshead, 25 minutes' drive. Nearby Carts Bog Inn, a traditional coaching inn with open fire, serves food and real ale.

OUT AND ABOUT
Hadrian's Wall, Hexham Abbey, Kielder Forest, Beamish Museum, Alnwick Castle and gardens.

PRICES PER PERSON PER NIGHT AND WHAT'S INCLUDED
B&B £64.00-£124.50 based on two sharing. Choice break (minimum two nights) dinner, B&B £74.50-£129.50 based on two sharing.

The Leconfield

VENTNOR, ISLE OF WIGHT 5 STAR
SILVER AWARD GUEST ACCOMMODATION

Wonderful sea views from on high at this luxury country house

Enjoying uninterrupted views across the English Channel from its elevated position 400 feet above the sea, the Leconfield is situated on St Boniface Down above the historic village of Bonchurch. The house offers a warm welcome, comfortable, luxury accommodation and excellent, freshly-prepared food.

Guest rooms have all the comforts you would expect from a five star country house including en suite, TV and hospitality tray and most have panoramic sea views. In addition there are two luxury rooms: the ground-floor Coral Reef with reserved parking, private entrance, large bathroom and dressing room; and the opulent Captain's Bridge with stunning bedroom, luxurious bathroom and balcony terrace with fantastic views.

This peaceful country house also features comfortable sitting rooms, a conservatory with spectacular views and heated outdoor pool with secluded suntrap open from May to September.

Fine dining in the Seascape Dining Room includes locally-farmed meat, fresh fruit, vegetables and locally-landed fish wherever possible. Ω

Matter of facts

CONTACT
Paul Judge
T +44 (0)1983 852196
E paul@leconfieldhotel.com
W leconfieldhotel.com
Address The Leconfield,
85 Leeson Road,
Upper Bonchurch,
Ventnor,
Isle of Wight PO38 1PU

RATING
VisitBritain 5 Star
Silver Award Guest
Accommodation

SLEEPING
12 double/twin rooms,
three of which are luxury
rooms, all en suite.

FOR THE FAMILY
Over 16s only; no dogs.

FACILITIES
Heated swimming pool
with sun terrace; fine
dining in the Seascape

Dining Room (special diets
and requests catered for);
sitting rooms; conservatory.

**NEAREST SHOPS, PUBS
AND RESTAURANTS**
Shops in Ventnor a mile
distant; Bonchurch Inn
200 yards; restaurants in
Ventnor or Shanklin, which
is three miles away.

OUT AND ABOUT
Appuldurcombe House and
falconry; Bonchurch pottery;
Ventnor botanical gardens;
Arreton Barns; Brading
Roman Villa; Amazon
World; Morton Manor.

**PRICES PER PERSON
PER NIGHT AND
WHAT'S INCLUDED**
B&B £43.00-£93.00
based on two sharing a
double room; half board
£58.00-£108.00 based on
two sharing a double room.

Linthwaite House Hotel

WINDERMERE, CUMBRIA
3 STAR GOLD AWARD HOTEL

Three Red Stars, three rosettes, in the top 200 ... the accolades abound

With stunning views over Lake Windermere from its hilltop perch, Linthwaite House Hotel enjoys one of the most spectacular and romantic settings in the Lake District. Set in 14 acres of private grounds with a private tarn, Linthwaite has been named one of the AA's top 200 British hotels with three Red Stars for consistently excellent customer service to go with its three Rosettes for outstanding, modern British cuisine with a daily-changing menu incorporating the best local ingredients.

Guest accommodation consists of 27 bedrooms with 'Ralph Lauren meets Raffles'-style interiors. All have private bath, shower, bathrobes, 12-channel TV, mini hi-fi, wireless Internet access, trouser press, tea and coffee tray, books and mineral water. Some rooms have lake views and king-size beds with canopies. There is a Level 1-accessible disabled room on the ground floor with its own access.

Whether it's drinks on the terrace overlooking Windermere in summer or comfy sofas in front of crackling log fires in winter, Linthwaite is a getaway for all seasons. Ω

Matter of facts

CONTACT
Reservations
T +44 (0)15394 88600
E stay@linthwaite.com
W linthwaite.com
Address
Linthwaite House Hotel,
Crook Road, Windermere,
Cumbria LA23 3JA

RATING
VisitBritain 3 Star
Gold Award Hotel

SLEEPING
27 individually-designed bedrooms, including suite with garden view, deluxe rooms with lake views and twin-bedded rooms.

FOR THE FAMILY
Large gardens.

FACILITIES
Lounge and conservatory; terrace; billiard room and mirror room; civil weddings (on-site wedding coordinator); practice golf hole; putting green; croquet lawn; in-room massage and facials; use of off-site spa.

NEAREST SHOPS, PUBS AND RESTAURANTS
Lakeland Ltd, Hayes Garden World and many independent craft shops in Bowness (one mile); many local restaurants and pubs serving food, including Masons Arms and Drunken Duck.

OUT AND ABOUT
Lake District; Hilltop (Beatrix Potter's house); Dove Cottage, Blackwell Arts and Crafts House.

PRICES PER PERSON PER NIGHT AND WHAT'S INCLUDED
Dinner, B&B £85.00-£180.00. Special offers regularly updated on website.

Little Holtby

NORTHALLERTON, NORTH YORKSHIRE
4 STAR SILVER AWARD B&B

Modern creature comforts await in farmhouse on historic route

This old farmhouse has origins going back to the Domesday Book and is said to have been a favourite stopping-off point for the Saxons, Vikings and Romans following the ancient trade routes north. The current house dates from the 18th century, but is much more focused on today's discerning traveller. If you are looking for somewhere special, somewhere with character and somewhere where the warmth of welcome and attention to personal comfort are paramount, then Little Holtby is right up your street.

The farmhouse faces south west and all its guest rooms have wonderful views over rolling countryside to the Yorkshire Dales. Two double rooms – one with a four-poster bed – and one twin-bedded room are offered to guests. One room adapts to accommodate a family and all have TVs, hot drinks tray and hairdryers. Two have en suite baths or showers and one has a private bathroom.

Log fires are lit on chilly evenings creating an excellent atmosphere in which to relax and unwind in the sitting room and in the dining room, where Aga-cooked breakfasts are served. Ω

Matter of facts

CONTACT
Dorothy Layfield
T +44 (0)1609 748762
E littleholtby@yahoo.co.uk
W littleholtby.co.uk
Address Little Holtby, Leeming Bar, Northallerton, North Yorkshire DL7 9LH

RATING
VisitBritain 4 Star
Silver Award B&B

SLEEPING
One twin room with private bathroom; one double room with en suite bathroom; one double room with en suite shower.

FACILITIES
Dining room; sitting room;

reduced green fees at local golf course.

NEAREST SHOPS, PUBS AND RESTAURANTS
Shops in market town of Bedale, a five minute drive away. Many restaurants and pubs within a few miles.

OUT AND ABOUT
Fountains Abbey and Studley Royal Water Garden; historic cities of York and Durham; Catterick Racecourse; Richmond Castle.

PRICES PER NIGHT AND WHAT'S INCLUDED
£30.00-£35.00 per person. Includes breakfast.

Llwyndu Farmhouse

Wonderful old features enhance farmhouse that overlooks the bay

With exposed oak beams, inglenook fireplaces and a stone spiral staircase, this late 16th century farmhouse exudes a sense of history in a magnificent location overlooking Cardigan Bay. A Grade II Listed building, Llwyndu Farmhouse provides comfortable accommodation combined with an informal and cheery welcome, good food and a selection of reasonably-priced wines and micro-brewery beers and ciders.

Guest accommodation respects the age and character of the building yet contains the latest home comforts. Several rooms are in the farmhouse and several more in the converted 18th century granary next to the house. All have en suite bathrooms and are comfortably appointed with TVs, drinks facilities and sofas.

Dining at Llwyndu is an experience with the candlelight and old lamps creating their own dancing patterns on the stonework, the huge inglenook and the ancient oak timbers. Excellent two and a three-course dinners are prepared to order using fresh ingredients from local producers or suppliers and include local Welsh black beef, superb lamb and a very good selection of Welsh cheeses. Ω

Matter of facts

CONTACT
Peter Thompson
T +44 (0)1341 280144
E intouch@
llwyndu-farmhouse.co.uk
W llwyndu-farmhouse.co.uk
Address Llwyndu
Farmhouse, Llanaber,
Barmouth, Gwynedd
LL42 1RR

RATING
VisitWales 4 Star
Guest Accommodation

SLEEPING
Seven bedrooms comprising four double/twin rooms, two four-poster rooms and the Granary suite, all en suite.

FOR THE FAMILY
Cots and highchairs available.

FACILITIES
Comfortable lounge; dining room serving two and three-course dinners every day except Sunday.

NEAREST SHOPS, PUBS AND RESTAURANTS
Barmouth, two miles away.

OUT AND ABOUT
Harlech Castle; Portmeirion; Mawddach Estuary and trail from Dolgellau to Barmouth; Barmouth Bridge; Cadair Idris; Rhinog Mountains; Llanfair Slate Caverns; arduous walks and scintillating scenery.

PRICES PER ROOM PER NIGHT AND WHAT'S INCLUDED
B&B £88.00-£94.00; dinner, B&B £144.00-£150.00 – all prices based on two sharing.

Lonmay Old Manse

BY FRASERBURGH, ABERDEENSHIRE
5 STAR B&B

Local produce is high on shopping list at recently refurbished manse

Built by the Church of Scotland in 1820, the manse has been comprehensively and sympathetically refurbished since coming into new ownership in 2002, transforming it into an elegant and spacious B&B with three large double or twin rooms with generous en suite facilities.

Situated in two acres of grounds next to the North East Coastal Trail between Peterhead and Fraserburgh, this hidden gem in an undiscovered corner of Scotland has spectacular and uninterrupted views of the countryside.

Hosts Pam and John place great emphasis on quality, locally-sourced produce and in addition to the imaginative and extensive breakfast menu, which includes fish, bacon and home-produced eggs, dinners are available by prior arrangement. In summer you can enjoy a game of croquet in the lovely walled garden while winter is the time to curl up in front of the open fire in the sitting room or the cosy log burner in the dining room which enhance the warm and secluded atmosphere that the manse offers. Ω

Matter of facts

CONTACT
Pamela Hall
T +44 (0)1346 532227
E info@lonmay.co.uk
W lonmay.co.uk
Address Lonmay Old Manse, Lonmay, by Fraserburgh, Aberdeenshire AB43 8UJ

RATING
VisitScotland 5 Star B&B

SLEEPING
One twin/super king-size double with en suite bathroom and separate shower; one king-size double with en suite bathroom; one king-size double with en suite shower.

FACILITIES
Evening meals from simple suppers to four-course dinners by prior notice; large, secluded garden; croquet; all rooms have thermostatically-controlled radiators, hairdryer, bathrobe, extra bedding, complimentary mineral water, toiletries and fresh flowers.

NEAREST SHOPS, PUBS AND RESTAURANTS
St Combs and Crimond village shops locally; Fraserburgh for general shopping. Pubs and restaurants in Lonmay, St Combs (five-minute drive) and Fraserburgh (10-minute drive).

OUT AND ABOUT
Loch of Strathberg nature reserve (Royal Society for the Protection of Birds); Kinnaird Head Lighthouse Museum; Fraserburgh; Cairnbulg Castle and Cairness House; beach walks at St Combs; woodland walks on doorstep; various links golf courses.

PRICES PER PERSON AND WHAT'S INCLUDED
B&B from £32.00 per night; four nights or more from £30.00 per night. Two-course simple supper from £18.00 per head; dinner £25.00-£30.00 per head.

Lonsdale Hotel

BOWNESS-ON-WINDERMERE, CUMBRIA
4 STAR SILVER AWARD GUEST HOUSE

No expense spared by owners to give visitors the best Lakes experience

Ideally situated for Lakeland, shops, bars and restaurants, the Lonsdale was built in Bowness in 1851, originally as a private gentleman's residence. It first became a guest house in 1973 and was acquired in the winter of 2003 by the present owners who immediately embarked on a £250,000 refurbishment and upgrade.

Guest accommodation consists of large, luxury, en suite bedrooms and includes family rooms which sleep up to five people, four-poster rooms and rooms with splendid views of Lake Windermere. All are decorated and finished to a high standard throughout and are equipped with TVs and videos, radios, alarm clocks, hairdryers and tea and coffee-making facilities.

The Lonsdale also has a breakfast dining room, a lounge where snacks and drinks are served at any time of the day and a licensed bar which serves draught and bottled beers and a wide selection of spirits and soft drinks at any time guests require them. The lounge also has a library of novels and board games for guests' use. Ω

Matter of facts

CONTACT
Stewart Kershaw
T +44 (0)1539 443348
E info@lonsdale-hotel.co.uk
W lonsdale-hotel.co.uk
Address
Lonsdale Hotel,
Lake Road,
Bowness-on-Windermere,
Cumbria LA23 2JJ

RATING
VisitBritain 4 Star Silver Award Guest House

SLEEPING
Three double rooms and seven family rooms, including four-poster, all en suite.

FOR THE FAMILY
Cots and highchairs available.

FACILITIES
Lounge; licensed bar; parking.

NEAREST SHOPS, PUBS AND RESTAURANTS
All within walking distance in Bowness.

OUT AND ABOUT
Bowness; Dove Cottage and the Wordsworth Museum; Ullswater and Penrith; Holehird Garden; Long Meg and Her Daughters; Brougham Castle; Furness Abbey.

PRICES PER NIGHT AND WHAT'S INCLUDED
Double room £70.00-£110.00 per room based on two people sharing; single occupancy of double room from £55.00. Includes breakfast.

Macdonald Holyrood Hotel

EDINBURGH 4 STAR HOTEL

Hospitality at its finest right in the heart of the Scottish capital

With Edinburgh Castle, the Royal Mile and Princes Street virtually on the doorstep, Macdonald Holyrood Hotel is perfectly placed for those wishing to explore the Scottish capital.

The 156 delightfully-appointed, en suite bedrooms offer a choice of classic or Club Floor rooms. All have air conditioning, data ports, cable TV, desk, minibar, tea and coffee-making facilities, complimentary mineral water, iron and ironing board and shoeshine service. In addition, guests of the Club Floor rooms have private lift access; a private library, lounge and bar and champagne and canapé reception every evening.

Leisure facilities include Vital, one of the UK's most contemporary health, fitness and beauty clubs with a 14-metre swimming pool, sauna, steam room, hydro spa, state-of-the-art gym and beauty treatment rooms.

The Macdonald Holyrood offers a choice of dining. The one AA Rosette Opus 504 serves beef from the finest Scottish herds. The menu is fresh and varied with creamed Arbroath smokie, cullen skink, wild sea bass, poached smoked haddock, fillet, ribeye chop and T-bone. Relaxed and informal dining and afternoon teas are available in the lounge. Ω

Matter of facts

CONTACT
Reservations
T +44 (0)131 528 8173
E holyrood@
macdonald-hotels.co.uk
W macdonald-hotels.
co.uk/holyrood
Address Macdonald
Holyrood Hotel,
81 Holyrood Road,
Edinburgh EH8 8AU

RATING
VisitScotland 4 Star Hotel

SLEEPING
156 en suite bedrooms,
including classic doubles
or twins and junior suites
and Club Floor doubles
and junior suites.

FOR THE FAMILY
Cots and highchairs
available.

FACILITIES
One AA Rosette restaurant;
lounge and bar serving
food; wedding ceremonies;

concierge service;
banquets for up to 150;
conference and events
facilities; 24-hour room
service.

**NEAREST SHOPS, PUBS
AND RESTAURANTS**
Many within walking
distance on the Royal Mile
and Prince's Street.

OUT AND ABOUT
Edinburgh Castle; Palace
of Holyrood House;
Scottish Parliament;
National Galleries of
Scotland; National
Museums of Scotland;
Playhouse and Kings
Theatres; Dynamic Earth.

**PRICES PER ROOM
PER NIGHT AND
WHAT'S INCLUDED**
£110.00-£240.00
(supplements may apply to
Club Floor and junior suite
rooms). Includes
continental breakfast.

Magnolia House

CANTERBURY, KENT 5 DIAMOND
GOLD AWARD GUEST ACCOMMODATION

Cathedral city is great centre for exploring the Garden of England

This late Georgian, family guest house offers first class B&B accommodation in a quiet, residential street just 10 minutes' stroll from Canterbury city centre. It is ideally located for exploring the city, coastline or the beautiful Kent countryside.

The professionally-designed guest bedrooms are all en suite and have TV, radio/alarm clock, hairdryer, robes, sewing kit and a fridge stocked with fresh milk for tea and fresh coffee-making facilities. There is even complimentary wine and mineral water to welcome you on your arrival. The ground-floor Garden Room (right) has a queen-sized four-poster and spacious bathroom and is ideal for that special occasion.

The guest sitting room is well stocked with books, magazines, board games and tourist information while a feature of any stay at Magnolia House is the full and varied breakfast. Choose from a traditional English breakfast, fish or a continental breakfast, all prepared using fresh, local produce wherever possible and served overlooking the attractive, walled garden. Ω

Matter of facts

CONTACT
Isobelle Leggett
T +44 (0)1227 765121
E info@magnoliahouse
canterbury.co.uk
W magnoliahouse
canterbury.co.uk
Address Magnolia House,
36 St Dunstan's Terrace,
Canterbury, Kent CT2 8AX

RATING
VisitBritain 5-Diamond
Gold Award Guest
Accommodation; AA 5
Stars.

SLEEPING
Seven rooms comprising
single, double and twin,
including The Garden
Room with queen-size
four-poster. All en suite.

FOR THE FAMILY
Children aged 12 and
over welcome.

FACILITIES
Guest sitting room with
books, magazines, games
and tourist information;
parking; wireless Internet
access; welcome tray.

**NEAREST SHOPS, PUBS
AND RESTAURANTS**
Comprehensive range
of shops, pubs and
restaurants in city centre.

OUT AND ABOUT
Canterbury Cathedral;
St Augustine's Abbey;
Marlowe Theatre and
Gulbenkian Theatre; St
Lawrence Cricket Ground;
The Westgate Gardens;
ideal base for exploring
coast and countryside.

**PRICES PER NIGHT
AND WHAT'S INCLUDED**
Single room £55.00-
£65.00; double room with
single occupancy £65.00-
£110.00; double room
with en suite bath and
shower £110.00; double
room with en suite shower
£95.00; four-poster suite
£125.00-£145.00.

Manorhouse

BURY ST EDMUNDS, SUFFOLK
5 STAR GOLD AWARD B&B

Inglenooks and beams galore in house overlooking the village green

Welcoming and relaxed, this award-winning, 15th century timbered longhouse, set in large gardens, overlooks Beyton's picturesque village green. Furnished with antiques, oak beams, inglenooks and fresh flowers, the house has four large, luxurious, en suite rooms with king-size or twin beds and sofas.

Two of the four individually-designed bedrooms are on the ground floor in the barn conversion. All rooms have tea and coffee-making facilities, TV, radio, alarm clock and hairdryer. Washing, drying and ironing facilities are available to guests along with the use of a fridge-freezer.

Ideally located four miles east of Bury St Edmunds and 35 minutes from Cambridge, Manorhouse provides an excellent choice of breakfasts which include fresh fruit compotes and home-made preserves. Special diets are catered for. The large dining room features an inglenook fireplace with 12th century pillars from Bury St Edmunds Abbey and beamed walls and ceilings. A 'where to eat' list can be found on the Manorhouse website. Ω

Matter of facts

CONTACT
Kay and Mark Dewsbury
T +44 (0)1359 270960
E manorhouse@
beyton.com
W beyton.com
Address Manorhouse,
The Green,
Beyton,
nr Bury St Edmunds,
Suffolk IP30 9AF

RATING
VisitBritain 5 Star
Gold Award B&B

SLEEPING
Two king-size double
rooms and two twin
rooms, all en suite.

FACILITIES
Laundry service;
garden; fridge-freezer;
parking.

**NEAREST SHOPS, PUBS
AND RESTAURANTS**
Nearest shops one mile;
two pubs with food within
walking distance in village;
several good local inns.

OUT AND ABOUT
Bury St Edmunds
Cathedral; Abbey Gardens;
Wyken Hall; Ickworth
House (National Trust).

**PRICES PER PERSON
PER NIGHT AND
WHAT'S INCLUDED**
King-size double/twin
room £32.00-£35.00.
Includes full English
breakfast.

Manor House Farm

UTTOXETER, STAFFORDSHIRE
4 STAR SILVER AWARD FARMHOUSE

Take a step back in time at Jacobean farmhouse close to Alton Towers

Manor House Farm is an enchanting, rambling Jacobean farmhouse with oak timbers, tapestry drapes and an amazing collection of oak furniture. Built mainly between 1580 and 1708, this 170-acre, Grade II Listed farm lies at the confluence of the Dove and Churnet valleys and offers a glimpse into days gone by with its oak-panelled dining room and antique furniture.

The bedrooms, all with four-poster beds and en suite bathrooms, have beautiful views over the extensive terraced gardens or the dramatic Weaver Hills. Open log fires in both sitting and dining rooms add to that fabulous old world charm in what is a unique house for the discerning guest who expects that little bit extra.

Manor House Farm prides itself on the quality of its breakfasts. The morning feast of home cooking is just the thing to set you up for a day at nearby Alton Towers or a tour of the many stately homes within easy reach. Ω

Matter of facts

CONTACT
Chris Ball
T +44 (0)1889 590415
E cm_ball@yahoo.co.uk
W 4posteraccom.com
Address
Manor House Farm,
Prestwood, Denstone,
Uttoxeter,
Staffordshire ST14 5DD

RATING
VisitBritain 4 Star Silver
Award Farmhouse

SLEEPING
Four bedrooms, three with four-posters, one with half-tester, all en suite.

FOR THE FAMILY
Children welcome.

FACILITIES
Guests' lounge; in-room TV; extensive garden; Victorian summer house; tennis; croquet; barbeques; on-site parking.

NEAREST SHOPS, PUBS AND RESTAURANTS
Shops nearby in Rocester, Uttoxeter and Ashbourne; pubs and restaurants in Denstone (one mile), Alton, Mayfield and Marston Montgomery.

OUT AND ABOUT
Alton Towers (two miles); Shugborough Hall; Haddon Hall; Chatsworth; Sudbury Hall; tranquil valleys of the Dove, Churnet and Manifold; pottery of Stoke-on-Trent; market towns of Ashbourne and Uttoxeter; good base for golf, swimming, cycling and pony trekking.

PRICES PER NIGHT AND WHAT'S INCLUDED
Double room £27.00-£30.00 per person based on two sharing; single room £34.00-£40.00. Includes breakfast.

Mansefield B&B

GREENLAW, BERWICKSHIRE 4 STAR SILVER AWARD B&B

Family atmosphere is key ingredient in warm welcome offered by owners

Informality within a warm, family atmosphere is the central theme of this B&B in a traditional, Scottish Georgian former minister's house.

Mansefield, in the small, historic Scottish border town of Greenlaw, is the family home of the Culham family. Owners Tim and Pippa Culham lead a busy life with school-age children and a small farm with chickens, horses, sheep and pigs. Guests have a drawing room all to themselves, and there's a garden, paddocks and 250 metres of riverbank on the Blackadder where you can fish.

The main part of the house contains a twin bedroom with private bathroom and a smaller overflow bedroom should families require it. There is also a double/twin bedroom with luxury en suite bathroom in a separate wing.

Breakfast – and dinner if you require it – is served in the drawing room and, dependent on availability, includes home baking, fresh coffee, cheese scones, eggs from the Culham's free-range hens, their own recipe pork and pheasant sausages, home-grown bacon and local honey. They also grow their own vegetables and use organic food when available. Ω

Matter of facts

CONTACT
Pippa and Tim Culham
T +44 (0)1361 810260
E timc@tesco.net
W aboutscotland.com
Address Mansefield B&B, 35 East High Street, Greenlaw, Berwickshire TD10 6YF

RATING
VisitScotland 4 Star Silver Award B&B

SLEEPING
One luxury, en suite, double/twin room; one twin room with private bathroom and smaller overflow bedroom for family use.

FOR THE FAMILY
Cots; large garden with trampoline.

FACILITIES
Guests' drawing room with TV games, chess, piano and wood-burning stove; washing machine; off-road parking; TV connections and tea and coffee-making facilities with fresh milk in all rooms.

NEAREST SHOPS, PUBS AND RESTAURANTS
Greenlaw village has a Post Office, two stores, a butcher, bank, chemist and two pubs. Various restaurants in the area.

OUT AND ABOUT
Abbeys at Kelso, Jedburgh, Melrose and Dryburgh; Mellerstain House; Manderston House; Floors Castle; Thirlestane Castle; Chain Bridge; Tweed River; Southern Upland Way (five miles) for walking; fishing; shooting; riding.

PRICES PER NIGHT AND WHAT'S INCLUDED
En suite double room £35.00 per person; twin room with private bath £30.00 per person; third room £25.00. Includes breakfast.

Mansefield House

LOCH LONG, ARGYLL & BUTE 4 STAR SELF-CATERING

A loch at the foot of the garden and mountains beyond provide great views

Close enough to Loch Long to hear the lapping of its waters at the foot of the garden and high enough to enjoy breathtaking views out to the Arrochar Alps, Mansefield House is a retreat of rare exception just 45 minutes from Glasgow.

A fine, Grade B Listed Victorian house in the Loch Lomond and the Trossachs National Park – Loch Lomond lies just two miles to the east – Mansefield House retains many original features and can accommodate up to 12 people. Large, gracious reception rooms with high ceilings and ornate cornicing lend themselves to entertaining, while the main character of the house is warm, comfortable and homely. A large dining room with wood-burning stove, large sitting room and spacious kitchen with range cooker comprise the main rooms of the house.

A fully-equipped laundry/drying room ensures that all your wet gear will be dry by morning. There is also a games room, complete with a half-size snooker table and doors leading to the patio and large private mature gardens. Ω

Matter of facts

CONTACT
Fiona Butcher
T +44 (0)1301 702956
or +44 (0)7958 771106
E accommodation@
mansefieldhouse.com
W mansefieldhouse.com
Address Mansefield House,
Arrochar, Loch Long,
Argyll & Bute, G83 7AG

RATING
VisitScotland 4 Star
Self-Catering

SLEEPING
Sleeps 12 – four doubles;
one twin; two guest beds.
Two en suite bathrooms,
one family bathroom and
one separate toilet.

FOR THE FAMILY
Cot and highchair provided.
Enclosed garden. Dogs
welcome (£20 supplement)

FACILITIES
Pottery studio behind
house; barbeque; wireless
broadband; CD, satellite TV,
DVD, video with additional
TV and video in games
room; parking for five cars.

NEAREST SHOPS, PUBS AND RESTAURANTS
There is a well-supplied
village shop, greengrocer,
Post Office, petrol station,
coffee shop and newsagent
in Arrochar. The renowned
Village Inn – a pub and à la
carte restaurant serving fine
Scottish fare and a wide
variety of real ales and
whiskies – is just 100
metres from Mansefield
House. Other excellent
restaurants in immediate
vicinity include The Loch
Fyne Oyster Bar, The
George in Inveraray and
Inver Cottage near Strachur.

OUT AND ABOUT
The immediate area has a
wealth of attractions,
including Inveraray Castle,
the glorious gardens of
Argyll and Bute, Charles
Rennie Mackintosh's Hill
House, and the Glengoyne
Whisky Distillery. Activities
such as walking, climbing,
golf, mountain biking, horse
riding, fishing, sailing and
various other watersports
are on the doorstep.

PRICES AND WHAT'S INCLUDED
Minimum two-night stays
start at £650.00. Weekly
rates from £850.00-
£1,600.00. Includes
heating, electricity and linen.

MapleLeaf Middlewick

HOLIDAY COTTAGES & B&B

GLASTONBURY, SOMERSET 4 STAR SELF-CATERING

Eight cottages amid spectacular scenery in area of myth and legend

In the shadow of the famed Glastonbury Tor, these eight comfortable, rustic cottages converted from an early 17th century, Grade II Listed farmstead exude peace and tranquillity in an area steeped in history, myth and legend.

Nestled in 16 acres of gardens, horse paddocks and a cider orchard, MapleLeaf Middlewick offers 15 miles of unrivalled views across Wells and its cathedral to the Cheddar Gorge and the Mendip Hills. Guests have use of the indoor heated swimming pool and may book the steam room or treatments in the 'pamper room'. Larger groups may wish to book the fabulous new function room. With its wooden floors, wood-burning stove, kitchen and tables to seat up to 36 it's ideal for dining, workshops, yoga, and so on.

Set around a courtyard with lawns and gardens, the cottages are a blend of old and new with natural stone and timber interiors, capped inglenook fireplaces and exposed beams. All cottages have wireless Internet access. Ω

Matter of facts

CONTACT
Amanda I'ons
T +44 (0)1458 832351
E middlewick@
btconnect.com
W middlewickholiday
cottages.co.uk
Address MapleLeaf
Middlewick Holiday
Cottages, Wick Lane,
Glastonbury,
Somerset BA6 8JW

RATING
VisitBritain 4 Star
Self-Catering

SLEEPING
Eight cottages with
between one and three
bedrooms sleeping up
to six people plus a cot.

FOR THE FAMILY
Plenty of space in which to
play; cots available.

FACILITIES
Heated indoor swimming
pool; treatment room with
qualified local therapists;
steam room; large function
room; ample parking;
wireless Internet access in
all cottages; the Wendy
Pottery is on site.

**NEAREST SHOPS, PUBS
AND RESTAURANTS**
Glastonbury, two miles,
where crystals and all
things new age sit
alongside traditional market
town retailers, while the
numerous cafés create the
perfect place for relaxed
dining. Wells is five miles
away.

OUT AND ABOUT
Glastonbury Abbey;
Glastonbury Tor; Chalice
Wells and Gardens; Rural
Life Museum; Wells
Cathedral; Bishop's Palace,
Wells; Wookey Hole Caves;
Cheddar Caves and Gorge;
Longleat; Stourhead;
Roman Baths, Costume
Museum and Royal
Crescent, Bath; Bristol Zoo;
Haynes Motor Museum;
Fleet Air Arm Museum; SS
Great Britain; Stonehenge.

**PRICES AND
WHAT'S INCLUDED**
£220.00-£770.00 per
week. Short breaks in low
season £154.00-£357.00
(Friday-Monday or
Monday-Friday). Includes
bed linen and towels.

Marlborough House

BATH, SOMERSET 4 STAR GUEST HOUSE

Organic foods a speciality at this friendly, period atmosphere B&B

Marlborough House is an enchanting and impressive Victorian stone house close to the centre of Georgian Bath. Built in 1876, the house is run in a friendly and informal manner and has well-proportioned and spacious rooms which are furnished with antiques to create a period atmosphere.

Its six bedrooms are handsomely furnished and contain either an antique wood four-poster or a Victorian brass and iron bed. Each room is unique in style and all are equipped with TV, direct-dial telephone, high-speed wireless Internet access, radio/alarm clock and organic herbal toiletries. You will even find a well-stocked hostess tray and a complimentary sherry.

Breakfasts are cooked to order and are served in either the elegant parlour or lovely dining room. Marlborough House specialises in organic foods, including a wide range of cereals, juices, yoghurts, fresh fruits and jams, English cheeses, eggs and milk and a selection of excellent breads and croissants, as well as fresh-roasted continental coffees and all manner of Fairtrade organic teas. Ω

Matter of facts

CONTACT
Peter Moore
T +44 (0)1225 318175
or +44 (0)7960 907541
E mars@
manque.dircon.co.uk
W marlborough-house.net
Address
Marlborough House,
1 Marlborough Lane,
Bath BA1 2NQ

RATING
VisitBritain and AA
4 Star Guest House;
Green Tourism Merit
Award.

SLEEPING
Six double/twin rooms,
some with four-posters
and all en suite.

FOR THE FAMILY
Children welcome; pets by
arrangement charged at
£10.00 per night.

FACILITIES
Parlour; dining room;
breakfast available by
room service.

**NEAREST SHOPS, PUBS
AND RESTAURANTS**
Many and varied a short
walk away in city centre.

OUT AND ABOUT
Bath Abbey and the Abbey
Heritage Vaults; Roman
Thermae Bath Spa;
Jane Austen Centre; Sally
Lunn's house; Stonehenge;
Wells; Glastonbury;
Lacock; Castle Combe;
Cheddar Gorge; Longleat.

**PRICES PER NIGHT
AND WHAT'S INCLUDED**
Double/twin rooms
£95.00-£125.00 based
on two sharing; additional
adults £10.00-£20.00,
children £5.00-£10.00.

Matfen Hall

MATFEN, NEWCASTLE UPON TYNE 4 STAR SILVER AWARD COUNTRY HOUSE HOTEL

High accolades go to fitness club, restaurant and the hotel overall

Charm and character are evident throughout Matfen Hall's 53 luxurious bedrooms, award-winning restaurant, dedicated conference suites and its acclaimed Spa and Leisure Club, recently voted No 1 in the Fitness Industry Association's FLAME awards.

Named Large Hotel of the Year 2006 in the Enjoy England Awards for Excellence, Matfen Hall is a magnificent country house hotel set in beautiful countryside. Its bedrooms are all en suite with satellite TVs, direct-dial telephones and all the amenities you would expect. Its premier and deluxe rooms are particularly spacious with seating areas and luxurious bathrooms and four-poster rooms are also available.

Matfen Hall offers fine dining in the form of the two AA Rosette Library and Print Room Restaurant, one of Northumberland's finest. Snacks are served in the Conservatory Bar overlooking the final green of the hotel's own golf course (there is also a nine-hole par three course) and excellent pub meals are available in the Keepers Lodge, the perfect 19th hole for golfers and non-golfers alike. Ω

Matter of facts

CONTACT
Reservations
T +44 (0)1661 855708
E reservations@matfenhall.com
W matfenhall.com
Address
Matfen Hall,
Matfen,
Newcastle upon Tyne
NE20 0RH

RATING
VisitBritain 4 Star Silver Award Country House Hotel

SLEEPING
53 en suite bedrooms comprising classic, deluxe and premier rooms and including four-poster rooms.

FOR THE FAMILY
Children over seven welcome.

FACILITIES
Award-winning leisure club and luxury spa; two AA Rosette restaurant; Conservatory Bar; 27-hole golf course plus nine-hole par three, golf academy, driving range and Keepers Lodge clubhouse; wedding ceremonies and receptions; conferences and events.

NEAREST SHOPS, PUBS AND RESTAURANTS
At Corbridge.

OUT AND ABOUT
Hadrian's Wall; Newcastle city centre (25 minutes); Newcastle International Airport (15 minutes).

PRICES AND WHAT'S INCLUDED
From £175.00 per room B&B. Special interest breaks available.

Melrose House

LONDON 4 STAR B&B

Easy access to London's shops and theatres plus Garden of England

Close enough to central London to get there in 15 minutes by train yet far enough away to escape the hustle and bustle and offer out-of-town pricing, Melrose House is a beautifully-restored Victorian townhouse with a warm, friendly atmosphere.

Located in a quiet suburb of southeast London, Melrose House was built in 1885 and has nine guest bedrooms which are a mix of single, double and family rooms, all with en suite or private bathrooms and all furnished to a high standard, complete with LCD TVs with Freeview. One room has a four-poster bed. Two of the double/twin rooms and a large family room situated in the new unit overlooking the courtyard garden with its large pond and seasonal flowers have the advantage of ground-floor access.

Breakfast of fruit juice, fruit, yoghurts, cereals, breads and scones, cheese, scrambled or boiled eggs, bacon, sausages and preserves is served in the airy dining room and the bright conservatory which looks on to the garden. Ω

Matter of facts

CONTACT
Frances Roberts
T +44 (0)208 776 8884
E melrosehouse@
supanet.com
W uk-bedandbreakfast.com
Address
Melrose House,
89 Lennard Road,
London SE20 7LY

RATING
VisitBritain 4 Star B&B

SLEEPING
Nine bedrooms comprising one single, one family and seven double/twin rooms.

FOR THE FAMILY
Not suitable for children under 12.

FACILITIES
Most rooms have tea and coffee-making facilities; hairdryer; personal safe and a trouser press. Garden with pond; conservatory; off-street parking.

NEAREST SHOPS, LOCAL PUBS, RESTAURANTS
Wide selection of shops, pubs and restaurants within a 10-minute walk.

OUT AND ABOUT
Easy access to central London and the Kent countryside. In the immediate vicinity are several golf clubs and sports centres; The Royal Watermen's Almshouses, built around 1840 to house retired Thames ferrymen; London's oldest working police station, built in 1872; Crystal Palace Park and National Sports Centre; Hornimans Museum; Down House, the home of Charles Darwin.

PRICES PER NIGHT AND WHAT'S INCLUDED
Single room £40.00-£50.00; double/twin £55.00-£65.00; triple room £70.00-£75.00; family room (sleeps four) £85.00-£90.00. Includes breakfast.

Mill of Blackhall

MENMUIR, ANGUS 4 STAR SELF-CATERING

Watermill carefully restored to provide a relaxing retreat close to attractions

This Grade II Listed watermill ground corn in the 16th century and was enlarged in the 17th century. Using the warm red sandstone from redundant farmsteads and internal architectural features recycled from the University of Aberdeen's old King's College Library and Marischal College Museum, it has now been converted into a house which retains features of previous eras, including the waterwheel.

Exposed beams, arched doorways and traditional flagstones, combined with period furniture, oriental rugs, timber floors and views over fields to a small trout stream, create a setting of character for a relaxing holiday close to numerous attractions.

Sleeping up to eight people, the mill has a large living room with inglenook fireplace and wood-burning stove; a big eat-in kitchen; three double/twin bedrooms, one en suite; a study/ bedroom with double sofa bed; a bathroom and a downstairs cloakroom. The large garden includes trees, lawns, shallow ponds and flagged and gravelled areas. The waterwheel is stationary and is secured by a chain. Ω

Matter of facts

CONTACT
Dr John Cummins
T +44 (0)1356 660211
E johnofblackhall@aol.com
W menmuir.org.uk/blackhall
Address
Mill of Blackhall,
Menmuir,
Angus DD9 7RJ

RATING
VisitBritain 4 Star
Self-Catering

SLEEPING
One double with en suite;
two twins, one with
washbasin; study/bedroom
with double sofa bed.

FOR THE FAMILY
Cot and highchair; large
enclosed garden; many
books and games.

FACILITIES
TV with Freeview; video;
radio; stone-built barbecue;
oil-fired central heating;
washer; tumble dryer;
microwave; dishwasher;
fridge and freezer.

**NEAREST SHOPS, PUBS
AND RESTAURANTS**
3.5 miles away in Brechin.

OUT AND ABOUT
Caledonian Steam Railway;
Glamis, Edzell and
Dunottar castles; Scone
Palace; Falkland Palace; a
large array of stone circles
and Pictish relics; the
House of Dun and the
Abbey of Arbroath. Many
day and half-day trips
including Balmoral and
various distilleries. Great
area for walking, angling
and shooting; golf
(Carnoustie, St Andrews
etc – golf equipment
provided); birdwatching;
glens and sandy beaches
in easy reach.

**PRICES PER WEEK
AND WHAT'S INCLUDED**
£375.00-£695.00. Short
breaks by arrangement.
Includes electricity, bed-
linen (duvets), towels and
welcome pack. Non-
smokers only.

Millness Croft Cottages

INVERNESS, INVERNESS-SHIRE 5 STAR SELF-CATERING

Croft-style luxury cottages in the heart of the Scottish Highlands

Cattle, sheep, chickens, wild deer, eagles, buzzards and pine martens on this 120-acre croft help make these luxury Millness Croft Cottages the perfect Highland hideaway.

Set in majestic scenery on the doorstep of four spectacular glens, the three cottages, Fraser, Grant and Chisholm, are built in traditional croft style but with the most modern comforts of home.

Overlooking the forest and river, each cottage is private and has been beautifully and tastefully decorated with excellent fixtures and fittings. Wood-burning stoves, solid oak floors, satellite TV, DVD, Internet access, spa baths, an in-house chef's service and a welcome package are among the many luxuries which make this a home-from-home. Each also has a private parking area, garden with barbeque and deck or patio with quality outdoor furniture.

Millness Croft Cottages enjoy a fantastic central location, ideal for exploring the whole of the Highlands. They are just 10 minutes from Loch Ness and 25 minutes from the wonderfully cosmopolitan city of Inverness with its International airport. Ω

Matter of facts

CONTACT
Justine Akeroyd
T +44 (0)1456 476761
E info@millnesscroft.co.uk
W millnesscroft.co.uk
Address
Millness Croft Cottages,
Glen Urquhart,
Inverness,
Inverness-shire IV63 6TW

RATING
VisitScotland
5 Star Self Catering

SLEEPING
Grant and Fraser cottages each have one double and one twin room; Chisholm cottage has a double room.

FOR THE FAMILY
Cot, baby bath, highchairs, booster seats, safety gates, toys, fire guards and baby bouncing seats are available free of charge.

FACILITIES
In-house chef's service for home-made meals, sourced locally and delivered direct to cottage; free broadband Internet; welcome pack including our free-range eggs, milk, bread, butter and a bottle of wine; complimentary toiletries; an essentials pack with tea bags, coffee, toilet rolls, washing up liquid and the like to help during the first few days.

NEAREST SHOPS, LOCAL PUBS, RESTAURANTS
At Cannich (five minutes) or Drumnadrochit (12 minutes) for a couple of 'supply-everything' shops and Post Office, plus doctor's surgery, a few pubs and restaurants and petrol stations. There are many pubs and restaurants in the area, most providing good, local food and drink, and usually with log fires.

OUT AND ABOUT
Loch Ness; Urquhart Castle; Inverness; Culloden battlefield; whisky routes; golf; both east and west coasts easily accessible.

PRICES PER WEEK AND WHAT'S INCLUDED
£500.00-£930.00. Includes all utilities, wood for burner, linen, towels, welcome pack and basic essentials. Special celebration packages available.

Millstream Hotel

BOSHAM, CHICHESTER, WEST SUSSEX
3 STAR GOLD AWARD HOTEL

Hotel that's cosy in winter and with a garden that's a delight in summer

A stone's throw from the shores where, legend has it, King Canute tried to turn back the tide, you will find this elegant hotel and restaurant, named after the millstream that meanders through its typically English country garden.

The 300-year-old property combines the elegance of a small country house with the charm of an 18th century malthouse cottage. It features a charming sitting room with deep-cushioned armchairs and grand piano, and a bar with a cosy, fireside setting and doors opening on to the lawns where you can sit beneath a sunshade on warmer days and listen to the chatter of the ducks. The two AA rosette restaurant offers modern British cooking where the emphasis is on freshness and seasonality of ingredients which are sourced locally. The superb food is complemented by a wide selection of wines from an established cellar.

The individually-furnished and decorated en suite bedrooms are all equipped with flatscreen TVs, radio/CD/alarm clocks, tea/coffee facilities, telephones, wall safes, trouser presses, hairdryers and wireless Internet. Ω

Matter of facts

CONTACT
Antony Wallace
T +44 (0)1243 573234
E info@
millstream-hotel.co.uk
W millstream-hotel.co.uk
Address The Millstream
Hotel and Restaurant,
Bosham Lane,
Bosham, Chichester,
West Sussex PO18 8HL

RATING
VisitBritain 3 Star
Gold Award Hotel

SLEEPING
35 single, double/twin,
four-poster rooms and
suites, all with en suite.

FOR THE FAMILY
Children's menu; baby-
listening; highchairs and
cots available.

FACILITIES
Restaurant (two AA Rosette);
licensed bar; sitting room
with grand piano; wireless
Internet access.

NEAREST SHOPS, PUBS AND RESTAURANTS
Farm shop one mile;
Chichester town centre
four miles.

OUT AND ABOUT
Fishbourne Roman Palace;
Chichester Festival Theatre;
Pallant House Gallery;
Goodwood House; West
Dean Gardens; Weald and
Downland Open Air
Museum of Historic Houses;
Chichester Harbour;
Tangmere Aviation Museum;
Petworth House and Park;
Uppark House and Garden.

PRICES PER PERSON PER NIGHT AND WHAT'S INCLUDED
Dinner, B&B from £82.00
to £105.00.

Millstr
Hotel
and
Restaura

Lunches
Dinner

Mitchell's of Chester

CHESTER, CHESHIRE 5 STAR SILVER AWARD B&B

Historic Chester is on your doorstep at this versatile Victorian B&B

This elegant, Victorian residence is located in a select residential area a 20-minute walk from the centre of historic Chester. Built in the 1850s, the house has steeply-pitched, slated roofs, a sweeping staircase and tall rooms with moulded cornices, providing a setting for many items of antique furniture. A large banqueting table forms the centrepiece of the dining room.

The lounge looks out and down on to unusual brick vaults tunnelling three metres under a quiet, well-maintained garden at the rear of the house. Mitchell's has book and video libraries each side of an open log fire in an original marble surround.

Bedrooms have been individually decorated, furnished in period style and include a fully-equipped shower room and toilet. They have individually-controlled central heating, TVs, refreshment trays, hairdryer, and clock/radios. Mitchell's has a wireless Internet connection for guests' use for a modest, returnable deposit.

There is a wide menu for breakfast, ranging from continental to full English. Vegetarian and special diets can usually be catered for by prior arrangement. Ω

Matter of facts

CONTACT
Helen and Colin Mitchell
T +44 (0)1244 679004
E mitoches@dialstart.net
W mitchellsofchester.com
Address
Mitchell's of Chester,
28 Hough Green, Chester,
Cheshire CH4 8JQ

RATING
VisitBritain 5 Star
Silver Award B&B

SLEEPING
Seven bedrooms, all
en suite.

FOR THE FAMILY
Cot and highchair
available.

FACILITIES
Wireless Internet; off-street
parking; iron and ironing
board available.

**NEAREST SHOPS, PUBS
AND RESTAURANTS**
In Chester city centre, a
20-minute walk away.

OUT AND ABOUT
Roman walled city of
Chester (pictured right);
Chester Racecourse; Chester
Zoo; Ellesmere Port Boat
Museum; Lady Lever Art
Gallery, Port Sunlight;
aquarium; North Wales.

**PRICES PER ROOM
PER NIGHT AND
WHAT'S INCLUDED**
Single room £40.00-
£42.00; double/twin room
£65.00-£72.00 based on
two people sharing; triple
room £87.00-£93.00;
four adults in a family
room £108.00-£116.00;
double/twin in family room
£70.00-£75.00. Includes
breakfast.

Nailey Cottages

BATH, SOMERSET 4 STAR SELF-CATERING

Working farm in an area of natural beauty is great wildlife retreat

If you like the idea of a 200-acre working farm in a largely undiscovered, unexploited Area of Outstanding Natural Beauty with a thriving wildlife community then you'll certainly like Nailey Cottages. A redundant farm building a stone's throw from the beautiful city of Bath has been superbly renovated to provide three cottages with a rustic feel but with fresh, contemporary styling.

Named after woods in the valley, Trulls, Dicknick and Longley are spacious and airy and feature cherry wood kitchens, English oak floors and bespoke furniture made by local craftsmen. Dark blue/black slate tiles clad the walk-in shower rooms and en suite bathrooms.

Longley and Dicknick, which each accommodate a maximum of six plus a cot, have wood-burning stoves in the dining rooms and upstairs galleried sitting rooms. Trulls accommodates a maximum of eight people plus cot and features a kitchen/dining room with stunning, uninterrupted panoramic views of the picturesque valley, and a living area with wood-burning stove and steps to the master double bedroom. Ω

Matter of facts

CONTACT
Mrs Brett Gardner
T +44 (0)1225 852989
E cottages@
naileyfarm.co.uk
W naileyfarm.co.uk
Address Nailey Cottages,
Nailey Farm,
St Catherine's Valley,
Bath BA1 8HD

RATING
VisitBritain 4 Star
Self-Catering

SLEEPING
Two two-bedroom cottages, each sleeping up to six, and one three-bedroom cottage sleeping up to eight.

FOR THE FAMILY
Farm animals; shared garden; books, toys and games; cots and highchairs available.

FACILITIES
Shared laundry with washing machine, tumble dryer, freezer, maps, guides and tourist information; in-cottage catering; holistic and Indian head massage; mini CD/radio systems and flatscreen TVs with DVDs and Freeview in each

cottage; barbeques and garden furniture available; ample parking space; stabling for horses.

NEAREST SHOPS, PUBS, AND RESTAURANTS
The thriving, ancient market town of Marshfield two miles away offers excellent shops and service and three historic pubs with food, wine and ale to suit every taste.

OUT AND ABOUT
Picturesque walks; city of Bath (15 minutes); Bristol (25 minutes); Castle Combe; Lacock; Longleat House and Safari Park; Westonbirt Arboretum; Bowood and Stourhead; the Cotswolds; 10 golf courses within easy reach.

PRICES PER WEEK AND WHAT'S INCLUDED
From £400.00-£850.00. Includes pure cotton percale bed linen, Egyptian cotton towels, one basket of logs, electricity, oil-fired central heating and hot water, welcome hamper, wireless Internet and VAT. Short breaks available.

New Inn

TRESCO, ISLES OF SCILLY
2 STAR SILVER AWARD HOTEL

Quality of the food puts this inn in the county's Delicious Dozen

One of only 12 pubs in Cornwall listed in the new *Eating Out in Pubs* Michelin Guide, the New Inn on Tresco in the Isles of Scilly stays open all year to give guests the opportunity to see migrant birds and fields of narcissi flowering, against the backdrop of empty beaches, deserted headlands and lush green fields.

The one AA Rosette restaurant provides an eclectic choice of dining, including a table d'hôte evening menu specialising in freshly caught seafood, Scillonian and Cornish seasonal produce and Tresco-reared beef. The wine list features a range of popular choices and a small selection of champagnes. Breakfast treats include smoked salmon and scrambled egg as an alternative to a full English or continental breakfast.

The en suite bedrooms are bright, airy, cosy and fully equipped. Two rooms have sun terraces overlooking the swimming pool and many have views of the sea over the picturesque harbour of New Grimsby. Ω

Matter of facts

CONTACT
Reception
T +44 (0)1720 422844
E newinn@tresco.co.uk
W tresco.co.uk
Address New Inn, Tresco, Isles of Scilly, Cornwall TR24 0QG

RATING
VisitBritain 2 Star Silver Award Hotel

SLEEPING
16 bedrooms, all en suite.

FOR THE FAMILY
Cot and highchair available.

FACILITIES
Swimming pool; Residents Bar; Driftwood Bar for light lunches and a wide range of Cornish and Scillonian ales; Pavilion Bar for fresh ground coffee and Cornish ice cream; beer garden with boules area; all-weather tennis court 500 yards from inn.

NEAREST SHOPS, PUBS AND RESTAURANTS
Tresco stores; two restaurants and bar meals in nearby Island Hotel.

OUT AND ABOUT
Tresco Abbey Garden; Gallery Tresco.

PRICES PER NIGHT AND WHAT'S INCLUDED
£70.00-£105.00 per person. Includes breakfast.

Oak Farm Barn

ROUGHAM, BURY ST EDMUNDS, SUFFOLK
4 STAR SILVER AWARD B&B

This newly-converted, beamed Suffolk barn with its stylish open-plan stairs and gallery is close to the heart of the village of Rougham. Originally built during the early 19th century, the barn is timber framed and roofed with traditional Suffolk pan tiles.

Many of the original oak beams are exposed, showing the rich oak grain and original craftsman's markings. Blended with this are hand-crafted solid oak doors and a stylish, traditional, open-plan oak staircase and landing walkway. A true family effort over an 18-month period has seen the building transformed into a unique experience for visitors.

The entrance hall floor incorporates the original floor bricks and the underfloor heating provides a warm welcome leading to three double or twin bedrooms, all with en suite facilities. Mobility-impaired guests are accommodated in the purpose-built twin room with access to wet room facilities.

The open staircase leads to the light and airy upstairs lounge and dining area which offers a relaxed country feel.

The three bedrooms are individually styled with handmade accessories and comprise a first-floor twin room with en suite bath and shower, a ground-floor, king-size double room with en suite shower

Restoration of original features transforms barn into visual delight

and a ground-floor twin room suitable for the less mobile with a large wet room with walk-in shower. All rooms have TVs and DVD players, hot drinks facilities and biscuits, alarm clocks, hairdryers, bath sheets and hand towels and toiletries.

The Barn stands in its own grounds and has ample off-road parking. As it is detached from the owners' house, guests can enjoy the benefits of being more independent. With their own door key they can come and go as they wish and can relax in the Barn throughout the day. There are two other areas where guests can relax – the main lounge on the first floor and the cosy seating area overlooking the patio.

Being in the heart of the countryside yet only 10 minutes from the centre of the local market town Bury St Edmunds, Oak Farm Barn is the ideal place to unwind and relax. Ω

Matter of facts

CONTACT
Rachel Balmer
T +44 (0)1359 270014
E oakfarmbarn@tiscali.co.uk
W oakfarmbarn.co.uk
Address Oak Farm Barn, Moat Lane, Rougham, Bury St Edmunds, Suffolk IP30 9JU

RATING
VisitBritain 4 Star Silver Award B&B

SLEEPING
Two twin rooms and one king-size double, all en suite.

FACILITIES
Guests' lounge; games, jigsaws, books and selection of DVDs; ample off-street parking.

NEAREST SHOPS, PUBS AND RESTAURANTS
Nearest shops 15 minutes' walk away; excellent selection of local pubs and restaurants.

OUT AND ABOUT
Bury St Edmunds with Abbey Gardens and Cathedral; historic wool town of Lavenham; Sutton Hoo Anglo-Saxon royal burial site; Ickworth House (National Trust).

PRICES PER ROOM AND WHAT'S INCLUDED
Double from £70.00 per night; single from £50.00 per night. Includes full English breakfast. Double/ twin room for October-March, two nights £115.00, including bottle of wine; three nights for the price of two £140.00, including bottle of wine.

Ocklynge Manor

EASTBOURNE, EAST SUSSEX 5 STAR B&B

Homemade delights and luxurious decor enhance ex-home of top illustrator

This 300-year-old former home of children's book illustrator Mabel Lucie Attwell sits in a secluded setting on three-quarters of an acre of land a mere 10-minute stroll from Eastbourne town centre. The site was once a monastery with 40 acres of farm land, as well as a 12th century Commandery for the Knights of St John of Jerusalem.

Today, Ocklynge Manor has a delightfully welcoming feel with beautiful gardens and three uniquely decorated and luxurious guest rooms, all with fridge, TV and DVD player, tea and coffee-making facilities, hairdryers, garden views and 100 per cent Egyptian cotton sheets.

The public areas are equally as opulent. Visitors can relax in the guest lounge, complete with grand piano, or in the first floor seating area at the end of the landing where floor-to-ceiling windows afford magnificent views over the gardens.

Start your Ocklynge Manor day with the smell of home-made bread and freshly-baked cakes, served with home-made jam and marmalade and a full English breakfast. Ω

Matter of facts

CONTACT
Wendy and David Dugdill
T +44 (0)1323 734121
E ocklyngemanor@
hotmail.com
W ocklyngemanor.co.uk
Address
Ocklynge Manor,
Mill Road,
Eastbourne,
East Sussex BN21 2PG

RATING
AA 5 Star Highly
Commended B&B

SLEEPING
One twin with en suite;
one double with private
shower; one double with
adjoining single and en
suite bath/shower.

FACILITIES
Walled garden and
orchard; wireless Internet.

**NEAREST SHOPS, PUBS
AND RESTAURANTS**
Many in town centre
within 10 minutes' walk.

OUT AND ABOUT
Beachy Head; South Downs
Way; Glyndebourne; Great
Dixter house and gardens;
Bodium Castle.

**PRICES PER PERSON
PER NIGHT AND
WHAT'S INCLUDED**
£35.00-£40.00 based
on two sharing. Single
occupancy from £45.00-
£50.00. Includes breakfast.

Old Bridge Hotel

HUNTINGDON, CAMBRIDGESHIRE
3 STAR GOLD AWARD HOTEL

Great food and drink underpin everything that's good in this hotel

This handsome 18th century building overlooks the River Ouse yet is only 500 yards from Huntingdon town centre. It has the atmosphere of a beautiful and luxurious hotel, yet is a busy meeting place for the local community. Historic Cambridge city centre is just 14 miles away.

All 24, individually-designed bedrooms have air-conditioning, bath with power shower, top-quality audio system and satellite TV. Many have Bang and Olufsen DVD players and two rooms have four-posters.

With two AA Rosettes and an award-winning wine list, the accent is very much on food and drink at the Old Bridge. The terrace is the main restaurant open every day serving a full menu, bargain lunches, snacks and sandwiches, while the dining room opens for dinner on Fridays and Saturdays as a very smart restaurant serving a full à la carte menu. Everything from bread and croissants to ice cream, pasta and black pudding is made in the Old Bridge's own kitchen and its real ales are highly acclaimed by the Campaign for Real Ale (CAMRA). Ω

Matter of facts

CONTACT
Reception
T +44 (0)1480 424300
E oldbridge@
huntsbridge.co.uk
W huntsbridge.com
Address Old Bridge Hotel,
1 High Street, Huntingdon,
Cambridgeshire PE29 3TQ

RATING
VisitBritain 3 Star
Gold Award Hotel

SLEEPING
24 en suite rooms,
comprising 18 doubles
and six singles.

FOR THE FAMILY
Children welcome; pets
by arrangement.

FACILITIES
Restaurant (two AA
Rosettes); separately
staffed business centre

with meeting facilities for
up to 18 and a conference
room for up to 50; civil
weddings for up to 80
guests; garden and
riverside patio; wireless
Internet access.

**NEAREST SHOPS, PUBS
AND RESTAURANTS**
500 yards to Huntingdon
town centre.

OUT AND ABOUT
University city of Cambridge
(14 miles); Grafham Water
for biking and sailing (five
miles); cathedral city of Ely
(20 miles).

**PRICES PER ROOM
PER NIGHT AND
WHAT'S INCLUDED**
Single rooms £95.00-
£120.00; doubles
£125.00-£180.00.
Includes breakfast.

Old Farm Cottages

NORWICH, NORFOLK 4 STAR SELF-CATERING

Six barn conversions – each with its own distinctive character – await your pleasure

Six delightful cottages, 15 bedrooms and the whole of beautiful, rural Norfolk as your playground; Old Farm Cottages are perfectly situated to extract the maximum enjoyment from the beautiful Broads National Park, the lovely north Norfolk coast and the stunning medieval city of Norwich.

The exclusive barn conversions have been tastefully and individually furnished and decorated to provided outstandingly comfortable and well-appointed accommodation for couples, families, groups and organised events. The individually-named cottages each have an enclosed patio area with barbeque and garden furniture, dishwasher, microwave, fridge-freezer, hairdryer, radio, CD, TV with Freeview and DVD players.

The cottages are:
Coach House (sleeps six): Elegance and charm have taken over this two-storey Victorian building which adjoins Ostlery – both of which are non-smoking from 2008.
Ostlery (sleeps four): The groom's quarters; a pretty two-storey cottage with wood-burning stove was originally part of the adjoining Coach House.
Granary (sleeps five): No more the grain store, now a compact, but comfortable, single-storey cottage adjoining Stables.
Mardlers (sleeps four): A Norfolk word meaning to meet and chat, this spacious and secluded cottage has its own walled garden with a lawn, paved patio and wood-burning stove.
Stables (sleeps six): A lovely view and beautifully beamed, this spacious, single-storey cottage was the original stable block.
Mast (sleeps four): This cosy, single-storey cottage has a wherry mast running the length of the eaves.

Matter of facts

CONTACT
Kay Paterson
T +44 (0)1692 536612
E mail@oldfarm cottages.fsnet.co.uk
W oldfarm cottages.com
Address Old Farm Cottages, Tunstead, Norwich, Norfolk NR12 8HS

RATING
VisitBritain 4 Star Self-Catering

SLEEPING
Six cottages, each sleeping four, five or six people.

FOR THE FAMILY
Play area with slide, swings and climbing frame; indoor games.

FACILITIES
Indoor swimming pool; fitness room; games room.

NEAREST SHOPS, PUBS AND RESTAURANTS
Post Office/village shop and pub with food 1.5 miles; other pubs with food by the river within two miles. Comprehensive facilities in Norwich city centre 10 miles away.

OUT AND ABOUT
Norfolk Broads; craft centre; city of Norwich; Norfolk coast. Full range of tourist leaflets in games room.

PRICES AND WHAT'S INCLUDED
Three days low season from £265.00 to one week high season £920.00. 10% reduction for two people only; 20% reduction for late bookings. Includes towels and linen.

Old Farm Cottages have plenty of indoor and outdoor activities to offer. The indoor, heated swimming pool is timetabled so each cottage has private use nearly every day plus shared time daily. The fitness room has running, rowing, cycling, walking, skipping, stepping and stretching equipment to keep you in shape, and the games rooms has table tennis, pool table, air hockey, table football and DVD library and a range of boxed games to keep you amused.

The children's play area is perfect for youngsters to have adventures on the climbing frames or play on the large grassed area while you enjoy a game of badminton or croquet.

In addition, there is a communal laundry room and, for large groups, arrangements can be made for additional services, such as outside catering, flowers, champagne, restaurant bookings and beauty treatments. Ω

185

The Old Farmhouse & The Granary

PENZANCE, CORNWALL 5 STAR SELF-CATERING

Situated on the south-facing courtyard of Chegwidden Farm, these two luxurious 17th century conversions are within easy walking distance of Porthcurno beach and the famous Minack Theatre.

The three-bedroomed Old Farmhouse has en suite master bedroom with four-poster and a family bathroom, a galleried hall upstairs and a large living area. The kitchen is equipped with microwave, washer/dryer, dishwasher, TV plus a DVD player and stereo system. The original bread oven has been kept as a feature and there is an eight-seater hot-tub in a private walled area.

The Granary has a well-equipped, open-plan kitchen/diner and a large, second floor sitting room with a multi-fuel fire. There is also a TV with a DVD player. There are two bedrooms: one twin which can be en suite to the large bathroom with a roll-top bath and a large separate shower, and a master bedroom with en suite shower. The Granary has a large, private walled courtyard with barbeque and an eight-seater hot tub. Ω

Numerous extras add to guests' enjoyment

Matter of facts

CONTACT
Viv Hall
T +44 (0)1736 810516
E halls@
chegwiddenfarm.com
W chegwiddenfarm.com
Address
Chegwidden Farm,
St Levan,
Penzance,
Cornwall TR19 6LP

RATING
VisitBritain 5 Star
Self-Catering

SLEEPING
Old Farmhouse has one
master bedroom with en
suite shower, one double
and one twin room; the
Granary has one master
bedroom with en suite
shower, one twin room
and a separate
bathroom.

FOR THE FAMILY
Cots and highchairs
available; pets welcome.

FACILITIES
Eight-seater hot tubs;
patio and barbecue area;
five acres of woodland
leading down the valley
to the cove at Penberth;
beauty treatments and
massage available.

**NEAREST SHOPS,
PUBS AND
RESTAURANTS**
Shops 1.5 miles away;
pubs and restaurants one
mile.

OUT AND ABOUT
Minack Theatre; St Ives
Tate Gallery; Eden Project;
many superb beaches,
including Porthcurno;
birdwatching at
Porthgwarra; day trips by
helicopter or ferry to the
Isles of Scilly; golf at Cape
Cornwall; coastal walks.

**PRICES PER WEEK
AND WHAT'S
INCLUDED**
£400.00-£950.00
per property. Special
romantic breaks
available. Includes bed
linen, towels, electricity,
heating and logs.

The Old Vicarage

PICKERING, NORTH YORKSHIRE 5 STAR
SILVER AWARD GUEST ACCOMMODATION

Perched on the edge of the Moors with panoramic views to the south

Country charm meets contemporary style in the Old Vicarage, a welcoming and relaxing home-from-home in the picturesque Yorkshire village of Newton upon Rawcliffe, complete with its village pub and duck pond. Whether you are looking for an active walking or cycling break, or simply wanting to recharge your batteries, then this is the place to do it.

All rooms have been extensively refurbished and feature flatscreen TVs, DVD players, Egyptian cotton sheets, fluffy towels and home-made biscuits. There is a spacious and inviting guest sitting room with wonderful views and a log fire, plus an elegant dining room.

Meals are prepared with care and attention using locally-sourced, seasonal produce and home-grown ingredients wherever possible. Breakfasts range from the traditional hearty meal to a more varied menu. And as a special treat, relax in the attractive garden seating area with views over the paddock and beyond and tuck into the complimentary tea and home-made cakes that are served each afternoon. Ω

Matter of facts

CONTACT
Neville and Barbara Hobbs
T +44 (0)1751 476126
E oldvic@toftlyview.co.uk
W toftlyview.co.uk
Address The Old Vicarage, Toftly View, Newton upon Rawcliffe, Pickering, North Yorkshire YO18 8QD

RATING
VisitBritain 5 Star Silver Award Guest Accommodation

SLEEPING
All bedrooms are en suite.

FOR THE FAMILY
Children over 10 welcome.

FACILITIES
Wireless Internet access; drying room; ample parking and lockable bike storage. Two-course evening meal available on Monday, Tuesday, and Thursday; stabling available within the village.

NEAREST SHOPS, PUBS AND RESTAURANTS
Mucky Duck Inn is within walking distance in Newton upon Rawcliffe and has a varied menu; shops and other pubs and restaurants are in Pickering, four miles away.

OUT AND ABOUT
North Yorkshire Moors; steam railway; coast; Castle Howard; historic city of York; Whitby (pictured opposite); TV's *Heartbeat* country.

PRICES PER NIGHT AND WHAT'S INCLUDED
£75.00-£95.00 per double room; £65.00-£80.00 single occupancy. Includes breakfast.

Outchester & Ross Farm Cottages

BAMBURGH, NORTHUMBERLAND 4 STAR SELF-CATERING

Stunning locations to enjoy in North-East

These 16 spacious cottages are on two outstanding farm sites in an Area of Outstanding Natural Beauty in a get-away-from-it-all location on Northumberland's stunning coastline. They are near the Farne Islands and Alnwick Gardens and between the village of Bamburgh and Holy Island, next to the 8,000-acre Lindisfarne National Nature Reserve.

Outchester Manor Cottages recently won the Northumbria Tourist Board 'Pride of Northumbria Award'. They consist of eight attractive cottages around three sides of a pretty courtyard garden. All are equipped to a very high standard and feature oil-fired central heating and a sitting room/kitchen/diner with French doors opening on to a patio with its own enclosed garden. There is also a detached cottage adjacent to the farm itself.

There are seven charming cottages at Ross, a working farm which grows Lindisfarne oysters, just like the monks of Holy Island did. These cottages are of varying sizes with an individual range of facilities, but all are centrally heated and have TVs and lawned gardens. Ω

Matter of facts

CONTACT
Shirley McKie
T +44 (0)1668 213336
E enquiry@rosscottages.co.uk
W rosscottages.co.uk
Address Outchester and
Ross Farm Cottages, Ross Farm,
Belford, Bamburgh,
Northumberland NE70 7EN

RATING
VisitBritain 4 Star Self-Catering

SLEEPING
16 cottages, each sleeping two, four or six people.

FOR THE FAMILY
Sand play yard and sand digger at Outchester, and the sky castle rope climbing frame at Ross, both surrounded by a large area of special silica play sand; cots and highchairs available.

FACILITIES
Home-grown Lindisfarne oysters; Outchester has facilities for the disabled.

NEAREST SHOPS, PUBS AND RESTAURANTS
The nearby villages of Belford and Bamburgh have a good range of village shops for groceries, and in the surrounding area there are excellent pubs and restaurants for eating out. There is a small supermarket in Belford and a good butcher in Bamburgh.

OUT AND ABOUT
Holy Island, on which stands Lindisfarne Castle and Priory; Alnwick Garden; castles at Bamburgh, Dunstanburgh and Alnwick, Warkworth, Chillingham, Norham and Etal; country houses at Cragside, Wallington Hall, Belsay, Paxton House, Manderston, Mellerstain and Floors Castle; historic towns of Berwick upon Tweed, Alnwick, Kelso and Edinburgh; Chain Bridge Honey Farm; Heatherslaw Railway.

PRICES PER WEEK AND WHAT'S INCLUDED
£259.00-£776.00 per cottage; includes electricity, heating, bed linen, hand and tea towels.

Park Farm

SAXMUNDHAM, SUFFOLK
4 STAR SILVER AWARD B&B

Comfortable and peaceful B&B offers many of nature's delights

Set in beautiful gardens regularly visited by barn owls and kingfishers, Park Farm is a delightful, peaceful house, a family home and a top-quality B&B close to the Suffolk coast. Its three spacious, comfortable and beautifully-dressed bedrooms comprise two twins with en suite shower rooms and one double with a private bathroom, newly refurbished with a lovely old cast-iron bath.

Breakfast is served in a pretty dining room and guests have their own sitting room with comfy sofas, open wood fire and a TV with video.

Park Farm caters for all tastes and diets. Breakfast can be as large as you like, with fruit juice, cereal, yoghurt or fruit compote, followed by a full English, toast and preserves. Bacon and sausages are supplied by a renowned local butcher, the mushrooms are grown in Suffolk, the eggs are from Park Farm's own chickens and the preserves are home-made in its kitchen. Visit at the right time and you may even be treated to raspberries and strawberries freshly picked that very morning from the garden. Ω

Matter of facts

CONTACT
Margaret Gray
T +44 (0)1728 668324
E mail@
sibtonparkfarm.co.uk
W sibtonparkfarm.co.uk
Address Park Farm,
Sibton, Saxmundham,
Suffolk IP17 2LZ

RATING
VisitBritain 4 Star
Silver Award B&B

SLEEPING
Two twin rooms with en suite showers; one king-size double with private bathroom.

FOR THE FAMILY
Children over 10 welcome.

FACILITIES
All bedrooms have tea and coffee-making facilities and a good selection of books and magazines.

NEAREST SHOPS, PUBS AND RESTAURANTS
Shops in Peasenhall and Yoxford (both 1.5 miles); excellent pubs with food at Yoxford (the Griffin) and Sibton (White Horse), both 1.5 miles.

OUT AND ABOUT
Dunwich, lost city of old (seven miles); Aldeburgh and Southwold; Framlingham Castle (nine miles); Minsmere, home of RSPB (four miles); Snape (eight miles).

PRICES PER PERSON AND WHAT'S INCLUDED
£35.00 per night for one or two nights; £32.00 per night for three or more nights; £200.00 per week. Includes breakfast.

Park Farm Cottages

SAXMUNDHAM, SUFFOLK
4 STAR SELF-CATERING

Same beautiful surroundings but maybe you prefer self-cater option

Like the idea of Park Farm (opposite) but would prefer to cater for yourself? Then these single-storey, imaginatively-converted farm buildings behind the house will appeal to you. Close to the unspoilt Suffolk coast, they are ideal for couples or family groups and offer peaceful walks to see the wildlife.

All four have wheelchair access, are centrally heated and feature well-equipped kitchens with fridge, cooker and microwave. The living areas have TV, DVD and CD players while zip-and-link beds are standard, meaning that guests can choose whether to have single beds or a six-foot double. Each property also features items of furniture made by local craftsmen.

Bluebell, Bonny and Buttercup are positioned round a flower-decked courtyard – a wonderful place for a sunny breakfast or a barbecue on warm summer evenings. Bertie has a 'drive-in' shower and sits on its own at the bottom of the garden with French windows opening on to a little garden with views of the fields beyond. Ω

Matter of facts

Most of these details appear in the Matter of facts shown on the page opposite. Where they differ ...

RATING
VisitBritain 4 Star Self Catering

SLEEPING
Three cottages each have two bedrooms and sleep four; one (Bluebell) has one bedroom and sleeps two.

FOR THE FAMILY
Cots and highchairs available; swings in garden.

FACILITIES
Games room with table tennis and small snooker table; all cottages have books and magazines, jigsaw puzzles, games and a folder with ideas about where to shop, things to do and places to eat.

PRICES PER WEEK AND WHAT'S INCLUDED
Bluebell £250.00-£340.00; Bonny £290.00-£420.00; Buttercup £310.00-£460.00; Bertie £320.00-£475.00. Three-day breaks available November-May. Includes heat, light, linen and towels.

Park House Hotel

MIDHURST, WEST SUSSEX 5 STAR HOTEL

Luxury bedrooms, quality food and a romantic setting add up to a great stay

Renowned for its relaxed atmosphere and intimate character, Park House is a beautifully-situated, country house hotel set in 10 acres of gardens at the foot of the South Downs. With staff who pride themselves in offering flexible, friendly and unobtrusive service, this lavishly-refurbished hotel gives a warm welcome to all who visit.

It is one of the best-kept secrets in West Sussex, offering stunning views of the surrounding, romantic, rolling hills and open fields. Every room has its own character and charm, including the sunlit dining area, where the menu has a reputation for quality.

The main house has 12 individual, en suite, bedrooms, including two family suites. The luxurious and spacious bedrooms benefit from high ceilings and large windows of Victorian architecture. Nestling within the grounds are Polo Cottage and Bay Tree Cottage. Both provide luxury and additional privacy for families or couples. All rooms have garden or downland views and are fitted to the highest standards.

A labour of love, the gardens are a cherished and much enjoyed feature of the hotel. Within the seclusion of the grounds, guests can enjoy many sporting activities. There are two grass tennis courts, a professionally-designed, six-hole pitch and putt course, croquet and putting lawns and an outdoor, heated swimming pool. The grounds also provide the perfect backdrop for marquees to accommodate larger events.

Park House offers fresh and wholesome cuisine, inspired by the culinary heritage of the countryside. Enjoy a meal in the intimate dining room, or perhaps take a seat in the conservatory area, admiring the scenery while you eat. The hotel is passionate about

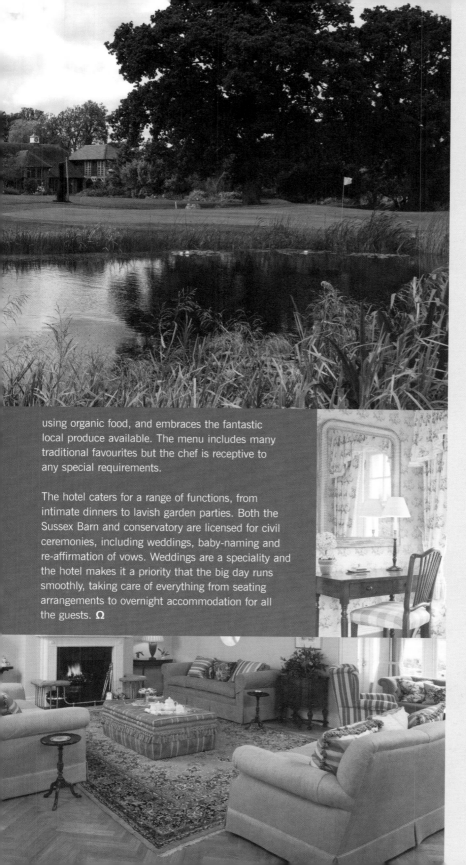

using organic food, and embraces the fantastic local produce available. The menu includes many traditional favourites but the chef is receptive to any special requirements.

The hotel caters for a range of functions, from intimate dinners to lavish garden parties. Both the Sussex Barn and conservatory are licensed for civil ceremonies, including weddings, baby-naming and re-affirmation of vows. Weddings are a speciality and the hotel makes it a priority that the big day runs smoothly, taking care of everything from seating arrangements to overnight accommodation for all the guests. Ω

Matter of facts

CONTACT
Rebecca Crowe
T +44 (0)1730 819000
E reservations@ parkhousehotel.com
W parkhousehotel. com
Address
Park House Hotel, Bepton, Midhurst, West Sussex GU29 0JB

RATING
AA 5 Star Hotel

SLEEPING
15 bedrooms comprising 13 double/twin rooms and two family rooms, all en suite.

FOR THE FAMILY
Cots, highchairs and baby monitors available; dogs permitted in two rooms.

FACILITIES
Six-hole pitch and putt course; outdoor heated pool; tennis courts; croquet and putting lawns; civil ceremonies; state-of-the-art boardroom for business meetings, conferences and seminars; wireless Internet access and videoconferencing facilities; complimentary shuttle to railway station.

NEAREST SHOPS, PUBS AND RESTAURANTS
Two miles away in Midhurst.

OUT AND ABOUT
Goodwood; Cowdray Park; Chichester; Petworth.

PRICES PER NIGHT AND WHAT'S INCLUDED
From £145.00-£290.00 per room. Includes breakfast.

Pelham House

LEWES, EAST SUSSEX 4 STAR SILVER AWARD GUEST ACCOMMODATION

Flavours of the world help add to piquancy of this 16thC townhouse

Elegance, history and design come together in this 16th century townhouse to create a hotel of style and distinction.

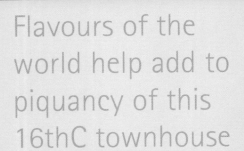

The 32 individually-designed bedrooms offer modern fittings and a high degree of comfort while preserving many original historic features. They are fitted with contemporary, handmade oak furniture, TVs, phones and high-speed data points and have en suite baths or luxury showers with a range of natural toiletries. Most overlook the pretty, south-facing garden, framed by views towards the South Downs.

The hotel's fine-dining restaurant is renowned for using unique and vibrant flavours from around the world. Every effort is made to use the highest quality, seasonal ingredients, which are complemented by a hand-picked wine list.

Pelham House is licensed to hold civil ceremonies in the beautiful 16th century Panelled Room or in the Terrace Room with lovely views of the garden. The experienced team aims to ensure that wedding celebrations are perfect, the food and wine inspiring and delicious, and that a truly warm welcome awaits all the guests. Ω

Matter of facts

CONTACT
Reception
T +44 (0)1273 488600
E reservations@
pelhamhouse.com
W pelhamhouse.com
Address Pelham House,
St Andrews Lane, Lewes,
East Sussex, BN7 1UW

RATING
VisitBritain 4 Star
Silver Award Guest
Accommodation

SLEEPING
32 bedrooms comprising
singles, doubles/twins and
deluxe doubles, all en suite.

FOR THE FAMILY
Garden.

FACILITIES
Conference centre with
nine meeting rooms
accommodating up to 180
delegates; Internet access
in all rooms; licensed for
civil ceremonies.

**NEAREST SHOPS, PUBS
AND RESTAURANTS**
All within walking distance
in Lewes town centre.

OUT AND ABOUT
Anne of Cleves' House;
Lewes Castle; Brighton.

**PRICES PER ROOM
PER NIGHT AND
WHAT'S INCLUDED**
Single rooms £90.00;
standard double/twin
rooms £110.00-£130.00;
deluxe rooms £150.00-
£200.00. Includes
breakfast.

Pentre Mawr
COUNTRY HOUSE

LLANDRYNOG, DENBIGH 5 STAR GOLD AWARD GUEST ACCOMMODATION

Energetic sports or even relaxing fishing – all are at romantic retreat

Pentre Mawr has been in the family of owners Graham and Bre Carrington-Sykes for 400 years. Set in 190 acres of meadows, park and woodland with fishing rights on the River Clwyd, the house has a lovely, romantic feel and is in an Area of Outstanding Natural Beauty.

There is a heated, salt-water swimming pool in the walled garden which is a great suntrap, plus a tennis court and croquet lawn. Breakfast is served in the morning room or on the Georgian terrace on warmer mornings while dinner is served in a formal, but distinctly unstuffy, dining room.

There are two lovely sitting rooms, all with comfy sofas and portraits of Graham Carrington-Sykes' ancestors, and, in keeping with the tradition at Sychnant Pass House (see page 227), all five recently-refurbished bedrooms, are named after T S Elliot's cats.

Exemplified by first-class hospitality and perfection without pomposity, Pentre Mawr is a haven of tranquillity with strong appeal for couples, parties or those seeking an ideal venue for a special occasion. Ω

Matter of facts

CONTACT
Bre Carrington-Sykes
T +44 (0)1824 790732
E info@pentremawr
countryhouse.co.uk
W pentremawr
countryhouse.co.uk
Address Pentre Mawr
House, Llandrynog,
Denbigh, LL16 4LA

RATING
AA 5 Star Gold Award
Guest Accommodation;
AA Dining Award.

SLEEPING
Five double bedrooms,
all en suite.

FOR THE FAMILY
Not suitable for children;
pets welcome.

FACILITIES
Heated outdoor pool,
tennis and croquet lawn;
three-acre gardens.

**NEAREST SHOPS, PUBS
AND RESTAURANTS**
All about one mile
distant.

OUT AND ABOUT
Denbigh Castle; Offas
Dyke; medieval town
of Ruthin.

**PRICES PER PERSON
PER NIGHT AND
WHAT'S INCLUDED**
B&B from £45.00;
dinner, B&B from £70.00
– both prices based on two
sharing.

The Pheasant Inn
BY KIELDER WATER

FALSTONE, NORTHUMBERLAND
4 STAR SILVER AWARD B&B

List the merits of country inns and see how many boxes this ticks

The Pheasant Inn is everyone's idea of what a country hostelry should be like but rarely is: ivy-clad stone walls; woody bars with beamed ceilings, plenty of brass fittings and cosy, open fires; fine wines and real ales; hearty, wholesome, home-cooked food; and peaceful, attractive rooms in which to rest your weary head at the end of a busy day.

Located in a national park in unspoilt Northumberland countryside, the buildings date from 1684 and were originally part of a farm before being converted in 1974. It now has eight, recently-refurbished guest rooms, all with en suite facilities, TVs and radio alarms, hairdryers, toiletries and tea and coffee-making facilities. All rooms are set around a pretty courtyard and barn and enjoy delightful countryside views.

The mellow dining room is the place to enjoy some of the best traditional home-cooked food in the area which is individually prepared, using fresh local produce. The varied and interesting menu includes game pies, salmon and local lamb as well as wonderful Northumbrian cheeses. Ω

Matter of facts

CONTACT
Robin, Walter or Irene Kershaw
T +44 (0)1434 240382
E enquiries@
thepheasantinn.com
W thepheasantinn.com
Address The Pheasant Inn, Stannersburn, Falstone, by Kielder Water, Northumberland NE48 1DD

RATING
VisitBritain 4 Star Silver Award B&B

SLEEPING
Four double, three twin and one family room which sleeps 4/5. All en suite.

FOR THE FAMILY
Play area alongside outside eating area.

FACILITIES
28-cover dining area; evening meals and bar meals.

NEAREST SHOPS, PUBS AND RESTAURANTS
In the nearby villages of Bellingham and Hexham a short distance away.

OUT AND ABOUT
Hadrian's Wall; Alnwick, Bamburgh and Chillingham castles; Kielder Water; Lindisfarne.

PRICES PER NIGHT AND WHAT'S INCLUDED
B&B – double room £85.00; single occupancy £50.00. Dinner, B&B £65.00 per person.

Raffles

BLACKPOOL, LANCASHIRE
4 STAR B&B

B&B consistently earns the highest accolades in top hotel guides

Raffles is the only Blackpool accommodation to have been listed continuously since 2001 in both the *Good Hotel Guide* and *Which? Guide to Good Hotels.* One of the resort's few B&Bs with a four star rating, Raffles is an exceptional house just minutes from Blackpool Tower.

With its free parking and five-minute stroll to all Blackpool's major venues and attractions, including the Winter Gardens, it is an ideal base for both holidaymakers and conference delegates.

Owners Graham and Ian have a real passion for their spick-and-span little gem. The standard of decor is high; the housekeeping exemplary. The atmosphere is relaxed from the moment you step through the door. All bedrooms are compact, but not small, and meticulously decorated with flair. There is even the option of three superior boutique suites with lounge, kitchen area and bedroom with en suite which sleep up to four people.

The adjoining, quintessentially English Raffles Tea Rooms serves good, traditional home-baked cakes and light meals. Evening meals are also served with menus to suit all tastes. Ω

Matter of facts

CONTACT
Graham Poole
T +44 (0)1253 294713
E enquiries@raffleshotel
blackpool.fsworld.co.uk
W raffleshotelblackpool.
co.uk
Address
Raffles Hotel and Tea Rooms,
73-77 Hornby Road,
Blackpool FY1 4QJ

RATING
VisitBritain 4 Star B&B

SLEEPING
17 en suite bedrooms and two superior family apartment suites which each sleep up to four.

FOR THE FAMILY
Cots and highchairs available.

FACILITIES
Breakfast room; English tea room; licensed bar; all bedrooms have TVs and tea/coffee facilities; free parking.

NEAREST SHOPS, PUBS AND RESTAURANTS
All within a five-minute walk in Blackpool town centre.

OUT AND ABOUT
Blackpool Tower and Circus; Winter Gardens; Pleasure Beach; Sea Life Centre; Sandcastle Waterworld; Ripley's Believe It Or Not; Solaris Centre; Blackpool Zoo Park; Model Village and Gardens; Karting 2000.

PRICES PER NIGHT AND WHAT'S INCLUDED
£32.00-£37.00 per person (reduced rates for three nights or more). Suites £120.00-£140.00. Includes breakfast.

SHOE
REPAIRS

KEY
CUTTING

WATCH
REPAIRS

Café Mauresque

GAP

Coffee
Shop
&
Take
Away

Coffee
Shop

THE
CITY ARMS
INN

Silver
Designs

CASEY'S

SHOP
TO LET

Blacks

GUY

CITY ARMS

FOOD SERVED
12-5
COFFEE

The cobbled streets of Canterbury leading to the cathedral.

The Relish

FOLKESTONE, KENT
5 STAR GUEST ACCOMMODATION

Little things can mean a lot at this well-named seaside oasis

An exquisitely-crafted, luxury guest accommodation where little touches make all the difference, The Relish in Folkestone's fashionable west end is an oasis of calm in one of East Kent's hidden havens.

Contemporary, boutique accommodation highlighted by state-of-the-art Hypnos beds for a sound night's sleep; high-pressure, rainforest-style showers; and luxury, organic Aveda toiletries set this hotel apart, as does the welcome glass of wine or beer on your arrival and the unlimited supplies of tea and coffee served with a home-made cake throughout your stay.

The period exterior has been carefully restored while the interiors are expressions of contemporary taste and include a dining room with views across the four-acre Augusta Gardens and a drawing room which features a small library, plenty of the latest magazines and an open fire in winter. On summer mornings your full English breakfast is best taken on the private, secluded terrace which traps the morning sun. Ω

Matter of facts

CONTACT
Sarah van Dyke
T +44 (0)1303 850952
E reservations@hotelrelish.co.uk
W hotelrelish.co.uk
Address The Relish, 4 Augusta Gardens, Folkestone, Kent CT20 2RR

RATING
AA 5 Star Guest Accommodation

SLEEPING
One single, three standard double, four large double and two luxury double rooms, all en suite.

FOR THE FAMILY
Cots, Z-beds, highchairs and baby-listening facilities.

FACILITIES
All rooms have a DVD/CD player and Freeview TV; broadband Internet; library with books, magazines and extensive DVD collection.

NEAREST SHOPS, PUBS AND RESTAURANTS
Town centre shops within a five-minute walk; plenty of good restaurants, including Italian, Chinese, Indian, Thai, Spanish, English and French cuisine, within a five to 15-minute walk. Mexican and fish restaurants within a 10-minute taxi ride.

OUT AND ABOUT
Cliff tops and the Leas Cliff Hall a short walk away; Romney, Hythe & Dymchurch Light Railway (six miles); Dover Castle (10 miles); Eurotunnel terminal (15 minutes' drive); Dungeness and Ashford's designer outlet shopping centre (30 minutes); Canterbury (45 minutes).

PRICES PER NIGHT AND WHAT'S INCLUDED
Single rooms from £59.00; double rooms £85.00-£130.00. £10.00 reduction for single occupancy of double room. Includes breakfast and VAT. Two-night minimum stay applies on summer weekends and most bank holidays.

The Residence

BATH, SOMERSET
5 STAR GOLD AWARD B&B

Staying in this luxury townhouse is like being at an exclusive club

A new concept in accommodation for Bath, the Residence combines the exclusivity of a private members' club with the service of a modern hotel within a large, luxury Georgian townhouse built in 1796.

Reputedly one of the homes of Ethiopian Emperor Haile Selassie during his exile in the 1930s, the Residence is now a luxury B&B with five rooms and one suite. Its aim is simple: to be the best home-from-home you ever had. Its style is relaxed and friendly but eager to please.

All rooms have unique minibars, large screen TVs, some with DVDs, and a cutting-edge sound system. Organic breakfasts, sourced locally and cooked to order, can be served any time of day. Room service is 24 hours and the restaurant opens Thursday, Friday and Saturday nights and for brunch on Saturdays and Sundays.

A modern conservatory bar with heated terrace and retractable canopy, a steam room and sauna and a beautiful garden ideal for outdoor dining complete the picture of this rather special B&B. Ω

Matter of facts

CONTACT
David Woodward
T +44 (0)1225 750180
E info@
theresidencebath.com
W theresidencebath.com
Address Weston Road,
Bath, Somerset BA1 2XZ

RATING
VisitBritain 5 Star
Gold Award B&B

SLEEPING
Six bedrooms, five en suite, one with private bathroom.

FACILITIES
Library; steam room; sauna; garden with summer house, boules piste and croquet; 24-hour room service; wireless Internet.

NEAREST SHOPS, PUBS AND RESTAURANTS
All within a 10-minute walk in Bath city centre.

OUT AND ABOUT
Bath's medieval abbey and the Abbey Heritage Vaults; Roman Baths; 18th century Pump Room; Jane Austen Centre; Sally Lunn's house; The Museum of East Asian Art; The Building of Bath Museum; Holbourne Museum of Art and Victoria Gallery.

PRICES PER ROOM PER NIGHT AND WHAT'S INCLUDED
£135.00-£270.00 midweek; £150.00-£300.00 at weekends. Christmas and New Year packages available.

Hotel Riviera

SIDMOUTH, DEVON
4 STAR GOLD AWARD HOTEL

Everything you would expect from a deluxe four star hotel

With its echoes of the South of France and prime position on Sidmouth seafront offering panoramic views, the Hotel Riviera is the choice for the discerning visitor in search of relaxation and quieter pleasures.

Handsome 18th and 19th century architecture abounds in elegant and exclusive Sidmouth and the hotel's fine Regency facade was once a terrace of three-storey houses. Inside is an alluring blend of old-fashioned service and present day comforts. The hotel has a long tradition of hospitality, a warm and friendly atmosphere and is perfect for unforgettable family holidays, long weekends, unwinding breaks and the spirit of the festive season.

Business meetings are also more assured of a successful outcome in the superb working environment of the self-contained conference suite. Whether you stay on holiday or on business, you will find the staff have a genuine desire to please and treat you to the kind of friendly, personal attention that can only be found in a privately-owned hotel of this quality.

All bedrooms are tastefully furnished and individually designed in keeping with the hotel's

character, and through its programme of continual refurbishment they are maintained to the highest standard. All twin, double and single bedrooms have a private bathroom with bath, toilet and shower en suite.

As you would expect from a deluxe, four star hotel, each room has a TV with video link, radio, direct-dial telephone, hairdryer and thoughtful touches such as flowers, bathrobes and complimentary toiletries. The hotel has full central heating during the cooler seasons and the public rooms are air-conditioned during the summer months.

Hotel Riviera has a proud reputation for its fine cuisine which has earned it two AA Rosettes. Discerning menus combine international dishes with the best English cooking and feature a selection of fresh local produce with an emphasis on seafood. The restaurant has an extensive à la carte menu as well as table d'hôte lunch and dinner menus. Light refreshments are available throughout the day in the Regency Bar, in the foyer or on the patio during summer. Entertainment is provided on many evenings by the hotel's resident pianist. Ω

Matter of facts

CONTACT
Reservations
T +44 (0)1395 515201
E enquiries@
hotelriviera.co.uk
W hotelriviera.co.uk
Address
Hotel Riviera,
The Esplanade,
Sidmouth,
Devon EX10 8AY

RATING
VisitBritain 4 Star Gold
Award Hotel; Restaurant
two AA Rosettes.

SLEEPING
26 rooms, all en suite.

FOR THE FAMILY
Reduced rates for
children sharing adults'
accommodation; cots
and highchairs available;
baby-listening service;
children's high teas.

FACILITIES
Two AA Rosette
restaurant; cocktail bar
open until midnight
with resident pianist;
wedding receptions,
parties and conferences;
room service.

NEAREST SHOPS, PUBS AND RESTAURANTS
Shops within a two-
minute walk; many pubs
and restaurants in
Sidmouth.

OUT AND ABOUT
Exeter Cathedral;
Killerton House and
Gardens; Bicton Gardens;
Beer Quarry Caves;
concessionary green fees
at Sidmouth Golf Club
and Woodbury Park Golf
and Country Club.

PRICES PER PERSON PER NIGHT AND WHAT'S INCLUDED
Bed and full English
breakfast from £94.00;
dinner, bed and full
English breakfast from
£109.00. Luxury three-
day breaks from £98.00.
Dinner, bed and full
English breakfast two-
night weekend breaks
from £195.00 per
person.

Rooke Country Cottages

CHAPEL AMBLE, WADEBRIDGE, CORNWALL 5 STAR SELF-CATERING

Tranquil Cornish cottages can cater for almost every guest combination

These seven five star cottages on a Duchy of Cornwall Farm are situated in 235 acres of beautiful Cornish countryside and offer the perfect retreat for those seeking peace and tranquillity. They have been thoughtfully converted to combine the traditional style of natural stone, slate flagstones, oak floors and beamed ceilings with modern comforts.

Fittings and fixtures are all high quality. Sitting rooms have subtle lighting, elegant soft furnishings, digital widescreen TV, DVD, hi-fi and homely log-burners and central heating for colder evenings. Kitchens are comprehensively equipped with dishwashers, washing machines and tumble dryers and a range of small appliances, including food processors, and the bedrooms, tastefully decorated with mellow furnishings, all feature beds with quality mattresses, pillows, duvets and linen.

The cottages vary in size and accommodate between two and eight guests each. All have private lawned gardens with individual barbecues, garden furniture and views of the unspoilt countryside as the perfect backdrop. Ω

Matter
of facts

CONTACT
Gill and Rob Reskelly
T +44 (0)1208 880368
E info@
rookecottages.com
W rookecottages.com
Address Rooke
Country Cottages,
Rook Farm,
Chapel Amble,
Wadebridge,
Cornwall, PL27 6ES

RATING
VisitBritain 5 Star
Self-Catering

SLEEPING
Seven cottages: one
sleeps two, two sleep
four, one sleeps five, one
sleeps six, one sleeps
seven and one sleeps
eight people.

FOR THE FAMILY
Cots; baby-sitting can
be arranged; children's
adventure garden.

FACILITIES
Private gardens with
barbeques and garden
furniture; midweek maid
service; parking for cars
and boats.

**NEAREST SHOPS, PUBS
AND RESTAURANTS**
All in the village of Chapel
Amble, a short walk away
through country lanes.
Rick Stein's Seafood
Restaurant at Padstow.

OUT AND ABOUT
North Cornwall coast
including sandy beaches
at Rock, Daymer Bay and
Polzeath; country houses
at Lanhydrock and
Pencarrow; the Lost
Gardens of Heligan; the
Eden Project; Bodmin
Moor; historic villages of
Tintagel and Boscastle.

**PRICES PER WEEK
AND WHAT'S INCLUDED**
From £407.00 low
season for one-bed
cottage to £2,596 high
season for four-bed en
suite cottage. Includes
electricity, linen, towels,
heating, mid-week maid
service and VAT.

Rothay Manor

AMBLESIDE, CUMBRIA
3 STAR SILVER AWARD HOTEL

Excellence in its cuisine is key to Small Hotel of the Year success

After 40 years in the custody of the Nixon family, Rothay Manor continues to set the pace in the Lake District by being named Small Hotel of the Year 2006 in the Cumbria for Excellence awards and by being one of only six hotels mentioned in the *Good Food Guide* in all 38 annual editions that have been published.

The 1825-built house is a Listed building which still retains many original features. It is set in attractive landscaped gardens 400 metres from the head of Lake Windermere.

Fresh flowers and antiques give the feel of a welcoming private house and the lounges are ideal for relaxing over afternoon tea or pre-dinner drinks.

Famed for its relaxed, comfortable and friendly atmosphere, the hotel has 16 individually-designed bedrooms and three suites. Two rooms have been adapted for use by the disabled.

Renowned for the excellent cuisine, the restaurant has one AA Rosette. Ω

Matter of facts

CONTACT
Reception
T +44 (0)15394 33605
E hotel@
rothaymanor.co.uk
W rothaymanor.co.uk
Address Rothay Manor,
Rothay Bridge, Ambleside,
Cumbria LA22 0EH

RATING
VisitBritain 3 Star
Silver Award Hotel

SLEEPING
16 rooms including one single and a mix of standard and superior rooms, all with en suite bath and shower. There are also three suites, two of which are in the grounds with private parking and one of which is fully wheelchair-accessible.

FOR THE FAMILY
Cots and highchairs free of charge; family rooms with video players; children's videos; children's high teas; baby-listening facilities.

FACILITIES
Restaurant open for morning coffee, lunch, afternoon tea and dinner; free use of nearby leisure club; all rooms have TV, hot drinks, radio and telephone.

NEAREST SHOPS, PUBS AND RESTAURANTS
400 yards away.

OUT AND ABOUT
Lake Windermere and the Lake District; Dove Cottage (home of William Wordsworth); Hill Top (home of Beatrix Potter); Brantwood (home of John Ruskin); the Aquarium of the Lakes; Lake cruises.

PRICES PER ROOM PER NIGHT AND WHAT'S INCLUDED
B&B – double from £140.00-£215.00; single from £90.00-£140.00.
Dinner B&B – double £205.00-£285.00; single £120.00-£175.00.

Roxburghe Hotel

EDINBURGH 4 STAR HOTEL

At the Roxburghe you can dine well, get fit and visit top shops nearby

The elegant, luxurious and traditionally-styled Roxburghe Hotel will appeal to both the traditionalist and the modernist with its 197 bedrooms and unique courtyard area at the centre of the hotel.

Seconds from George Street and Princes Street and a short stroll from Edinburgh Castle, the Roxburghe Hotel's guest rooms are all fully en suite with sumptuous soft furnishings, a comfortable working area, wireless Internet, satellite TV, direct-dial telephone and second phone point, personal voicemail, tea and coffee-making facilities, hospitality tray and a hairdryer.

The one AA Rosette Melrose Restaurant offers a classically British style of cooking, Scottish specialities prepared from the best of national produce and a wide choice of international cuisine, complemented by wines from the vineyards of both the old and the new world.

The Vital Health, Fitness and Beauty Club has a 12 metre indoor pool, sauna and steam rooms and fully-equipped gym. It offers classes from pilates to body pump and step to body combat, and a full range of beauty treatments. Ω

Matter of facts

CONTACT
Reservations
T +44 (0)131 527 4669
E roxburghe@
macdonald-hotels.co.uk
W macdonald-
hotels.co.uk/roxburghe
Address
The Roxburghe Hotel,
38 Charlotte Square,
Edinburgh EH2 4HQ

RATING
VisitBritain 4 Star Hotel

SLEEPING
197 en suite bedrooms,
including classic doubles
or twins, superior rooms,
executive rooms and one
full suite.

FOR THE FAMILY
Cots and highchairs
available.

FACILITIES
One AA Rosette Melrose
Restaurant; Melrose Lounge
and Bar; Consort Bar;
wedding ceremonies and
receptions; 12m swimming
pool; Technogym; sauna
and steam room; dance
studio; three beauty
treatment rooms.

**NEAREST SHOPS, PUBS
AND RESTAURANTS**
Minutes away on
Princes Street and
George Street.

OUT AND ABOUT
Edinburgh Castle; Palace of
Holyrood House; Scottish
Parliament; National
Galleries of Scotland;
National Museums of
Scotland; Playhouse and
Kings Theatres; Our
Dynamic Earth; Royal
Yacht Britannia.

**PRICES PER ROOM
PER NIGHT AND
WHAT'S INCLUDED**
£110.00-£240.00
(supplements may apply to
superior rooms, executive
rooms and suites). Includes
full Scottish breakfast.

Royal Duchy Hotel

FALMOUTH, CORNWALL 4 STAR HOTEL

Plenty to entertain visitors every night in the town's only four star hotel

From its prime seafront location, Falmouth's only four star hotel enjoys dramatic views across the bay. Its 43 delightful bedrooms are well appointed and each has en suite bathroom, satellite TV, radio and direct-dial telephone.

Dining is one of the hotel's great pleasures. Chefs in the Panoramic restaurant, which overlooks beautiful Falmouth Bay, have earned the Royal Duchy two AA Rosettes for their varied menus and fine cuisine, prepared using the best local produce. Coffee is served throughout the day in the Cocktail Bar and Sun Lounge, lunch on the terrace and devastating Cornish cream teas in the afternoon for those who can manage them.

Afterwards it's time to relax in the indoor heated swimming pool, sit back in the sauna or enjoy a game of snooker or table tennis. But make sure you recharge your batteries for the nightly entertainment, which includes cabaret, comedy, music, bingo and a full family-oriented programme during the school holidays. Ω

Matter of facts

CONTACT
Reservations
T +44 (0)1326 214001
E reservations@
royalduchy.com
W royalduchy.com
Address
The Royal Duchy Hotel,
Cliff Road, Falmouth,
Cornwall TR11 4NX

RATING
AA 4 Star Hotel

SLEEPING
43 bedrooms including a mix
of single and double/twin
rooms, all en suite.

FOR THE FAMILY
Playroom in school holidays;
baby-listening; children's high
teas; family entertainment.

FACILITIES
Heated indoor pool; sauna;
snooker and table-tennis rooms;
nightly entertainment; civil

weddings; fresh flowers,
chocolates, slippers with
bathrobes and binoculars in
all deluxe rooms; 24-hour
room service.

NEAREST SHOPS, PUBS
AND RESTAURANTS
All within 5-10 minutes' walk.

OUT AND ABOUT
National Maritime Museum;
the Eden Project; National
Maritime Aquarium; Tate St
Ives; Flambards Theme Park;
the National Seal Sanctuary;
Paradise Park, Hayle; Heritage
sites; various gardens;
beaches; golf courses.

PRICES PER PERSON
PER NIGHT AND
WHAT'S INCLUDED
Low season – B&B from
£83.00; dinner, B&B from
£98.00. High season – B&B
from £95.00; dinner, B&B
from £110.00

Royal Lancaster Hotel

WEST LONDON
4 STAR SILVER AWARD HOTEL

Life of luxury by Hyde Park with the West End on your doorstep

Few city centre hotels can boast a better location than the Royal Lancaster: 416 rooms over 18 floors with 600 acres of Kensington Gardens and Hyde Park across the road and Marble Arch, Oxford Street, Bond Street and London's West End just a few minutes away by taxi or Underground.

There is a vast choice of rooms on offer, from standard doubles and twins to superior rooms with stunning views over the London skyline, the larger deluxe and executive rooms and a range of luxury suites. All share double-glazed tranquillity in an air-conditioned environment and, in addition to essentials like satellite TV, American oak furniture, tea and coffee-making facilities and in-room safe, they each have a desk with universal power sockets, Internet access, direct-dial telephone and an en suite marble bathroom with power shower.

Two award-winning restaurants feature some of the finest authentic Thai cuisine in the Nipa Restaurant and top-quality, seasonal British produce, bought daily, simply cooked and stylishly presented in the Island Restaurant and Bar. Ω

Matter of facts

CONTACT
Reservations
T +44 (0)207 262 6737
E book@
royallancaster.com
W royallancaster.com
Address
Royal Lancaster Hotel,
Lancaster Terrace,
London W2 2TY

RATING
VisitBritain 4 Star
Silver Award Hotel

SLEEPING
416 rooms comprising 331 standard/superior rooms, 38 deluxe rooms, 25 executive rooms and 22 suites. All have en suite marble bathrooms.

FACILITIES
Two restaurants; 24-hour lounge bar; 24-hour room service; dry cleaning and valet service; car park (fee payable); 24-hour business centre; conference and banqueting facilities; 24-hour concierge.

NEAREST SHOPS, PUBS AND RESTAURANTS
Shops, pubs and restaurants a short walk away in Paddington area; a few minutes by taxi or Underground (Lancaster Gate Underground Station is adjacent to hotel) to Oxford Street, Bond Street and the West End.

OUT AND ABOUT
Hyde Park; Kensington Palace; Marble Arch; West End; Paddington Station for Heathrow Express (20 minutes).

PRICES AND WHAT'S INCLUDED
See website for latest offers.

The Royal Oak

EAST LAVANT, WEST SUSSEX 5 STAR GOLD AWARD INN & 5 STAR SELF-CATERING

Award-winning inn offers a successful mixture of B&B and self-catering

Set in beautiful Goodwood country, this 18th century inn has luxury B&B accommodation in the main house and Sussex barn, along with two flint period cottages 40 yards away providing self-catering.

Situated just a few minutes from Chichester city centre, guest accommodation at the Royal Oak is arranged around a charming courtyard and consists of six, individually-styled rooms, each with up-to-the-minute, en suite facilities, flatscreen TVs and CDs and a complimentary library of DVDs. All bathrooms are luxuriously fitted with power showers and a selection of L'Occitane toiletries.

The restaurant has earned a wide reputation for its menu featuring a combination of French, Mediterranean and New English cuisine with wines to match.

The recently-added, self-catering cottages each comprises two bedrooms, a stunning bathroom, fully-fitted kitchens with wine cellars and front parlour with warm glowing stove, large flatscreen TV and DVD, Bose audio system, broadband Internet and iPod docking stations. Both have private gardens with patio. Ω

Matter of facts

CONTACT
Hayley Edgar
T +44 (0)1243 527434
E enquiries@
royaloaklavant.co.uk
W royaloaklavant.co.uk
Address Royal Oak,
Pook Lane,
East Lavant, Chichester,
West Sussex PO18 0AX

RATING
Inn – VisitBritain 5 Star
Gold Award; Self-Catering
cottages – Quality Tourism
5 Star.

SLEEPING
The Royal Oak has six
single and double rooms,
each with en suite; the
two, two-bedroom, self-
catering cottages sleep
three and four people
respectively.

FACILITIES
Restaurant; Sky TV;
broadband Internet access;
private parking.

**NEAREST SHOPS, PUBS
AND RESTAURANTS**
Shops in Chichester city
centre three miles away;
pubs and restaurants
adjacent to the Royal Oak.

OUT AND ABOUT
Goodwood; Chichester;
beach (eight miles); golf;
flying.

**PRICES PER NIGHT AND
WHAT'S INCLUDED**
Single £75.00-£85.00
per room; Sussex barn
£95.00-£125.00 per
room; double/twin in main
house £80.00-£155.00
per room; deluxe flint
cottage £125.00-£160.00
per room. Includes full
English breakfast,
newspaper and VAT. Self-
catering cottages –
Blackberry from £130.00;
Mulberry from £160.00;
both cottages available
from £380.00 for two-
night weekend.

Rye Lodge

RYE, EAST SUSSEX
3 STAR GOLD AWARD HOTEL

Pamper yourself with breakfast in bed or be picked up by Rolls-Royce

Elegant surroundings, a relaxed atmosphere and service second to none are to be found perched on the East Cliff of Rye in the form of Rye Lodge Hotel.

The hotel enjoys panoramic views across the estuary and Romney Marshes yet is close to the town centre with its cobbled streets, quaint old shops, tea rooms, pubs and restaurants and is within a stone's throw of the Landgate, an ancient monument built in 1326 as the entrance to Rye.

The luxury bedrooms are all en suite and there is room service – with the bonus of breakfast in bed. The elegant, marble-floored Terrace Room Restaurant serves superb cuisine and fine wines; you can take afternoon tea, light snacks or pre-dinner cocktails in the lounge bar; and there is an indoor pool, sauna and aromatherapy steam cabinet in which to relax. And as a special treat, you can arrive in style in the hotel's chauffeur-driven Rolls-Royce, which can collect you from your home, station, port or airport. It can also take you for a drive in the Sussex countryside. Ω

Matter of facts

CONTACT
Carol Swaine
T +44 (0)1797 223838
E info@ryelodge.co.uk
W ryelodge.co.uk
Address Rye Lodge Hotel, Hilder's Cliff, Rye, East Sussex TN31 7LD

RATING
VisitBritain 3 Star Gold Award Hotel

SLEEPING
12 double rooms and six twin rooms, all en suite.

FOR THE FAMILY
Extra beds for children.

FACILITIES
Leisure centre with pool, spa bath, sauna and aromatherapy steam cabinet; chauffeur-driven Rolls-Royce service.

NEAREST SHOPS, PUBS AND RESTAURANTS
A short walk away in Rye High Street.

OUT AND ABOUT
Museum; the Ypres Tower (castle); Landgate; town wall; beach; Hastings; Leeds Castle; Battle and Canterbury.

PRICES PER NIGHT AND WHAT'S INCLUDED
B&B – single occupancy £75.00-£105.00; double room £100.00-£200.00. Dinner, B&B £79.50-£119.50 per person (minimum two-night stay).

Saunton Sands Hotel

NR BRAUNTON, DEVON 4 STAR HOTEL

A wide exercise choice awaits those who enjoy the fine cuisine

Set high above Saunton's lovely three-mile beach and overlooking the natural wonder of the Braunton Burrows World Heritage Site, the hotel's magnificent location affords one of the most dramatic coastal views in the West Country.

Many of its 90 stunning, tastefully-furnished bedrooms overlook Saunton Beach and all have en suite facilities and satellite TV. The public rooms, designed very much with visitors in mind, include the Cocktail Bar with its relaxing atmosphere; the Terrace Lounge with its wide choice of tasty snacks, delicious meals and traditional cream teas; and the social heart of the hotel, the Lounge Bar, with live music and entertainment throughout the year. Saunton Sands' great cuisine has earned it an AA Rosette. There are also self-catering apartments available.

For those who take relaxation seriously, there is a health and beauty salon; an indoor pool with a safe area for toddlers plus a heated outdoor pool; a sauna and solarium; pool and table tennis tables; and, for the particularly energetic, tennis and squash courts. Ω

Matter of facts

CONTACT
Reception
T +44 (0)1271 892001
E reservations@
sauntonsands.com
W sauntonsands.com
Address The Saunton Sands
Hotel, Saunton, nr Braunton,
Devon EX33 1LQ.

RATING
AA 4 Star Hotel

SLEEPING
90 single, double/twin and
deluxe bedrooms.

FOR THE FAMILY
Children's teas; outdoor play
area; OFSTED-approved
playroom; toddlers' area in
indoor pool.

FACILITIES
Two swimming pools; sauna
and solarium; gym; pool
and table tennis; billiard
room; tennis and squash
courts; putting green;
health and beauty salon;
hairdressing salon.

**NEAREST SHOPS, PUBS
AND RESTAURANTS**
Gift shop in hotel; shops in
Croyde (one mile) and
Braunton (1.6 miles). Pubs
and restaurants one mile.

OUT AND ABOUT
North Devon beaches;
Woolacombe; Croyde;
Barnstaple; Exmoor
National Park; Lundy
Island; cycling; fishing;
many golf courses.

**PRICES PER PERSON
PER NIGHT AND
WHAT'S INCLUDED**
Room only £82.00-
£144.00; B&B £87.00-
£150.00. Dinner, B&B from
£100.00-£175.00. See
website for special offers.

Sea Tree House

LYME REGIS, DORSET 4 STAR SELF-CATERING

Views over film-set harbour help add to the romance of elegant apartments

Sea Tree House is a romantic hideaway overlooking Lyme Regis' famous Cobb harbour. The three-storey house dates back more than 200 years and has been lovingly restored by present owner David Parker. Here you can relax in Georgian elegance in spacious, one-bedroom, completely private self-catering apartments and enjoy magnificent views.

Within the calm and gentle atmosphere of Sea Tree House, all the apartments are different but share the same standards of furnishings and elegant decor. Arranged on each floor, they all have individual kitchens and bathrooms and each can accommodate up to four people.

The kitchens are fully equipped with extras such as washer/dryers and dishwashers. Large, bright sitting rooms overlook the sea through south-facing bay windows and the setting sun lights the raised dining areas with their panoramic views as a prelude to candlelight. With beautiful Lyme Regis, the setting for the movie *The French Lieutenant's Woman*, on the doorstep, Sea Tree House is ideal for couples wanting to celebrate an anniversary or special occasion in style. Ω

Matter of facts

CONTACT
David Parker
T +44 (0)1297 442244
E seatree.house@
ukonline.co.uk
W lymeregis.com/
seatreehouse
Address Sea Tree House,
18 Broad Street, Lyme
Regis, Dorset DT7 3QE

RATING
VisitBritain 4 Star
Self Catering

SLEEPING
Two apartments each
sleeping up to four people.

FOR THE FAMILY
Children welcome; pets
accepted.

FACILITIES
All apartments have fully
equipped kitchens and TVs;
private parking; wireless
Internet by arrangement.

**NEAREST SHOPS, PUBS
AND RESTAURANTS**
Boutique and general
shops, top-class
restaurants and friendly
inns and pubs are all on
the doorstep.

OUT AND ABOUT
The Thomas Hardy Trail;
the Philpot Museum; the
Heritage Jurassic Coast of
Dorset; the Town Mill
(working watermill); the
Marine Theatre and the
Smugglers Trail.

**PRICES PER WEEK AND
WHAT'S INCLUDED**
Low season £215.00-
£365.00; high season
£415.00-£595.00.
Includes central heating
and lighting, all bed linen
(duvets), bath towels and
hand towels.

Spanhoe Lodge

UPPINGHAM, RUTLAND 5 STAR GOLD AWARD B&B

Spanhoe earns high praise in print for its all-round quality

As the only five star, gold-awarded accommodation provider in this picturesque part of England, Spanhoe Lodge's key ingredients for success are quality and a very warm welcome. It is situated in the centre of the country, five minutes' drive from the A1 and on the border with the tiny, unspoilt county of Rutland.

Its additional eight new luxury en suite rooms are individually styled and offer various options for guests. They include king-size doubles, twins, self-catering, family rooms and a fully-accessible room for the mobility impaired with wheel-in wet room and dedicated car parking just feet from the door. All rooms have a TV, a wide range of toiletries and a full hospitality tray and guests have the use of a full-size snooker room.

Spanhoe Lodge has recently added a hot tub, licensed bar and a restaurant offering traditional British fare. Its gourmet breakfasts have earned it an AA Egg Cup award and the property has also been included in the *Best Bed & Breakfast Guide* and featured in the *Which? Magazine Editor's Top 20 B&Bs*. Ω

Matter of facts

CONTACT
Jennie Bell
T +44 (0)1780 450328
E jennie.spanhoe@
virgin.net
W spanhoelodge.co.uk
Address Spanhoe Lodge,
Laxton Road, Harringworth,
Northamptonshire NN17 3AT

RATING
VisitBritain 5 Star
Gold Award B&B

SLEEPING
12 ground-floor bedroom
comprising four doubles,
four twins, two family
rooms, one self-catering
and one disabled room, all
en suite.

FOR THE FAMILY
Children welcome;
high/low chairs and cots
available; pets by
arrangement.

FACILITIES
In-room TV and DVD,
tea and coffee-making
facilities, trouser press,
ironing facilities, hairdryer
and Internet access;
1.7-acre site; garden with
patio and decked area;
snooker room; hot tub;
licensed bar; restaurant
(special diets catered for);
picnic lunches; conference/
meeting facilities; on-site
parking with access for
large vehicles, such as
horse boxes.

**NEAREST SHOPS, PUBS
AND RESTAURANTS**
Shops in Uppingham;
10 pubs with food within
five-mile radius; nearby
Stamford has restaurants
with all types of cuisine.

OUT AND ABOUT
Rockingham Motor
Speedway; Rutland Water;
Burghley House;
Rockingham Castle Park;
Jurassic Way (walking);
riding in village; fishing,
golf and cycle hire nearby.

**PRICES PER ROOM
PER NIGHT AND
WHAT'S INCLUDED**
Double/twin rooms from
£75.00; single occupancy
(Sunday-Thursday) from
£55.00. Discounts for
stays of three nights or
more. Includes gourmet
breakfast.

The Stables

Historic values are respected but there is no shortage of modern facilities

This architect-designed house with a beautiful interior combines the best of contemporary design while respecting the historical architecture of one of England's finest medieval towns. It is the perfect location for a short break, whether it is of the action-packed and outdoors variety or a feet-in-front of the fire kind.

Enjoying an excellent location in the historic town centre at Wyle Cop, the Stables is fully equipped and furnished to the highest standards. The property looks out on to a black and white Tudor building and features a vaulted ceiling in the living room, underfloor heating and oak floors.

Sleeping up to four adults, the two bedrooms contain a double and two single beds and both rooms are en suite. There is a TV, DVD and CD player, dining space for six and a kitchen equipped with dishwasher, cooker, microwave, fridge and a number of small appliances.

The Stables is an ideal base from which to explore Shrewsbury with its 660 Listed buildings, many linked by ancient passageways. Ω

Matter of Facts

CONTACT
Miriam Doyle
T +353 1 679 1551
E info@pka.ie
W holidaylettings.co.uk/
rentals/shrewsbury/15905
Address The Stables,
48A Wyle Cop,
Shrewsbury, Shropshire.
Booking address
1 Johnson Place,
Dublin 2, Ireland.

RATING
VisitBritain 4 Star
Self-Catering

SLEEPING
One double and one twin
room, both with en suite.

FOR THE FAMILY
Cot and highchairs
provided.

FACILITIES
Secure parking.

NEAREST SHOPS, PUBS AND RESTAURANTS
All within a two-minute
walk in Shrewsbury town
centre.

OUT AND ABOUT
River Severn; the Dingle
sunken gardens;
Shrewsbury's 660 Listed
buildings; Acton Burnell
Castle; Attingham Park
(National Trust mansion
and park); Coleham
Pumping Station;
Haughmond Abbey;
Shrewsbury Castle and
Abbey; Wroxeter Roman
City; Shrewsbury Museum
and Art Gallery;
Shrewsbury Music Hall.

PRICES PER WEEK AND WHAT'S INCLUDED
£300.00-£600.00.
Includes linen and
towels.

Steele's Mill

PENRITH, CUMBRIA
SELF-CATERING AWAITING GRADING

Restored mill is perfect spot for views of river's varied wildlife

This newly-restored corn mill sits in a quite, idyllic setting on the banks of the River Lyvennet in Cumbria. It includes a viewing balcony where you can relax, take in the wonderful views and become acquainted with the inhabitants of the river, which include kingfisher, dipper, brown trout, heron and the occasional otter.

A mill has stood on the present site since at least 1327 and every effort has been made to preserve its history, including retaining the original mill workings such as millstones, applewood cogs and mill gearing. The three-storey, freestanding building has been sensitively restored by local craftsmen using local materials. Local oak has been used for fittings, such as floors and staircases, and there is handmade oak furniture in the two bedrooms.

Steele's Mill is family-run with a friendly welcome and service. An ideal base for an active outdoor or touring holiday, it has a high standard of accommodation, including a fully-fitted kitchen/dining area which houses the original mill workings behind a glass feature. Ω

Matter of facts

CONTACT
Margaret Addison
T +44 (0)1931 714226
E wendyaddison@
yahoo.com
W steelesmill.co.uk
Address Steele's Mill,
Kings Meaburn, Penrith,
Cumbria CA10 3BU
Booking address
Keld, Kings Meaburn,
Penrith, Cumbria CA10 3BS

RATING
Self-Catering
awaiting grading

SLEEPING
One double and one twin
room, both with en suite.

FOR THE FAMILY
Pets welcome; grass/livery
available for horse.

FACILITIES
Free fly-fishing in River
Lyvennet; patio/garden
area; private car parking.

**NEAREST SHOPS, PUBS
AND RESTAURANTS**
Shops in Appleby (five
miles) and Penrith (10
miles), and wide selection
of pubs and restaurants.
The White Horse Inn,
within walking distance in
Kings Meaburn, serves
good, home-cooked food.

OUT AND ABOUT
The Lake District National
Park; Carlisle to Settle
Railway; Pennine Way
(coast-to-coast walk);
Horse racing (Carlisle);
sport and leisure centres
(Appleby and Penrith).

**PRICES PER WEEK
AND WHAT'S INCLUDED**
High season £750.00;
mid season £680.00;
low season £540.00.
Short breaks from
£350.00-£450.00.
Includes linen, towels
and fuel.

The Strathdon

BLACKPOOL 4 STAR GUEST ACCOMMODATION

'Simply a nice place to stay' is how owners sum up this little gem

Situated next to Blackpool Promenade, The Strathdon is a small, unpretentious, four star establishment where cleanliness and customer care are paramount and value for money is exceptional.

The 10 cosy, centrally-heated bedrooms all have en suite facilities and are decorated to a high standard. The Strathdon is exclusively for couples and families and serves good home cooking in a comfortable restaurant with individual tables. There is a fully-licensed bar/lounge with flatscreen TV.

It has been assessed for the fifth year running by Quality in Tourism through VisitBritain and given four stars for guest accommodation with an executive summary that says 'the owners are to be congratulated on the standard of cleanliness and hospitality'.

A recently highly-commended Hotel of the Year finalist in the Blackpool Tourism Awards, its proprietors, Lisa and Eddie, describe The Strathdon as 'simply a nice place to stay', but guests, many of whom are repeat visitors, will tell you it's much more than that… Ω

Matter of facts

CONTACT
Lisa
T +44 (0)1253 343549
E stay@
strathdonhotel.com
W strathdonhotel.com
Address
Strathdon Hotel,
28 St Chads Road,
South Shore,
Blackpool FY1 6BP

RATING
VisitBritain 4 Star
Guest Accommodation

SLEEPING
10 bedrooms, all en suite.

FOR THE FAMILY
Children welcome; large family rooms available.

FACILITIES
Licensed lounge/bar with newspaper, magazines and board games; in-room TV, tea and coffee-making facilities, hairdryer, toiletries; ironing facilities available.

NEAREST SHOPS, PUBS AND RESTAURANTS
Shop with papers and provisions 100 yards; market, restaurants and pubs within 10-15 minutes' stroll.

OUT AND ABOUT
Blackpool Tower and Circus, Winter Gardens and Pleasure Beach all within 15-minute stroll; two of the best working men's clubs and Blackpool Football Club's Bloomfield Road ground are five minutes' walk away.

PRICES PER PERSON AND WHAT'S INCLUDED
£112.00-£115.00 per week; £64.00-£69.00 Monday-Friday; £51.00-£75.00 Friday-Monday; £19.00-£25.00 per day. Includes a choice breakfast menu. Optional pre-booked evening meal (when available) £8.00.

Swan Hotel

LAVENHAM, SUFFOLK 4 STAR HOTEL

Favourite haunt of World War II flyers now offers more peaceful pursuits

Ancient oak beams and inglenook fireplaces blend with luxurious furnishings and fabrics in this 14th century, quintessentially English country retreat which was once central to Lavenham's wool trade.

Its has 51 enchanting bedrooms where oak beams and original medieval wall paintings proliferate. Ranging from standard double rooms to mezzanine suites and four-poster beds, they all have their own unique character and layout and are named after local villages.

The Swan's dining options embrace the informal Garden Bar Restaurant, the historic Old Bar, the elegant two AA Rosette Gallery Restaurant and the tranquil garden. The Swan's inspired menus are made using fresh, locally-sourced ingredients. The Old Bar houses a wonderful collection of memorabilia, including a wall signed by British and American airmen stationed at Lavenham during World War II.

Licensed for civil wedding ceremonies, the Swan can cater for up to 90 guests. The medieval courtyard, tranquil garden and minstrels' gallery offer the perfect backdrop for celebrations. Ω

Matter of facts

CONTACT
Alice Iles
T +44 (0)1787 247477
E info@theswanatlavenham.co.uk
W theswanatlavenham.co.uk
Address The Swan Hotel, High Street, Lavenham, Suffolk CO10 9QA

RATING
AA 4 Star Hotel

SLEEPING
51 en suite bedrooms ranging from singles and standard doubles to mezzanine suites.

FACILITIES
Each bedroom has TV and CD/DVD player; suites and feature rooms provide use of bathrobes.

NEAREST SHOPS, PUBS AND RESTAURANTS
Within walking distance in Lavenham.

OUT AND ABOUT
Market towns of Lavenham and Sudbury; cathedral city of Bury St Edmunds; Newmarket racecourse; Constable and Gainsborough country; craft shops and galleries.

PRICES PER PERSON PER NIGHT AND WHAT'S INCLUDED
From £60.00 for a single room to £135.00 for a suite. Includes breakfast.

Swinton Park

MASHAM, NORTH YORKSHIRE
4 STAR GOLD AWARD HOTEL

Top restaurant, every country pursuit and a castle – it all adds up to a super mix

Dating from the 1600s, Swinton Park is a magnificent ancestral castle set in 200 acres of parkland with five lakes, gardens, woodland and its own deer herd. Samuel's, its three AA Rosette restaurant, is one of the highest rated in North Yorkshire and Cumbria and among the top 10 per cent in the country.

There are five spacious and elegant reception rooms and 30 spacious, individually-designed bedrooms. Guests are able to enjoy Jo Malone luxury bath and body products. Four suites on three circular floors include one with a splendid Victorian rainbath in the turret. Guests eat in sumptuous surroundings in Samuel's with its ornate, gold-leaf ceiling, mahogany panelling and portraits of Samuel Cunliffe-Lister, after whom it is named. The conservatory houses a charming spa with Jacuzzi, sauna and five beauty treatment rooms.

Every country pursuit imaginable is on offer, including golf, fishing, shooting including clay pigeons, horse-riding course, moorland pony trekking, walking, mountain biking, croquet, an off-road driving course, falconry and even model yacht and coracle racing. The four-acre walled garden is the largest at any UK hotel and Swinton Park runs a year-round cookery school. Ω

Matter of facts

Reception
T +44 (0)1765 680900
E enquiries@ swintonpark.com
W swintonpark.com
Address
Swinton Park,
Masham,
North Yorkshire
HG4 4JH

VisitBritain 4 Star Gold Award Hotel

SLEEPING
30 en suite double/ twin rooms, including four suites.

FOR THE FAMILY
Playroom; swings; slides; bicycles; goody

bag; cots, beds and highchairs.

FACILITIES
Riding; fishing; golf; falconry; clay pigeon shooting; spa and treatment rooms; cookery school.

NEAREST SHOPS, PUBS AND RESTAURANTS
Market town one mile.

OUT AND ABOUT
Newby Hall; Castle Howard; Fountains Abbey.

PRICES PER NIGHT AND WHAT'S INCLUDED
£150.00-£350.00 per room. Includes full Yorkshire breakfast. Spa, golf and walking packages available throughout year.

Walking in Snowdonia.

Sychnant Pass Country House

CONWY 5 STAR GOLD AWARD GUEST ACCOMMODATION

Superb scenery, great food and rooms with direct access outdoors

The Snowdonia National Park provides the glorious backdrop to this award-winning country house, characterised by lovely sitting rooms with log fires, beautiful pictures and wonderful food. Among the accolades it has collected in recent years are the Booker Prize for Excellence 2002, AA Best Guest Accommodation in Wales 2004 and the RAC Little Gem Award for six consecutive years.

Sychnant Pass House is a substantial Victorian property set in three acres with an indoor, heated, salt-water swimming pool and a gym, sauna and solarium. Its 12 guest rooms – all named after T S Elliot's cats – include galleried suites, rooms with balconies and private terraces and decks. Some of the suites have four-poster beds and two of the ground floor rooms have French windows which open on to private patios. Two other suites have private decking and hot tubs.

Freshly-produced, mouth-watering meals using good-quality, seasonal ingredients, bought locally wherever possible, are served in the candlelit restaurant, which is also open to non-residents. Ω

Matter of facts

CONTACT
Bre Carrington-Sykes
T +44 (0)1492 596868
E bre@sychnant-pass-house.co.uk
W sychnant-pass-house.co.uk
Address
Sychnant Pass House,
Sychnant Pass Road,
Conwy LL32 8BJ

RATING
AA 5 Star Gold Award;
1 AA Rosette.

SLEEPING
12 en suite rooms comprising seven suites, two superior rooms and three standard rooms.

FOR THE FAMILY
Children's play area; DVDs and videos; high teas and babysitting by arrangement; pets welcome.

FACILITIES
Indoor pool, gym, sauna and solarium; weddings. All rooms have tea and coffee-making facilities; fridges; TV/DVD/videos; CD and radio alarms; bath robes; large, soft towels; iron and ironing board.

NEAREST SHOPS, PUBS AND RESTAURANTS
All about 1.5 miles away.

OUT AND ABOUT
Conwy Castle; Penrhyn Castle; Bodnant Gardens; five golf courses; river and sea sports and walking in Snowdonia National Park.

PRICES PER PERSON PER NIGHT AND WHAT'S INCLUDED
B&B from £47.50; dinner, B&B from £77.50 – both prices based on two sharing.

Ta Mill

LAUNCESTON, CORNWALL
4 STAR SELF-CATERING

Get back to nature close to beautiful Bodmin Moor

Ta Mill is a secluded, rural hideaway set in a peaceful hollow of 45 acres on the fringes of Bodmin Moor in an Area of Outstanding Natural Beauty. It consists of a beautiful, 17th century house, traditional stone and slate Cornish cottages with an abundance of charm, and seven select, detached two-bedroomed lodges. These are superbly situated and overlook wildlife ponds or the unspoilt valley where magnificent birds of prey can be seen swooping and nesting swallows spotted.

A babbling brook meanders through the grounds, linking Ta Mill's two wildlife ponds before continuing through a picturesque valley of blossoming gorse and dramatic stone outcrops.

The location couldn't be more perfect for touring both Devon and Cornwall.

Ta Mill House sleeps nine and each of the five cottages sleep between two and seven guests. Accommodation includes TV, video and DVD; CD hi-fi with radio; patio furniture and a kitchen with cooker, microwave and fridge. There is an on-site laundry room with washing and drying facilities. Ω

Matter of facts

CONTACT
Helen Shopland
T +44 (0)1840 261797
E helen@tamill.co.uk
W tamill.co.uk
Address Ta Mill,
St Clether, Launceston,
Cornwall PL15 8PS

RATING
VisitBritain 4 Star Self-
Catering (lodges 3 Star).

SLEEPING
Ta Mill House sleeps nine
in four bedrooms, all
en suite; cottages sleep
between two and seven;
lodges each sleep four in
two bedrooms.

FOR THE FAMILY
Outdoor play area; ample
lawns; cots and highchairs;
one small dog allowed
in specific lodges except
in August.

FACILITIES
Nine hole pitch 'n' putt in
an acre of meadowland;
games room with table
tennis, pool table and gym
equipment; free video and
DVD library; communal
lawns and mature gardens;
laundry.

**NEAREST SHOPS, PUBS
AND RESTAURANTS**
On-site shop for basic
supplies; small shops four
miles; supermarket six
miles. Nearest family-
orientated pub/restaurant
is Wilsey Downs Hotel two
miles away.

OUT AND ABOUT
Boscastle; Tintagel Castle;
Crackington Haven;
Bodmin Moor; Tamar Otter
Park; Lanhydrock (National
Trust) and Pencarrow
House and Gardens.

**PRICES PER WEEK
AND WHAT'S INCLUDED**
From £188.00 for Pump
Cottage (sleeps two/three)
to £1,150.00 for Ta Mill
House (sleeps nine). Short
breaks in Pump Cottage
from £132.00 for three/
four nights, any day start,
out of season. Includes
bed linen.

Tall Ships

CHARLESTOWN, CORNWALL
5 STAR B&B

Put the wind back in your sails with a relaxing break at Tall Ships

This newly-refurbished cottage offers self-contained, B&B accommodation overlooking the garden and a Victorian villa within the grounds of Tall Ships, a recently-built house just 500 yards from the sea in a beautiful harbourside village.

Standing in a walled garden with complete privacy, the centrally-heated cottage is bright and airy with a comfortable double bed, leather suite, washroom and toilet and separate shower. Breakfast is served in the cottage at a time to suit guests. Tall Ships uses only local produce, such as the kippers and haddock, while the all-Cornish ingredients for the full English breakfast are supplied by a local butcher and bread by the local baker.

The cottage can accommodate two people. Guests have the facility to make their own fresh coffee and tea and there is also a small fridge for items such as cold drinks. The cottage is equipped with a 70-channels TV and a VHS/DVD player. There is also a radio, hairdryer, iron and ironing board. Two bicycles are available for guests to use. Ω

Matter of facts

CONTACT
Nick Gay
T +44 (0)1726 871095
E tallshipscharlestown
@tiscali.co.uk
W cornwalltoday.co.uk
Address Tall Ships,
Eleven Doors,
Charlestown,
Cornwall PL25 3NZ

RATING
VisitBritain 5 Star B&B

SLEEPING
Cottage with one double room, washroom and toilet with separate shower.

FOR THE FAMILY
Pets by arrangement.

FACILITIES
Laundry facilities; disabled access; parking.

NEAREST SHOPS, PUBS AND RESTAURANTS
Shops and seven restaurants within walking distance.

OUT AND ABOUT
Eden Project; Clay Museum; Restormel Castle; Bodmin Moor; Lanhydrock House; minutes away from Lost Gardens of Heligan; South West Coast Path; four golf courses minutes away.

PRICES PER PERSON PER NIGHT AND WHAT'S INCLUDED
£30.00-£50.00. Single occupancy supplement £40.00. Includes full English breakfast.

Thirty Two

CHELTENHAM, GLOUCESTERSHIRE
5 STAR GOLD AWARD B&B

Listed townhouse puts you on the doorstep of best in Cheltenham

Overlooking Imperial Gardens in a landmark Listed Regency terrace, Thirty Two is a small privately-run boutique B&B in an unrivalled location within two minutes' walk of Cheltenham's best shops, restaurants and bars.

Thirty Two aims to offer all guests a home-from-home. Its four, superbly-designed bedrooms feature an eclectic mix of furnishings and contain king-size or super king-size beds with pocket-sprung mattresses, luxurious Egyptian cotton linens, goosedown duvets and pillows, beautiful natural stone bathrooms, rain showers, Penhaligon's toiletries and fluffy white robes, ensuring your stay will be a memorable one. There is also free wireless Internet access throughout the building.

Choose to start the day with healthy home-made muesli and fresh juice or relax and enjoy a hearty, home-cooked breakfast, freshly prepared using the best local produce.

The guests' drawing room with its three huge windows overlooking Imperial Gardens provides the perfect setting to sit and watch the sun go down over the rooftops of the Ladies' College. Ω

Matter of facts

CONTACT
Jonathan Sellwood
T +44 (0)1242 771110
E stay@thirtytwoltd.com
W thirtytwoltd.com
Address Thirty Two,
32 Imperial Square,
Cheltenham,
Gloucestershire GL50 1QZ

RATING
VisitBritain 5 Star
Gold Award B&B

SLEEPING
Four double rooms, all with king-size or super king-size beds and en suite rain showers; two with baths.

FOR THE FAMILY
Children over eight welcome.

FACILITIES
All rooms have flatscreen TV and DVD/CD player and hot drinks facilities; free wireless Internet access.

NEAREST SHOPS, PUBS AND RESTAURANTS
Within a two-minute walk in town centre.

OUT AND ABOUT
Chapel Spa, Lido and Leisure Centre in the town centre; Cheltenham Racecourse; Regency Cheltenham; Sudeley Castle; the Cotswolds.

PRICES PER ROOM PER NIGHT AND WHAT'S INCLUDED
£139.00-£189.00.
Includes breakfast.

Thornham Hall

EYE, SUFFOLK 5 STAR SILVER AWARD GUEST ACCOMMODATION

Indulge yourself a little and use a stately home as if it were your own

Renowned for magnificent views over the ancient parkland in which it is situated, Thornham Hall has been the baronial home of the Hennikers since the 18th century. The present building, which dates from the 1950s, reflects its Tudor, Georgian and Victorian predecessors with its open fires, spacious rooms, fine porcelain and Henniker family portraits.

The Restaurant at Thornham Hall, located in the old coach house, serves traditional English food with modern flair. In 2004 Les Routiers named The Hall the best accommodation in Central and East Anglia and in 2005 The Restaurant won the coveted Les Routiers National award for Best Restaurant of the Year.

This is the chance to use a stately home with a wonderful, friendly atmosphere as your own for the duration of your stay. Accommodation in the main hall comprises three double bedrooms, dining room, drawing room and study. Outside, the hall's Victorian kitchen garden has been restored as a walled orchard in ancient woodland. A paradise for walkers, there are 13 miles of woodland and rural walks on the estate. Ω

Matter of facts

CONTACT
Lesley Henniker-Major
T +44 (0)1379 783314
E hallrestaurant@aol.com
W thornhamhall
andrestaurant.com
Address Thornham Hall,
Thornham Magna, Eye,
Suffolk IP23 8HA

RATING
VisitBritain 5 Star
Silver Award Guest
Accommodation

SLEEPING
Three double rooms,
all en suite.

FOR THE FAMILY
Toys and games; videos;
DVDs; ample open space.

FACILITIES
Study with TV, DVD,
videos, board games and
a wide range of books;
award-winning restaurant;

civil weddings in the
Thornham Walled Garden.

**NEAREST SHOPS, PUBS,
AND RESTAURANTS**
Nearest shops 2.5 miles;
pubs and restaurants
within walking distance.

OUT AND ABOUT
Villages of Thornham
Magna and Parva;
Thornham Parva's 9th
century thatched church
with its medieval triptych;
market towns of Eye and
Diss; Framlingham Castle;
Minsmere; Suffolk coast;
wool towns of Long
Melford and Lavenham;
Ickworth House and park;
Bury St Edmunds
Cathedral and Abbey.

**PRICES PER NIGHT AND
WHAT'S INCLUDED**
Double room £100.00 per
couple. Includes breakfast.

Three Chimneys Farm

GOUDHURST, KENT 4 STAR SELF-CATERING

Amazing hideaway with superb leisure facilities on the edge of a forest

Set in glorious countryside at the end of a one-mile farm track in the heart of the Weald of Kent, Three Chimneys Farm is a perfect hideaway for a relaxing country holiday.

Hop farming on this traditional Kent farm, dating from the 16th century, ceased in the 1970s and the oast houses and other outbuildings have been converted to five cottages with outstanding views. Three Chimneys is still a working farm with sheep and cattle grazing in the fields.

Located in beautiful grounds and gardens on the edge of Bedgebury Forest, the cottages sleep between two and eight adults. They are stylishly and individually furnished and have wood-burning stoves, dishwashers, washer/dryers, electric ovens and hobs, fridge freezers, microwave ovens, toasters, videos, stereos, satellite TVs, wireless Internet and telephones.

Some have an enclosed garden and some have a balcony or private patio, but all have use of the well-kept grounds in which there is a badminton net, croquet and tennis court.

There is an unfenced pond in the grounds, 200 yards from the cottages. Ω

Matter of facts

CONTACT
Marion Fuller
T +44 (0)1580 212175
or +44 (0)7785 734639
E marionfuller@
threechimneysfarm.co.uk
W threechimneysfarm.co.uk
Address
Three Chimneys Oast,
Goudhurst,
Kent TN17 2RA

RATING
VisitBritain 4 Star
Self Catering

SLEEPING
Five cottages sleeping
two-eight/nine plus a cot.

FOR THE FAMILY
Children's play area; baby
sitters available.

FACILITIES
Extensive grounds with
badminton, croquet and
tennis court; unfenced
pond; barbeques on
request; ample parking.

NEAREST SHOPS, PUBS AND RESTAURANTS
Nearest shops two miles;
nearest pub with food one
mile across the forest and
many more within five miles.

OUT AND ABOUT
Village of Goudhurst; riding
in Bedgebury Forest;
fly-fishing on Bewl Water;
Sissinghurst Gardens;
Bodium Castle; Scotney
Castle; Ightham Mote;
several golf courses.

PRICES PER WEEK AND WHAT'S INCLUDED
One bedroom cottage
£295.00-£320.00; two
bedroom cottage £425.00-
£500.00; three bedroom
cottage £550.00-£775.00;
five bedroom cottage
£600.00-£1,000.00.
Includes bed linen (duvets),
tea towels, oven gloves and
electricity from May to
October (charged at cost
during winter).

Tides Reach Hotel

SALCOMBE, DEVON 3 STAR GOLD AWARD HOTEL

Former military base has everything visitors need to enjoy a little R&R

Three generations of the Edwards family have, over 40 years, turned this former World War II US Marines' barracks and Royal Navy training base into a modern hotel where the accent is on caring, friendly service in elegant, comfortable surroundings.

Built in 1936, this idyllic seaside retreat offers superb sea views and a totally-relaxing atmosphere. Small enough to retain the personal touch, but large enough to have the best facilities, the hotel has 32 en suite rooms, all but two of which have sea views and the majority with balconies. All the lounges, cocktail bar and restaurant have great views over the safe, sandy, clean beach of South Sands immediately in front of the hotel.

Award-winning cuisine specialises in local produce, particularly seafood, and is complemented by an extensive, carefully-selected and balanced wine list. Leisure facilities include an indoor pool with lush foliage giving a tropical atmosphere, sauna, spa bath, beauty salon, hairdresser, squash court, snooker table and a fully-equipped gym and fitness room. Ω

Matter of facts

CONTACT
John Edwards
T +44 (0)1548 843466
E enquiries@tidesreach.com
W tidesreach.com
Address Tides Reach Hotel, South Sands, Salcombe, Devon TQ8 8LJ

RATING
VisitBritain 3 Star
Gold Award Hotel

SLEEPING
32 bedrooms comprising single, double/twin and suites, all en suite.

FOR THE FAMILY
Children over eight welcome.

FACILITIES
Indoor pool; sauna; spa bath; beauty salon; hairdresser; squash court; snooker table; gym and fitness room; sheltered garden with ornamental lake; all bedrooms have TV, radio, direct-dial telephone, hairdryer and bathrobes.

NEAREST SHOPS, PUBS AND RESTAURANTS
Three-quarters of a mile away in Salcombe.

OUT AND ABOUT
South Devon Coastal Footpath; Dartmoor National Park; the Eden Project; Salcombe Estuary.

PRICES PER PERSON PER NIGHT AND WHAT'S INCLUDED
Dinner, B&B £85.00-£165.00. Winter promotion (November, February and March) dinner, B&B from £62.00.

Tom's Barn

ASHBOURNE, DERBYSHIRE
5 STAR SELF-CATERING

Modernised barn lets you experience rural life at its comfortable best

Tom's Barn is perfect for couples of all ages who are enchanted to find modern comfort within the charming shell of a traditional 18th century limestone farm building.

It is attached to the owners' house, Orchard Farm, which is set on the edge of the beautiful Peak Park village of Parwich. On the one side there is open countryside with fields of cows and a myriad of walks; on the other it is a five minute stroll to the village shop, pub and church. Next door is Douglas's Barn, a new five star barn conversion for two, meaning two couples can holiday together, entertain each other to meals yet retain their privacy.

Inside, the atmosphere is instantly warm and welcoming. Light streams through the huge window in the gable end of the high-walled sitting room; the log burner, generously-equipped kitchen, two-seater whirlpool bath and king-size bed with down and feather mattress topper all promise total relaxation and indulgence! No wonder everyone keeps returning. Ω

Matter of facts

CONTACT
John and Marion
Fuller-Sessions
T +44 (0)1335 390519
E tom@tomsbarn.co.uk
W tomsbarn.co.uk
Address Tom's Barn,
Orchard Farm, Parwich,
Ashbourne, Derbyshire
DE6 1QB

RATING
VisitBritain 5 Star
Self-Catering

SLEEPING
One double bedroom
en suite.

FOR THE FAMILY
Babies welcome but not
suitable for toddlers,
children or disabled people;
dogs permitted; stabling for
horses can be arranged.

FACILITIES
Off-road parking; both
barns have their own
garden area; Cycles and
tennis racquets available
for guests' use; Weber

barbecue; wireless Internet
access; Freeview TV, two
TVs, one with video, DVD,
CD/radio.

**NEAREST SHOPS, PUBS
AND RESTAURANTS**
Excellent village shop and
pub serving food, both less
than half a mile away.

OUT AND ABOUT
Dovedale; Peak District;
Chatsworth; Haddon Hall;
Kedleston Hall; Carsington
Water; market towns of
Ashbourne, Leek,
Bakewell and Matlock;
spa town of Buxton;
picturesque walks from
the property.

**PRICES PER WEEK
AND WHAT'S INCLUDED**
£395.00-£510.00 per
cottage. Three or four-
night winter short breaks
available at approximately
70% of weekly rate.
Includes all linen, towels,
cleaning materials and
basic kitchen ingredients.

Tone Dale House

WELLINGTON, SOMERSET 5 STAR SELF-CATERING

Listed villa has all you need to host a special gathering of family or friends

This impressive, Grade II Listed palladian-style villa is set in four acres of wonderful landscaped grounds through which runs a mill stream alongside a once-thriving but now silent woollen mill.

The house, built in 1797 by Thomas Fox, and gardens have been carefully restored by the current owners. Extremely comfortable and furnished to a high standard, the elegant house is full of antiques and family memorabilia. An ideal venue for celebrations of all kinds, including birthdays, anniversaries and reunions, Tone Dale has 16 bedrooms – 11 in the main house and five in the converted stables – which can sleep up to 31 guests. There are two dining rooms – one seating 31, the other 16 – and a total of nine bathrooms, including four en suite.

The main house also features a 40-foot long grand hall, off which is a fully-equipped kitchen, together with a scullery and jam room. There is also a games room (pictured below) with table tennis, pool and roulette. Ω

Matter of facts

CONTACT
Claire Bendall
T +44 (0)1823
662673
E claire@
thebighouseco.com
W thebighouseco.com
Address Tone Dale
House, Wellington,
Somerset TA21 0EZ

RATING
VisitBritain 5 Star
Self-Catering

SLEEPING
16 rooms comprising
six doubles, three
twins and seven with
zip and link beds.
Four rooms have en
suite facilities and
there are five other
bathrooms.

FOR THE FAMILY
Games room; on-site
croquet, badminton
and boules.

FACILITIES
Archery, pistol
shooting, laser clays,
bouncy castles, hot
tubs, massage,
beauty treatments
and catering can be
arranged on-site; civil
wedding ceremonies.

**NEAREST SHOPS,
PUBS AND
RESTAURANTS**
Shops, pubs and
restaurants half a
mile away plus many
country pubs within
five miles.

OUT AND ABOUT
Out and about:
Seaside (40 minutes);
Exmoor (20 minutes);
many National Trust
houses and gardens
nearby.

**PRICES PER NIGHT
AND WHAT'S
INCLUDED**
Two nights midweek
£2,995.00; three-
night weekends
£4,950.00.
Includes gas,
electricity and logs
for open fires.

Tower House 1066

ST LEONARDS-ON-SEA, EAST SUSSEX
4 STAR SILVER AWARD GUEST ACCOMMODATION

Take in the sea air and escape life's battles at friendly guest house

Tower House offers the personal and friendly atmosphere of a privately-owned guest house with the ambience of a country house. It is situated in the quiet heart of St Leonards-on-Sea yet is only three-quarters of a mile from the seafront and close to Hastings.

Every bedroom is individually decorated and all have en suite facilities, some with bath and shower. All rooms have TVs, Egyptian cotton bedding and fluffy white towels.

Meals, including breakfast, are freshly prepared using locally-sourced ingredients where possible or vegetables from Tower House's own garden. Special diets are catered for as the chef is qualified in diet/nutrition.

You can relax with a pre-dinner drink from the bar in the spacious conservatory. The stunning gardens capture the sun until late evening and provide the perfect place to unwind in summer.

The comfortable lounge contains a real fire where you can curl up in front of the TV or read a book. Perhaps you can try one of the themed weekends to while away the winter blues. Ω

Matter of facts

CONTACT
Louise Tester
T +44 (0)1424 427217
E reservations@
towerhousehotel.com
W towerhousehotel.com
Address Tower House 1066,
28 Tower Road West,
St Leonards-on-Sea,
East Sussex TN38 0RG

RATING
VisitBritain 4 Star
Silver Award Guest
Accommodation

SLEEPING
Four double rooms, one single, two twin, two four-poster, one family room.

FACILITIES
Licensed bar; conservatory; gardens; free wireless Internet; rooms on ground floor; evening meals by prior arrangement; light snacks available; unrestricted parking.

NEAREST SHOPS, PUBS AND RESTAURANTS
All within walking distance.

OUT AND ABOUT
Seafront; the old towns of Hastings, Battle, Rye and 1066 country all within 30-minute drive; London and Brighton just over an hour away.

PRICES PER NIGHT AND WHAT'S INCLUDED
Double/twin room £65.00-£79.00 per room; single occupancy of double/twin room £49.50-£59.00. Includes breakfast. Discounts for three nights or more. Please contact Tower House for further details. Open all year.

Trafford Bank

INVERNESS 5 STAR GUEST HOUSE

Examples of fine art and co-owner's interior design skills abound

Once the residence of the Bishop of Moray and Ross-shire, this 1873-built, award-winning guest house in the capital of the Highlands is now a celebration of Scottish art and modern technology. Refurbished from top to bottom by Lorraine Freel and Koshal Pun, the house retains many original features and mixes antique furniture with contemporary pieces, some designed by Lorraine herself, an accomplished interior designer.

Featuring a unique interior design, the house resembles a mini art gallery, packed with paintings and sculptures by Scottish artists. Indeed, Scottish products feature throughout the house and include Anta pottery and soft furnishings, Arran aromatic products and Skye soap. The five bedrooms are packed with up-to-date technology, including flatscreen digital TVs, DVDs and CDs, free wireless Internet connections and iPod docking stations, and nice little touches like hospitality trays, sherry decanters and silent mini-fridges.

Individually-prepared breakfasts are made using local ingredients and served in a stunning conservatory overlooking the mature gardens. Ω

Matter of facts

CONTACT
Lorraine Freel
T +44 (0)1463 241414
E info@trafffordbank
guesthouse.co.uk
W traffordbank
guesthouse.co.uk
Address Trafford Bank
Guest House, 96 Fairfield
Road, Inverness IV3 5LL

RATING
AA 5 Star Guest House

SLEEPING
Five family/twin/double
rooms, all en suite.

FOR THE FAMILY
Cots and highchairs
available.

FACILITIES
Hi-tech bedrooms with
digital flatscreen TVs and

iPod docking stations;
mature gardens; ample
parking space.

**NEAREST SHOPS, PUBS,
AND RESTAURANTS**
Supermarket two minutes'
walk away; town centre
shops, pubs and
restaurants within 10-
minute walking distance.

OUT AND ABOUT
Loch Ness; Culloden
battlefield; Cawdor Castle;
Glen Affric; Black Isle.

**PRICES PER NIGHT
AND WHAT'S INCLUDED**
Double room £40.00-
£48.00 per person based
on two sharing. Single
occupancy of double room
£60.00-£75.00. Includes
breakfast.

Treverbyn Vean Manor

THE WEST WING

LISKEARD, CORNWALL 5 STAR GOLD AWARD GUEST ACCOMMODATION

Take your leisure in surroundings where war leaders made their plans

This World War II home of Lord Beaverbrook, where he met Churchill and Montgomery in secret, is the work of Victorian architects George Gilbert Scott and William Burges. Situated in 40 acres of riverside and woodland walks, Treverbyn Vean Manor is an impressive Grade II Listed, neo-Gothic manor house built in 1856.

The Great Hall, where cream teas are served, features a minstrels' gallery, log fire and stone mullion windows, while the elegant dining and sitting rooms have elaborate ceilings and carved doors. Drinks may be enjoyed on the long terrace overlooking the woods or in the hall.

The two large, comfortable, centrally-heated bedrooms have views of the woods through leaded windows, glorious en suite bathrooms and six-foot beds made up with fine linen and Egyptian cotton sheets.

The full Cornish breakfast is accompanied by fresh orange juice, yoghurts, fresh fruits and cereals. Wherever possible, dishes are prepared using organic, locally-produced food, including fish and shellfish from Cornish coastal waters and meat and poultry from local farms. Ω

Matter of facts

CONTACT
Anthony and Carolyn Hindley
T +44 (0)1579 326105
E ahindley@mac.com
W treverbynvean.co.uk
Address The West Wing, Treverbyn Vean Manor, Twowatersfoot, Liskeard, Cornwall PL14 6HN

RATING
VisitBritain 5 Star Gold Award Guest Accommodation

SLEEPING
Two large double rooms with six-foot beds and en suite bathrooms with roll-top baths.

FACILITIES
Great hall; dining room; sitting room; magnificent gardens.

NEAREST SHOPS, PUBS AND RESTAURANTS
Trago Mills, family shopping and leisure parks; London Inn, St Neot; Tapenades, Liskeard; Food For Thought in Fowey; Trawler's on the Quay, Mawgan's and Barclay House in Looe; Jamie Oliver's Fifteen Cornwall at Watergate Bay; Rick Stein's seafood restaurants at Padstow.

OUT AND ABOUT
The Eden Project; The Lost Gardens of Heligan; many historic houses and gardens, including Trelissick, Trerice, Antony, Lanhydrock, Cotehele, Prideaux Place, Pencarrow, Boconnoc House and Caerhays; both north and south Cornish coasts within easy reach; three golf courses; coastal paths; trout fishing; nearby beaches.

PRICES PER NIGHT AND WHAT'S INCLUDED
£50.00-£60.00 per person. Includes full Cornish breakfast and cream tea or coffee/tea on arrival.

Ty'n Rhos
COUNTRY HOUSE

CAERNARFON, GWYNEDD
5 STAR COUNTRY HOUSE

Top Welsh produce is used to provide a culinary feast

The magnificence of Snowdon and the beauty of Anglesey provide the backdrop to Ty'n Rhos Country House, a special place in the land of myth and legend with a rather special culinary offering.

Quality furnishings and fittings are standard in all 14 individually-designed, en suite bedrooms. Two double/twin rooms on the ground floor open on to the garden where you can enjoy the views of Snowdon and Anglesey while you play croquet.

Proprietor/chef Martin James and his team use only the best local produce to prepare dishes that leave the kitchen, including meat from local farmers and butchers, freshly-caught local fish, and, in the summer, vegetables and herbs straight from the garden. Breakfast is a memorable affair with home-made rolls and preserves, freshly-squeezed orange juice, kedgeree in winter, kippers, smoked haddock and poached egg. All this is in addition to its fine dining restaurant where talented chefs prepare home-made chutneys and delicious sauces to complement the meals.

Two carp-stocked lakes; log fires in winter; a colonial-style conservatory; a stylish lounge; attractive, individual cottages in the courtyard and even a helipad are among the remarkable features of this stylish and romantic venue. Ω

Matter of facts

CONTACT
Janet James
T +44 (0)1248 670489
E enquiries@tynrhos.co.uk
W tynrhos.co.uk
Address Ty'n Rhos, Seion, Llanddeiniolen, Caernarfon, Gwynedd LL55 3AE

RATING
VisitWales 5 Star Country House

SLEEPING
14 en suite bedrooms including single, double/twin and four superior rooms, two of which have patio doors opening on to the garden. All superior rooms have super king-sized zip-and-link beds that can convert to twins.

FACILITIES
Digital flatscreen TVs; tea and coffee-making facilities; carp-stocked fishing lake; restaurant overlooking garden; helipad; wireless Internet.

NEAREST SHOPS, PUBS AND RESTAURANTS
Nearest shops are two-three miles away; there is a number of pubs and restaurants within a five-mile radius of the property.

OUT AND ABOUT
Medieval castles (including Caernarfon); National Trust properties; slate and copper mines; handicrafts; golf courses; sailing and other watersports.

PRICES PER ROOM AND WHAT'S INCLUDED
Bed and full Welsh breakfast, first night – single £75.00, standard double £110.00 (single occupancy £80.00); superior king-size double or twin £140.00 (single occupancy £100.00). Reductions for stays of two nights or more. Three-course dinner £32.50 per person.

Underleigh House

HOPE VALLEY, DERBYSHIRE 5 STAR GOLD AWARD B&B

Award-winning B&B takes great care of Peak District explorers

Tucked away on a private lane in magnificent walking country amid glorious Peak District scenery, this former cottage and barn, dating from 1873, has been tastefully converted to a B&B of exceptional quality.

Run with enthusiasm and offering everything the discerning walker requires, Underleigh House has six bedrooms, all with en suite shower or bath, superior beds and quality duvets.

After a day in the Peak Park, relax in the beamed lounge with its log fire on chilly days, or on the terrace surrounded by flowers. In the morning experience the delicious breakfasts served in house-party style around a large oak refectory table in the flagstoned dining hall. Homemade specialities include muesli, breads, several fruit compotes and porridge gently simmered overnight in the Aga. Tasty sausages, eggs and black pudding are local, as are the traditional, soft Derbyshire oatcakes.

Winner of Derbyshire's Best Breakfast award, Underleigh also won the Gold Award for Best B&B at the East Midlands Enjoy Excellence Awards in 2006. Ω

Matter of facts

CONTACT
Vivienne and Philip Taylor
T +44 (0)1433 621372
E info@
underleighhouse.co.uk
W underleighhouse.co.uk
Address Underleigh
House, off Edale Road,
Hope, Hope Valley,
Derbyshire S33 6RF

RATING
VisitBritain 5 Star
Gold Award B&B

SLEEPING
Six bedrooms comprising
four doubles, one twin and
one newly-refurbished
suite, all en suite.

FACILITIES
All rooms have TV with
DVD, tea/coffee facilities,
radio/alarm clock and
hairdryer. There is a DVD
library for guests to use
free of charge.

**NEAREST SHOPS, PUBS
AND RESTAURANTS**
Nearest shops are one mile
away in Hope village;
others are in Castleton and
Hathersage. There is an
excellent variety of pubs
and restaurants within a
five-mile radius, the nearest
being the Cheshire Cheese
just over half a mile away.

OUT AND ABOUT
Castleton caves;
Chatsworth; Haddon Hall;
Lyme Park; Bakewell; the
'plague village' of Eyam;
Hardwick Hall.

**PRICES PER NIGHT AND
WHAT'S INCLUDED**
Single room £50.00-
£55.00; double/twin room
£70.00-£90.00. Reduced
rates for stays of three
nights or more (excluding
bank holidays). Includes
full English breakfast.

The Valley

TRURO, CORNWALL
5 STAR SELF-CATERING

Cornwall's chic country retreat is just the place to unwind

A secluded hamlet of contemporary holiday villas where switching-off comes as standard. Set in 13 acres of conservation countryside, The Valley is Cornwall's undiscovered secret.

Combining the service of a five star hotel with the intimacy of your own villa, the stunning development, designed by award-winning architects, features a selection of local stone, slate and cedar in five different contemporary designs with no two properties being exactly alike. Specialist interior designers have ensured each one is luxuriously fitted and equipped to be both stylish and comfortable. Hand-crafted emperor-sized beds to sleep in and Villeroy and Boch crockery to eat from combine to create the self-catering version of heaven!

Enjoy landscaped gardens, indoor and outdoor swimming pools, spa pool, gym, tennis court and squash court with golf, fishing, sailing and cycling nearby. Indulge in exquisite food and drink in the stylish ambience of Café Azur. Ω

Matter of facts

CONTACT
Booking office
T +44 (0)1872 862194
E info@the-valley.co.uk
W the-valley.co.uk
Address The Valley, Bissoe Road, Carnon Downs, Truro, Cornwall, TR3 6LQ

RATING
VisitBritain 5 Star
Self-Catering

SLEEPING
46 villas comprising five individual designs, each sleeping up to four or six guests.

FOR THE FAMILY
Stairgates, cots and highchairs available free of charge; pets charged at £20.

FACILITIES
Restaurant; landscaped gardens; indoor and outdoor pools; spa pool; gym; tennis and squash court; games room.

NEAREST SHOPS, PUBS AND RESTAURANTS
A few minutes' drive away.

OUT AND ABOUT
Roseland Peninsula; the Eden Project; National Maritime Museum; cathedral city of Truro; Killiow Park Golf Club; cycling along the old Mineral Tramways from the ancient quays to the harbour at Portreath; surfing on Cornwall's north coast; sailing on the south coast; pottering around in of the county's many sub-tropical gardens.

PRICES PER WEEK AND WHAT'S INCLUDED
From £545.00, or £310.00 for a weekend. Includes bed linen, towels, electricity and VAT.

Vanilla Cottage

NR USK, MONMOUTHSHIRE
5 STAR SELF-CATERING

Idyllic retreat in the midst of a golfers' paradise

This gem of a 19th century, stone-built cottage, one of a pair perched above the banks of the River Usk, enjoys an idyllic, quiet, rural location yet has easy access to the A40, M4, M5 and M50.

Situated on the Usk Valley Walk, the cottage adjoins two golf courses and is a mere 10 minutes' drive away from Celtic Manor, venue of the 2010 Ryder Cup. In fact, there are 20 golf courses within easy reach.

Vanilla Cottage is stylishly furnished with a modern twist. It contains a sitting room with cosy wood-burner and a mixture of antique and modern furniture, satellite TV and DVD player; and a fully-fitted, flag-tiled kitchen and dining area, comprehensively equipped with full-size electric oven and grill, halogen hob, fridge and freezer, dishwasher, washer/dryer and quality cookware, crystal glasses and cream tea set.

Up the steeply twisting stairs there is a romantic double bedroom with four-poster and second TV and DVD; a small single bedroom and a sparkling bathroom with shower and whirlpool bath.

The cottage garden has been planted to be attractive all year round and contains a suntrap terrace with lavender hedge, quality patio furniture, barbecue, and off-road parking for one car. Ω

Matter of facts

CONTACT
Fiona Wilton
T +44 (0)1600 860341
E fionawilton@ btopenworld.com
W vanillacottage.com
Address Kemeys Commander,
nr Usk, Monmouthshire
Booking address
Ty Gwyn, Catbrook, Chepstow,
Monmouthshire NP16 6ND

RATING
VisitWales 5 Star Self-Catering

SLEEPING
One double room with a five-foot,
four-poster bed and one single
room. Separate bathroom.

FOR THE FAMILY
No children under four, except
babes in arms; well-behaved
dogs/cats welcome (£20 per
week each).

FACILITIES
Gated garden; two TVs with Sky
and DVD players; CD/radio hi-fi;
Egyptian cotton bed linen; low-
allergy duvets and pillows; cotton
robes and bath towels; spa-style
cosmetics; patchwork quilts;
payphone; safe; Internet access.
Guests receive special discount at
health and beauty spa 12 minutes'
drive away.

**NEAREST SHOPS, PUBS
AND RESTAURANTS**
Small farm shop in summer 400
yards away, otherwise nearest shops
are three miles; exceptional choice
of 20 eateries, some of which are
either AA, Taste of Wales, *Telegraph*
Perfect pub, CAMRA or other award
winners within four-mile radius; a
riverside pub 300 yards away;
Abergavenny Food Festival (six
miles) each September.

OUT AND ABOUT
Tintern Abbey; Roman remains at
Caerleon; Blaenarvon World
Heritage Centre; ancient castles at
Usk, Chepstow, Caldicot, Raglan
and Skenfrith; Brecon Beacons;
Hay on Wye; racing at Chepstow,
Hereford and Cheltenham.

PRICES AND WHAT'S INCLUDED
From £199.00 for low season
short break to £500.00 for high
season week. Includes bed linen,
towels, oil central heating,
electricity, Sky TV. Indulgent short
breaks available in spring, autumn
and Advent.

Venn Farm

PLYMOUTH, SOUTH DEVON
4 STAR GUEST ACCOMMODATION

Make the most of village life while taking in South Devon's delights

This 700-acre working farm has been in the same family for more than six generations. Conveniently located in the middle of Brixton, a small village in the beautiful South Hams, Venn Farm is the perfect base for exploring South Devon.

The cosy old farmhouse contains period features, bric-a-brac accumulated over generations and a country garden to enjoy. All rooms are furnished to an exceptionally high standard with quality furniture and king-size beds. All have a TV, alarm clock, hairdryer, hot drinks facilities and controllable heating.

Two converted, beamed, stone barns with galleried bedrooms in the courtyard offer a greater degree of privacy and independence. With solid oak floors, doors and staircases, they represent the ultimate in barn conversions. Modern fittings and furnishings offer stylish comfort and all modern conveniences in buildings dated 1853. One has a small patio area with table and chairs, perfect for morning coffee or a relaxing glass of wine.

Venn Farm is renowned for its breakfasts prepared with the best local ingredients and home-made bread and preserves. Ω

Matter of facts

CONTACT
Mrs Pat Cane
T +44 (0)1752 880378
E pat.cane@ukonline.co.uk
W vennfarm.co.uk
Address Venn Farm, Brixton, Plymouth, South Devon PL8 2AX

RATING
VisitBritain 4 Star Guest Accommodation

SLEEPING
Five en suite bedrooms, one with a patio.

FOR THE FAMILY
Cots and highchairs; slide and trampoline; no pets.

FACILITIES
Country garden; self-catering cottages available.

NEAREST SHOPS, PUBS AND RESTAURANTS
General store, a famous chip shop, garage, restaurant and a 200-year-old inn within short walk in Brixton.

OUT AND ABOUT
Beach; moors; Pennywell Farm; Plymouth (five miles); ancient Plymouth Barbican; Marine Aquarium; Eden Project.

PRICES PER PERSON PER NIGHT AND WHAT'S INCLUDED
Double room £27.50, twin £30.00 and suite £35.00 based on two people sharing. Reductions for longer stays. Includes breakfast.

Waitby School

KIRKBY STEPHEN, CUMBRIA
5 STAR SELF-CATERING

A lesson in how to mix original features with modern facilities

Built in 1680, this Grade II Listed schoolhouse has been lovingly restored by a local family into a simple, stylish, luxury holiday cottage for all seasons. Set in an idyllic location amid some of England's most stunning countryside, Waitby School sleeps six or seven comfortably in its three bedrooms.

Many original features have been retained, but 21st century luxuries have been artfully incorporated. These include underfloor heating, a Jacuzzi, quality oak and slate flooring, a wood-burning stove, hand-crafted Buttermere slate surfaces in the hand made, fully-fitted and equipped kitchen and two luxury bathrooms, a flatscreen TV with Sky and Bose sound system, a comprehensive DVD and CD collection and a carefully-selected library of books. The former main classroom is now the oak-floored, open-plan living area with original wall panelling.

Completing the picture of what is truly an all-year-round holiday home are large gardens, enclosed by drystone walls and containing a storage shed converted from the former boys' toilets, complete with wooden seat! Ω

Matter of facts

CONTACT
Cumbrian Cottages (agents)
T +44 (0)1228 599960
E info@waitbyschool.com
W waitbyschool.com
Address Kirkby Stephen, Cumbria
Booking address Cumbrian Cottages, Atlantic House, Fletcher Way, Parkhouse, Carlisle, CA3 0LJ

RATING
VisitBritain 5 Star Self-Catering

SLEEPING
Sleeps up to seven in three double bedrooms. Ground-floor master bedroom has en suite with Jacuzzi.

FOR THE FAMILY
Safe, enclosed garden; children's DVD library; cot and highchair available.

FACILITIES
Fully-fitted kitchen with Whirlpool appliances, including cooker, fridge, freezer, washing machine, tumble dryer, microwave and dishwasher plus full range of quality crockery, glassware and utensils; kitchen also has flatscreen TV, sound system and Sky; off-road parking for four cars.

NEAREST SHOPS, PUBS AND RESTAURANTS
Kirkby Stephen, 1.5 miles away, has an impressive array of shops selling art and antiques, along with many good pubs and restaurants.

OUT AND ABOUT
Many walks, including Wainwright's coast-to-coast path, the Northern Viaducts Road and the Poetry Path; Kirkby Stephen Church; Brough Castle; Castlerigg Stone Circle; Lammerside Castle; Long Meg and her daughters (Neolithic stone circle); Pendragon Castle; Shap Abbey; Acorn Bank Garden and Watermill; Sowerby Crossbank Nature Reserve.

PRICES AND WHAT'S INCLUDED
£420.00-£1,000.00 per week; short breaks £350.00. Includes luxury linen and towels, weekly maid service, welcome gift and luxury toiletries.

Wallett's Court
COUNTRY HOUSE HOTEL, RESTAURANT AND SPA

DOVER, KENT 3 STAR SILVER AWARD HOTEL

Food and facilities to stimulate all the senses at ancient manor house

The walls of this ancient manor house, nestling in wild, open landscape in White Cliffs country, positively exude 400 years of history. Climb the Jacobean staircase to one of the three four-poster bedrooms or stroll across the courtyard to one of 14 contemporary rooms housed in converted Kentish hay barns, stables and cowsheds, surrounding the manor.

Modern comforts abound, with crisp cotton linen, flatscreen digital TVs, DVD and CD players and broadband wireless Internet standard in all rooms. Lose yourself in bubbles at bath time or get energised in the shower with luxurious Essential Elements bath treats.

Enjoy breakfast in the conservatory, the library or in bed, take lunch in the lounge by the fire in winter or on the terrace in summer and dine in the oak-beamed restaurant in the evening. Drink where and when you like – champagne in the bath, sundowners at cocktail hour, great whites and elegant reds with dinner. Chill, feel alive, de-stress, shine and glow with a massage or beauty treatment in your own cabin in the woods on the edge of the grounds overlooking the rolling hills.

With Wallett's Relax you can energise, uplift, restore and feel the energy flow through your body in the sauna, steam room and hydrotherapy pool. With Wallett's Active you can take a dip in the indoor swimming pool and feel the force of the counter-current swim trainer and hydrotherapy jet. Invigorate yourself with a session in the gym, breathe in the sea air on the all-weather floodlit tennis court, on the croquet lawn or the boules court, or test your aim on the clay-pigeon shooting range. And with Wallett's Talk you can get together for a pow-wow, private meeting, party or brainstorming session in the Adam Room or the Conservatory.

Dining at Wallett's Court is a gastronomic delight with food designed to appeal to all five senses through imaginative menus created and developed by teamwork, extensive research and investigation into creative culinary processes.

Just 10 minutes from the Port of Dover, Wallett's Court is the perfect hotel in which to stay if you are touring Kent, starting your cruise or continental holiday early or just spending some time relaxing in luxurious surroundings. Ω

Matter of facts

CONTACT
Reservations
T +44 (0)1304 852424
E mail@wallettscourt.com
W wallettscourt.com
Address Wallett's Court Country
House Hotel, Restaurant and Spa,
Westcliffe, St Margaret's-at-Cliffe,
Dover, Kent CT15 6EW

RATING
VisitBritain 3 Star
Silver Award Hotel

SLEEPING
Three double rooms with
four-poster beds; two suites;
14 contemporary single and
double rooms, all en suite.

FOR THE FAMILY
Baby-sitting/child-minding service.

FACILITIES
Restaurant; garden; tennis court;
sauna; fitness centre; spa and
wellness centre; massage; Jacuzzi;
Turkish/steam bath; indoor
swimming pool; room service;
library; meeting/banquet facilities;
business centre; laundry and
dry cleaning; wireless Internet
services; safety deposit box;
parking.

NEAREST SHOPS, PUBS
AND RESTAURANTS
Comprehensive shopping and
a wide range of pubs and
restaurants in Dover, a
10-minute drive away.

OUT AND ABOUT
Dover Castle; Walmer and Deal
Castle; Dover Museum and
Roman Painted House; Samphire
Hoe; the Channel Tunnel;
Calais (45 minutes by Seacat,
75 minutes by ferry); Canterbury;
Sandwich; walks in White Cliffs
country.

PRICES PER ROOM PER NIGHT
AND WHAT'S INCLUDED
Sunday-Friday inclusive, single
rooms £109.00-£139.00;
double rooms £129.00-£169.00.
Includes full English breakfast,
use of spa and VAT. Saturdays
dinner B&B rate from £209.00.

Waren Lea Hall

BAMBURGH, NORTHUMBERLAND
4 & 5 STAR SELF-CATERING

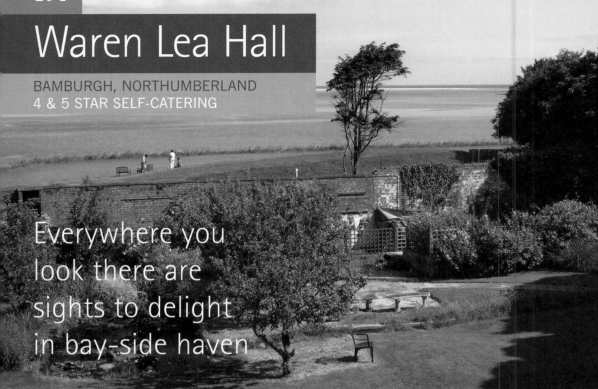

Everywhere you look there are sights to delight in bay-side haven

This gracious old residence, set in two acres of shore-lined parkland in beautiful Budle Bay, an area of Outstanding Natural Beauty and a Site of Special Scientific Interest for its birdlife, comprises three individual, self-catering properties which together accommodate up to 28 guests. This idyllic coastal retreat offers 360-degree panoramic views of the sea and hills, and is famed for its wildlife.

Waren Lea Hall, the beautifully-furnished main building, has high ceilings, chandeliers, sash windows, fireplaces and polished wooden floors and offers breathtaking views from every room. A warm, welcoming reception hall with a log-burning stove leads to a fine, galleried staircase while the large drawing room and dining room lead on to a floodlit terrace with views across the secluded, walled garden and tranquil pond to Holy Island. The ground floor also contains a large, superbly-equipped kitchen/breakfast room with ample cooking facilities, plus a twin bedroom and a cloakroom with shower.

Upstairs, there is a family bathroom and five further bedrooms, including an en suite master bedroom with four-poster and an en suite family room with king-size double bed and two singles.

Ghillie's View, which sleeps up to 10 people, is the former home of the ghillie, who looked after the fishing on the Waren Lea Hall estate, which included the salmon and sea trout runs on the River Waren. Luxuriously furnished throughout with polished wooden floors in the hall and reception rooms, the delightful guest accommodation is all on a single floor. This consists of a master bedroom with a four-poster bed and en suite shower room, a family bedroom with a double and two single beds and an en-suite bathroom, and two further twin bedrooms and a family bathroom.

The fully-equipped kitchen/dining room, which combines modern kitchen facilities with traditional pine furniture, and the semi-circular drawing room, with French windows opening on to a balcony, have views across the river and bay.

The two-bedroomed **Garden Cottage,** which forms the terrace wing of Waren Lea Hall, is furnished with high-quality fabrics and pine furniture and features polished wooden floors throughout. It has a pretty living room and a small, well-equipped kitchen/dining room. Guest accommodation, which, like Ghillie's View, is on a single floor, consists of a double and a twin bedroom, one of which is en suite, and a separate family shower room. Ω

Matter of facts

CONTACT
Carolynn and David Croisdale-Appleby
T +44 (0)1494 725194
or +44 (0)7901 716136
E croisdaleappleby@ aol.com
W selfcateringluxury.co.uk
Address Bamburgh, Northumberland
Booking address Abbotsholme,
Hervines Road, Amersham,
Buckinghamshire HP6 5HS

RATING
VisitBritain 5 Star – Waren Lea Hall;
4 Star – Ghillie's View and Garden Cottage;
all Self-Catering

SLEEPING
Waren Lea Hall sleeps up to 14 in five
double/twin rooms and one family room (two
en suite); Ghillie's View sleeps up to 10 in
three double/ twin rooms and one family
room (two en suite); Garden Cottage sleeps
up to four in two double/twin rooms
(one en suite).

FOR THE FAMILY
Children very welcome; no pets but quality
kennelling available locally.

FACILITIES
All have oil-fired central heating, ample
parking, private telephone, TV, videos,
radios, automatic washer/dryers,
dishwashers, microwaves and garden
furniture; each property is looked after by its
own housekeeper and the caretaker is on
site most days. Catering chef available.

NEAREST SHOPS, PUBS AND RESTAURANTS
The nearby villages of Belford and
Bamburgh have a good range of village
shops for groceries, and in the surrounding
area there are excellent pubs and
restaurants for eating out. There is a small
supermarket in Belford and a good butcher
and greengrocer in Bamburgh.

OUT AND ABOUT
Farne Islands; Holy Island (Lindisfarne);
castles at Bamburgh, Alnwick,
Dunstanburgh, Warkworth, Chillingham,
Norham and Etal; country houses at
Cragside, Wallington Hall, Belsay, Paxton
House, Manderston, Mellerstain and Floors
Castle; historic towns of Berwick upon
Tweed, Alnwick, Kelso and Edinburgh; Chain
Bridge Honey Farm; Heatherslaw Mill and
Steam Railway; Alnwick Garden.

PRICES PER WEEK AND WHAT'S INCLUDED
Waren Lea Hall £1,260.00-£2,362.00;
Ghillie's View £440.00-£1,377.00; Garden
Cottage £221.00-£589.00. Includes towels,
bed linen (duvets), heating and power. Short
breaks Friday-Monday or Monday-Friday
available at 75% of weekly price.

251

The Washington Mayfair

CENTRAL LONDON 4 STAR HOTEL

Traditional-style hotel lies at the centre of London's tourist attractions

Two minutes from Green Park Underground station in the heart of Mayfair lies the traditionally-styled Washington, a hotel which opened in 1813 – the year after Napoleon's retreat from Moscow – and which now combines luxurious quality with professional and unobtrusive service.

Occupying one of London's finest locations, Curzon Street, the hotel's fine English furniture, handwoven oriental carpets and Italian marble create a tranquil oasis in the busy West End.

Each of the Washington Mayfair's 171 bedrooms has distinctive art deco styling with handmade furniture of burred oak and soft furnishings of fine fabrics. All rooms are individually air conditioned and have a range of amenities, including minibars, room safes and computer-controlled security locking.

Dine in the most elegant of surroundings in the award-winning Madison's Restaurant, which offers superb, international cuisine with thoughtfully-designed and daily menus, or relax with a light meal or snack, served all day in the jazz piano lounge and bar. The hotel also has extensive, hi-tech conference facilities, and guests have the opportunity to unwind in a state-of-the-art gym. Ω

Matter of facts

CONTACT
Reservations
T +44 (0)207 499 7000
E reservations@ washington-mayfair.co.uk
W washington-mayfair.co.uk
Address Washington Mayfair Hotel, 5 Curzon Street, Mayfair, London W1J 5HE

RATING
VisitBritain 4 Star Hotel

SLEEPING
171 rooms, comprising classic, executive, state rooms and suites, all with en suite facilities.

FOR THE FAMILY
Children's menu and highchairs available.

FACILITIES
Restaurant; piano lounge; gym; conference facilities and business services; 24-hour room service; high speed Internet access with wireless connectivity; in-room TV with CNN, cable channels and radio, minibar, trouser press, hairdryer, international direct-dial telephone, room safe, bathrobes and hospitality tray.

NEAREST SHOPS, PUBS AND RESTAURANTS
Many in immediate area; Bond Street and Oxford Street a few minutes' walk away.

OUT AND ABOUT
Buckingham Palace, Green Park; Piccadilly; Royal Academy of Arts; Simpsons; West End theatres.

PRICES PER NIGHT AND WHAT'S INCLUDED
Classic room £240.00 + VAT; George Washington Suite £450.00 + VAT. Rates valid for single/ double occupancy. Weekend rates include full English breakfast.

The Weary
AT CASTLE CARROCK

BRAMPTON, CUMBRIA 4 STAR SILVER AWARD RESTAURANT WITH ROOMS

Tired and needing to chill out? The Weary is an aptly-named refuge

The Weary is a 300-year-old country inn with a 21st century mission: to be an unpretentious oasis of luxury for chilled-out indulgence. Even the bathrooms have TVs, giving soap operas a whole new meaning.

Surrounded by beautiful Cumbrian countryside, The Weary is designed for those who like the idea of a rural break but need to know they will have the chance to relax. The fabulous bedrooms are equipped with plenty of cushions and pillows, Egyptian cotton sheets, flatscreen TVs, DVDs, Bang & Olufsen phones and Tivoli radio alarms. The bathrooms, equally as big as the bedrooms, contain fantastic, walk-in monsoon showers, and, of course, television, so you can soak in the bath and watch your favourite TV programme at the same time. Luxury rooms have Jacuzzis big enough for three!

Food is a passion at The Weary. Named Cumbrian Restaurant of the Year 2004 and now with a Silver Award, the inn serves meals that are well presented without being overdone and portions are hearty, using local produce wherever possible. Chose from à la carte or probably the best bar food in the area. Ω

Matter of facts

CONTACT
Ian and Gill Boyd
T +44 (0)1228 670230
E relax@theweary.com
W theweary.com
Address The Weary
at Castle Carrock,
Brampton,
nr Carlisle,
Cumbria CA8 9LU

RATING
VisitBritain 4 Star
Silver Award Restaurant
with Rooms

SLEEPING
Five double rooms,
all en suite.

FACILITIES
All rooms have luxury en suite facilities, TV and DVD, Bang & Olufsen telephone, ironing facilities tea/coffee facilities and hairdryer; flatscreen TV in bathrooms; monsoon showers; Gilchrist and Soames bathroom products; spa baths in select rooms; private residents lounge; breakfast room; licensed restaurant; conference facilities; secure parking.

NEAREST SHOPS, PUBS AND RESTAURANTS
Shops in the village and in Brampton, three miles away. Many pubs and restaurants in surrounding villages within three-miles.

OUT AND ABOUT
Hadrian's Wall; Gelt Woods RSPB nature reserve; Talkin Tarn Country Park; Lanacost Priory; historic Carlisle; Rheged Centre; Carrock Fell.

PRICES PER ROOM PER NIGHT AND WHAT'S INCLUDED
Deluxe twin/double from £105.00; luxury twin/double from £125.00; single occupancy from £79.00. All include breakfast. Midweek and weekend breaks for dinner, B&B (minimum two nights) are also available.

Westcott Barton

BARNSTAPLE, NORTH DEVON
4 STAR GUEST ACCOMMODATION

Secluded valley hideaway with a welcome from the shire horses

Situated in its own secluded valley with beautifully laid-out gardens and its own wood and stream, Westcott Barton is the site of a historic Saxon farmstead mentioned in the Domesday Book.

The decor of the main farmhouse, a Grade II Listed Devon longhouse, is grand, yet comfortable and welcoming. A large barn opposite is regularly used for functions and weddings and boasts a dual-level layout with a dance floor and bar. There are relics from the farm's working life, including a waterwheel and threshing machine.

Accommodation comprises four doubles and a twin room, one of which is on the ground floor. All have en suite bath or shower, TV, DVD and organic tea and coffee facilities.

There is an orangery with a verandah which overlooks the gardens – perfect for tea and scones or an evening aperitif. With four friendly shire horses and bordered by a meandering stream, the two-acre formal gardens are laid to lawns and flowerbeds and lead to 80 acres of pastureland and a large, well-stocked fishing lake. Ω

Matter of facts

CONTACT
Howard Frank
T +44 (0)1271 812842
E westcott_barton@
yahoo.co.uk
W westcottbarton.co.uk
Address Westcott Barton,
Middle Marwood,
Barnstaple,
North Devon EX31 4EF

RATING
VisitBritain 4 Star
Guest Accommodation

SLEEPING
Two double rooms in main house, two doubles and one twin in stone cottages, all en suite.

FOR THE FAMILY
No children under 12; no pets.

FACILITIES
Book and film library for residents; occasional art

exhibitions and music events.

NEAREST SHOPS, PUBS AND RESTAURANTS
Full amenities in Braunton and Barnstaple; nearest pub with food is The Crown in West Down.

OUT AND ABOUT
Woolacombe and Croyde beaches; Lundy Island; Exmoor; Braunton Burrows (UK's largest sand dunes); Tarka Trail; RHS Rosemoor; Royal Society for the Protection of Birds' Chapel Wood Reserve; Marwood Gardens.

PRICES PER NIGHT AND WHAT'S INCLUDED
Guest house rooms £45.00 per person. Stone barn rooms from £45.00 per person. Includes breakfast.

Wethele Manor

LEAMINGTON SPA, WARWICKSHIRE
5 STAR GUEST HOUSE

Farmhouse has a restful atmosphere yet is close to four motorways

This 16th century farmhouse with its large garden, apple orchard and pond enjoys an idyllic, rural location on a peaceful, 250-acre private estate within easy reach of the M6, M40, M45 and M69 motorways.

Decorated with antiques in a traditional style and retaining many original features, such as an inglenook fireplace, a well, stone floors and an old dairy, Wethele Manor provides a homely, restful atmosphere. Bedrooms are spacious and beautifully appointed. All have pocket sprung-mattresses and the double beds are king-size.

Each room has been individually decorated and features a luxury, en suite bathroom with large bath and power shower and several have enchanting, original features such as fire places, elm and oak wooden floors and exposed beams. All rooms have TV, direct-dial telephones, ISDN lines for laptop computers and a hostess tray with complimentary items.

Full English and continental breakfasts, along with pre-booked, three-course evening meals, are served in Wethele Manor's dining room with its superb views over open countryside. Ω

Matter of facts

CONTACT
Simon Moreton
T +44 (0)1926 831772
or +44 (0)7932 156806
E simonmoreton@
wethelemanor.com
W wethelemanor.com
Address
Wethele Manor Farm,
Weston-under-Wetherley,
nr Leamington Spa,
Warwickshire CV33 9BZ

RATING
VisitBritain
5 Star Guest House

SLEEPING
Nine en suite rooms
comprising five king-size
doubles (two with four-
posters), two twins and
two family rooms that can
each sleep up to five.

FOR THE FAMILY
Large gardens and
country walks over
250-acre estate.

FACILITIES
Sitting room (the old
dairy) with selection of
reading material and local
information; conference
facilities; civil wedding
ceremonies; all rooms
have TV, direct-dial
telephones, ISDN lines for
Internet access, tea and
coffee-making facilities
and complimentary bottled
mineral water.

**NEAREST SHOPS, PUBS
AND RESTAURANTS**
Shops 1.5 miles away;
pubs and restaurants
within walking distance.

OUT AND ABOUT
Ideal for Warwick Castle,
Leamington Spa, Stratford-
upon-Avon, Heritage Motor
Museum, farm shops with
play areas, Stoneleigh
Abbey and numerous
stately homes.

**PRICES PER NIGHT AND
WHAT'S INCLUDED**
Single room £65.00-
£80.00; double £70.00-
£95.00; family room
£110.00-£125.00.
Includes full English
breakfast.

Witch Hazel

WYMONDHAM, NORFOLK
4 STAR SILVER AWARD B&B

Generous hospitality and good food await those who want to experience Norfolk

This spacious, detached house is situated in a peaceful location in a rural village overlooking open countryside. With floodlit, off-road parking and a large, secluded garden to relax in, guests can be assured of a warm welcome – along with tea or coffee and home-made cakes – from hosts Eileen and Peter Blake, who pride themselves on attention to detail.

Accommodation comprises three fully-fitted, centrally-heated bedrooms, all with en suite bath or shower, TV with teletext, fridge, radio/alarm clock, tea and coffee-making facilities and hairdryer.

The spacious Primrose Room has a seating area and three-foot twin beds which can be locked together to make a super-king if required. The room overlooks the front of the property with a view stretching for miles across open countryside. The Bluebell Room is also spacious with a double bed, basin and dressing table plus an en suite bathroom with large bath and fitted cupboards. The Poppy Room is a double with en suite shower room overlooking the koi pond.

The superb, open-plan lounge/dining room opens on to the landscaped gardens. Eileen and Peter grow their own fruit and vegetables which they use to prepare breakfast and to make their own preserves. Breakfast is cooked to order from a menu and served at a communal table where guests can chat about plans for the day ahead.

Home-cooked evening meals are available by arrangement and, because Witch Hazel is not licensed, guests are welcome to bring their own wine.

Whether you are visiting Norfolk for pleasure or on business, you can't fail to be impressed by the generous hospitality and good food that accompanies a stay at Witch Hazel.

Wicklewood is a small village with a fully-restored windmill close to the historic market towns of Wymondham, Hingham and Diss. And with many sports and leisure facilities close by and Norfolk within easy reach, Witch Hazel is the ideal base for touring the Norfolk Broads or simply walking in lovely countryside. Ω

Matter of facts

CONTACT
Eileen and Peter Blake
T +44 (0)1953 602247
E witchhazel@
tiscali.co.uk
W witchhazel-
norfolk.co.uk
Address Witch Hazel,
55 Church Lane,
Wicklewood,
Wymondham,
Norfolk NR18 9QH

RATING
VisitBritain 4 Star
Silver Award B&B

SLEEPING
Two doubles and one twin room, all en suite.

FOR THE FAMILY
No children under 15; no pets.

FACILITIES
Lounge/dining room;

large garden; floodlit parking.

NEAREST SHOPS, PUBS AND RESTAURANTS
Shops in nearby Wymondham; extensive shopping in Norwich. Cherry Tree pub with food within walking distance in Wicklewood.

OUT AND ABOUT
Mid Norfolk Railway; Historic Wymondham; Thorncroft Clematis Nursery; many golf clubs including Barnham Broom and the Norfolk Golf Clubs.

PRICES PER NIGHT AND WHAT'S INCLUDED
Double/twin room £25.00-£27.00 per person; single occupancy £34.00-£36.00. Includes breakfast.

Woodlands
COUNTRY HOUSE (CORNWALL)

PADSTOW, CORNWALL
5 STAR SILVER AWARD B&B

Breakfasts so good and varied there's even a recipe book!

This comfortable and informal B&B guest house enjoys farmland views in a rural setting sweeping down to Trevone Bay.

A large Victorian house on the north Cornish coast, Woodlands Country House has eight double and twin rooms, including two ground-floor rooms suitable for less able guests. All rooms are individually and stylishly decorated and have en suite shower and/or bath, digital TV with DVD, clock radio, telephone with modem access, tea, coffee and hot chocolate, a fridge with fresh milk, hairdryer, iron and ironing board and a selection of current magazines.

Guests can relax in the splendid Blue Room, enjoy a drink from the honesty bar and play a game of chess or Cornish Monopoly.

Woodlands' breakfasts are a speciality. 'It's the only meal we do, so we make sure we do the best', say proprietors Pippa and Hugo Woolley, who use local products wherever possible, including their own recipe sausages and local, free-range eggs. With daily specials available, such as kedgeree and eggs benedict, Woodlands even has a recipe book of its own breakfasts. Ω

Matter of facts

CONTACT
Pippa and Hugo Woolley
T +44 (0)1841 532426
E info@
woodlands-padstow.co.uk
W woodlands-padstow.co.uk
Address
Woodlands Country House,
Treator, Padstow,
Cornwall PL28 8RU

RATING
VisitBritain 5 Star
Silver Award B&B

SLEEPING
Eight rooms comprising
three principal double
rooms, one large
double/twin, two
double/twin rooms suitable
for disabled guests, one
twin room and one small
double/single. All have en
suite shower or bath.

FOR THE FAMILY
Children's breakfast menu;
teddy bears; highchairs and
booster chairs; children's
books and videos.

FACILITIES
Croquet lawn; table tennis
shed; wireless Internet
access; computer station
with Internet access for
guest use; off-road parking;
large, lawned paddock for
children and animals.

NEAREST SHOPS, PUBS AND RESTAURANTS
Many shops in Padstow;
Padstow farm shop (10
minutes' walk); huge
selection of restaurants in
Padstow and St Merryn,
including Rick Stein
Seafood Restaurants, and
several very good pubs.
Woodlands provides an
eating and drinking guide.

OUT AND ABOUT
Prideaux Place – 10
minutes' walk; the
Camel Trail for cycling and
walking; offshore fishing
and boating from Padstow;
golf at Trevose GC or
Merlin GC (discounts on
green fees for Woodlands'
guests); Eden Project –
45 minutes' drive; Cornish
Birds of Prey and Crealy
Leisure Park – both 10
minutes' drive.

PRICES PER PERSON PER NIGHT AND WHAT'S INCLUDED
£42.00-£64.00. Single
occupancy supplement
£12.00. Includes breakfast,
morning newspaper and
VAT. From 1 November
to 1 May, excluding Easter
week, three nights for the
price of two (Sunday-
Thursday).

Woodlands
COUNTRY HOUSE (CUMBRIA)

IREBY, CUMBRIA
4 STAR GUEST HOUSE

Take in the rolling hills and the Lakes as you unwind and feel at ease

Formerly a vicarage, Woodlands is a comfortable Victorian house full of charm and character and a friendly place in which to relax, unwind and feel at peace. Situated in a traditional farming area, Woodlands is an ideal base from which to enjoy the unspoilt scenery of the northern Lakes and the Solway coast.

There is ample parking and a 1.5-acre garden containing mature specimen trees which attract a wide variety of birds and other wildlife. The grounds overlook the rolling hills of the Northern Fells.

The house has full central heating with open fires and log-burning stoves in the lounges. All bedrooms are en suite with comfortable beds, TV, large, fluffy towels and a hospitality tray with home-made shortbread. The cosy snug and bar contain a large selection of books and games.

The wide breakfast choice ranges from light continental to a traditional, cooked Cumbrian offering. The excellent four-course dinner offers a variety of menu choices of home-cooked food prepared using fresh, local ingredients wherever possible. Ω

Matter of facts

CONTACT
Judith Willis
T +44 (0)1697 371791
E stay@
woodlandsatireby.co.uk
W woodlandsatireby.co.uk
Address
Woodlands Country House,
Ireby,
Cumbria CA7 1EX

RATING
VisitBritain
4 Star Guest House

SLEEPING
Seven en suite rooms, including ground-floor rooms, super king-size doubles, standard double/twin rooms and family rooms. Three bedrooms at Mobility Level 1.

FOR THE FAMILY
Well-behaved children welcome; children's meals portions; baby-listening; travel cot; well-behaved dogs permitted in some ground-floor rooms (£10.00 per pet per stay).

FACILITIES
Large grounds; snug and bar with books and games; ample parking.

NEAREST SHOPS, PUBS AND RESTAURANTS
Shops in Caldbeck (six miles) and market towns of Keswick and Cockermouth (both 12 miles); Lion pub with good food within walking distance in Ireby; other pubs and eateries in nearby villages and in Keswick.

OUT AND ABOUT
Lakes and mountains, including Little Binsey and Bassenthwaite Lake; Keswick on Derwentwater; Caldbeck Common; Whitehaven; Maryport; St Bees; Solway Firth.

PRICES PER NIGHT AND WHAT'S INCLUDED
B&B – double/twin room £76.00-£120.00; three or more nights £72.00-£110.00; seven or more nights £60.00-£90.00. Single occupancy £38.00-£75.00. Family room for three people £90.00-£132.00. Dinner £22.00 per person. Dinner, B&B – three-night package for two people £320.00-£420.00; seven-night package for two people £660.00-£900.00.

Yellowtop Country Park

FOGGATHORPE, EAST YORKSHIRE 4 STAR SELF-CATERING

Every lodge enjoys a lakeside view in park at the foot of the Yorkshire Wolds

Ducks quacking, fish splashing, skylarks singing … you're in Yellowtop country, sitting lakeside on a 10-acre private park close to your stylish, self-catering lodge, one of only 20 equipped with every home comfort.

Situated at the foot of the Yorkshire Wolds between historic York and beautiful Beverley, Yellowtop Country Park offers excellent coarse fishing for anglers of all abilities on its own two-and-a-half-acre lake, fully stocked with roach, rudd, tench, all types of carp, including crucian, and the odd bream.

Spacious, well-appointed one and two-bedroom Russian redwood lodges, some with hot tubs and some with four-posters but all with lakeside views, offer superb comfort for year-round holidays. At the end of the day when you need a good night's sleep, curl up on a top-of-the-range memory foam or pocket-sprung mattress on all double and king size beds. Ω

Matter of facts

CONTACT
Paula Jessop
T +44 (0)1430 860461
E paulayellowtop@aol.com
W yellowtopcountry.co.uk
Address
Yellowtop Country Park,
Foggathorpe, York,
East Yorkshire YO8 6PZ

RATING
VisitBritain 4 Star
Self-Catering

SLEEPING
20 one and two-bedroom lodges, some with four-posters and some with outdoor hot tubs.

FOR THE FAMILY
Cots and highchairs available (£10.00 per week). Pets £30.00 per week (small dogs only in certain lodges).

FACILITIES
Fishing in 2.5 acre lake (charges may apply); laundry; all lodges feature free wireless Internet, TV, CD/hi-fi, kitchen including

microwave; bath with overhead shower;, bed linen and duvets; verandah; garden furniture and barbecue stands.

NEAREST SHOPS, PUBS AND RESTAURANTS
The local village, two miles away, has a good selection of pubs and eateries, deli, bakers, butchers and two mini-markets.

OUT AND ABOUT
Castle Howard; Harewood House; Wolds Way Lavender; Eden Camp Modern History Theme Museum; Burton Agnes Hall; Lotherton Hall; Goathland to Pickering steam train; Howden; Beverley; York.

PRICES PER WEEK AND WHAT'S INCLUDED
Lodges £260.00-£687.00 per week; short breaks £172.00-£453.00. Includes bed linen, gas/electric heating and electricity.

Yewfield

HAWKSHEAD, CUMBRIA
4 STAR B&B & SELF-CATERING

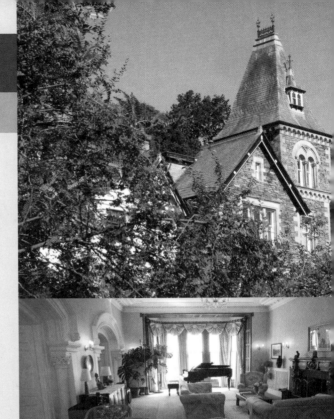

Delightful views and vegetarian breakfasts on the menu for guests

Situated in more than 30 acres of organic land, this impressive house is set in a quiet, elevated position with panoramic views over the Vale of Esthwaite, Lake Windermere and the fells beyond. With its Gothic architecture dating back to 1859, Yewfield is a former award-winning hotel which is now a private residence with six rooms available for B&B on a vegetarian basis.

Double and twin rooms are individually appointed to a high standard. All are en suite with TV, radio and tea and coffee-making facilities. The king-size or luxury twin room at the front of the house has superb views overlooking the Vale of Esthwaite. A lounge and library area are available for guests to use. Yewfield offers a wholefood continental buffet, including fresh fruits, muesli, cereals, home-baked bread, yoghurt, preserves, coffee and teas, and a fully-cooked breakfast. The grounds include organic vegetable gardens, orchards, a herb patio and a mixed border.

Yewfield also has four excellent self-catering apartments available and regularly hosts classical concerts featuring exceptional musicians from around the world. Ω

Matter of facts

CONTACT
Derek Hook
T +44 (0)1539 436765
E derek.yewfield@
btinternet.com
W yewfield.co.uk
Address Hawkshead Hill,
Hawkshead, Ambleside,
Cumbria LA22 0PR

RATING
VisitBritain 4 Star
B&B & Self-Catering

SLEEPING
Six double rooms, all
en suite.

FOR THE FAMILY
Children under nine
and pets cannot be
accommodated in the main
house but are welcome in
the self-catering apartments.

FACILITIES
30 acres of grounds with
nature trail; classical
concerts; abundance of
wildlife; private lake (no
fishing).

NEAREST SHOPS, PUBS AND RESTAURANTS
Hawkshead is just over
a mile away with a few
shops and three pubs that
serve food. Ambleside is
4.5 miles away with many
shops, good restaurants
and inns.

OUT AND ABOUT
Many attractions in the
area – Wordsworth's home,
Dove cottage; Ruskin's
house; Beatrix Potter
World; Zeffirelli's award-
winning cinema in
Ambleside – with live
music in the bar; Theatre
by the Lake in Keswick.

PRICES PER PERSON PER NIGHT AND WHAT'S INCLUDED
From £30.00-£55.00.
Breakfast included.

Yorke Lodge

CANTERBURY, KENT
4 STAR SILVER AWARD GUEST HOUSE

Grab a book and relax at B&B close to the centre of Canterbury

A quintessential Victorian villa built in 1887, Yorke Lodge offers a home-from-home atmosphere with all the modern conveniences the discerning traveller requires. A 10-minute stroll from Canterbury city centre, this family-run B&B provides first class service and friendly attention.

All bedrooms are individually decorated and furnished to the highest standards and are complete with bathroom and toiletries, remote-controlled TV, radio/alarm, hairdryer, tea and coffee-making facilities. Accommodation includes a single room, a twin bedded room and a choice of double rooms, including two with king-size four-posters. Yorke Lodge also has a well-stocked library with a huge range of books.

A conservatory opens out on to a beautiful sun terrace where breakfast can be served on warm summer mornings. Otherwise, breakfast is served in an elegant dining room that is home to a collection of Royal Jubilee, household, toy and tobacco memorabilia. All produce is locally sourced and there are also cereals, fruits and yoghurts for those preferring a lighter breakfast. Ω

Matter of facts

CONTACT
Vicky O'Shea
T +44 (0)1227 451243
E enquiries@
yorkelodge.com
W yorkelodge.com
Address Yorke Lodge,
50 London Road,
Canterbury, Kent CT2 8LF

RATING
VisitBritain 4 Star Silver
Award Guest House

SLEEPING
One single room, one twin room, four standard double rooms and two superior double rooms with king-size four posters, all en suite. Extra beds can be added to superior double rooms to accommodate families of three or four.

FACILITIES
Conservatory; sun terrace; library; dining room; private off-street parking.

NEAREST SHOPS, PUBS AND RESTAURANTS
Excellent shopping and a wealth of restaurants and pubs are available in Canterbury city centre a 10-minute stroll away.

OUT AND ABOUT
Canterbury Cathedral; St Augustine's Abbey; Marlowe Theatre and Gulbenkian Theatre; St Lawrence Cricket Ground; The Westgate Gardens; many famous gardens and castles in Kent; coast 15 minutes; convenient for day trips to France and Belgium.

PRICES PER NIGHT AND WHAT'S INCLUDED
Single room from £55.00 per person; double room from £90.00 per room. Includes full English breakfast and VAT.

Indexes

Animal friendly

Page

Armsyde, Padstow, Cornwall 30
Ascot House, York, N Yorkshire 32
The Ayrlington, Bath, Somerset 34
Battlesteads Hotel, Hexham, Northumberland 39
Brayscroft House, Eastbourne, Sussex 55
Brighton Marina Holiday Apartments, Brighton,
   Sussex 56
Brills Farm, Lincoln, Lincolnshire 58
Broadoaks Country House, Windermere, Cumbria 59
Cherrygarth Cottages, Slingsby, Yorkshire 72
Church Farm Country Cottages,
   Bradford-on-Avon, Wiltshire 73
Cliff Barns, Narborough, Norfolk 74
The Coach House at Crookham, Cornhill-on-Tweed,
   Northumberland 78
Cossington Park, Bridgwater, Somerset 86
The Cove, Penzance, Cornwall 89
Cressbrook Hall, Buxton, Derbyshire 90
Damerons Farm, Ipswich, Suffolk 93
Fairfield Gardens, Bowness-on-Windermere,
   Cumbria 105
Faweather Grange, High Eldwick, Yorkshire 106
Foxes Reach, nr Tintern, Monmouthshire 109
Foxgloves, Wigton, Cumbria 110
Gallon House, Knaresborough, N Yorkshire 112
Glebe House, Chippenham, Wiltshire 114
Green Lawns Hotel, Falmouth, Cornwall 120
Grimblethorpe Hall Country Cottages, nr Louth,
   Lincolnshire 122
Groomes Country House, Bordon, Hampshire 123
Harbour Heights, Dartmouth, Devon 127
Highgate House, Creaton, Northampton 135
Hob Green Hotel, Harrogate, N Yorkshire 136

Hornby Hall, Penrith, Cumbria 142
Isle of Eriska Hotel, by Oban, Argyll 144
Jeakes House, Rye, E Sussex 145
Kingfisher Barn, Abingdon, Oxfordshire 149
Kingston Estate, Totnes, Devon 150
Kingston House, Totnes, Devon 152
Lakelovers, Bowness-on-Windermere, Cumbria 155
Llwyndu Farmhouse, Barmouth, Gwynedd 161
Mansefield B&B, Greenlaw, Berwickshire 168
Mansefield House, Arrochar, Argyll and Bute 169
Marlborough House, Bath, Somerset 171
Mill of Blackhall, Menmuir, Angus 174
Old Bridge Hotel, Huntingdon, Cambridgeshire 183
Old Farm Cottages, Norwich, Norfolk 184
The Old Farmhouse & The Granary, Penzance,
   Cornwall 186
Park House Hotel, Midhurst, W Sussex 194
Pentre Mawr Country House, Llandrynog,
   Denbigh 197
Raffles, Blackpool, Lancashire 199
Rooke Country Cottages, Wadebridge, Cornwall 206
Rye Lodge Hotel, Rye, E Sussex 214
Sea Tree House, Lyme Regis, Dorset 218
Spanhoe Lodge, Harringworth,
   Northamptonshire 219
The Stables, Shrewsbury, Shropshire 220
Steele's Mill, Penrith, Cumbria 221
Swan Hotel, Lavenham, Suffolk 223
Sychnant Pass Country House, Conwy 227
Ta Mill, Launceston, Cornwall 228
Thornham Hall, Eye, Suffolk 232
Three Chimneys Farm, Goudhurst, Kent 233
Tides Reach Hotel, Salcombe, Devon 234
Tom's Barn, Ashbourne, Derbyshire 235
Trafford Bank Guest House, Inverness,
   Inverness-shire 239

The Valley, Truro, Cornwall	243
Vanilla Cottage, nr Usk, Monmouthshire	244
Woodlands Country House, Padstow, Cornwall	260
Yellowtop Country Park, Foggathorpe, E Yorkshire	262
Yorke Lodge, Ambleside, Cumbria	264

Children welcome

Minimum age is shown in brackets. The figure 0 signifies children of any age. Some houses welcome both very young children and those above a certain age which is denoted by the word "varies".

	Page
17 Northgate, Oakham, Rutland (0)	14
33/2 Queen Street, Edinburgh (0)	15
40 York Road, Tunbridge Wells, Kent (12)	16
6 & 15 Stonegate Court, York, N Yorkshire (0)	17
8 Clarendon Crescent, Leamington Spa, Warwickshire (4)	18
Abbey Court, Shrewsbury, Shropshire (0)	21
Allt y Golau, Felingwm Uchaf, Carmarthenshire (0)	24
Alma Mater, Lymington, Hampshire (15)	26
The Apartments, SW London (0)	27
The Apartments – Oxford, Oxfordshire (0)	28
Armsyde, Padstow, Cornwall (0)	30
Ascot House, York, N Yorkshire (0)	32
Barbican House, York, N Yorkshire (10)	36
Barncastle, Stroud, Gloucestershire (0)	38
Battlesteads Hotel, Hexham, Northumberland (0)	39
Beacon Hill Farm, Morpeth, Northumberland (0)	40
Beech Farm Cottages, Kendal, Cumbria (0)	42
The Bentley Kempinski, SW London (5)	44
Berkeley House, Tetbury, Gloucestershire (0)	45
Bethany House, Tunbridge Wells, Kent (4)	46
Bidwell Farm Cottages, Upottery, Devon (0)	47
Black Boys Inn, Hurley, Berkshire (12)	48
Blaize Cottages, Lavenham, Suffolk (varies)	49
Blenheim Lodge, Bowness-on-Windermere, Cumbria (0)	50
Blue Hayes, St Ives, Cornwall (10)	51
The The Blue Rooms, York, N Yorkshire (0)	52
Bowling Green Hotel, Plymouth, Devon (0)	54
Brayscroft House, Eastbourne, Sussex (10)	55
Brighton Marina Holiday Apartments, Brighton, Sussex (0)	56
Brills Farm, Lincoln, Lincolnshire (12)	58
Broadoaks Country House, Windermere, Cumbria (0)	59
Bruern Stables, Chipping Norton, Oxfordshire (0)	60
Bush Nook, Gilsland, Cumbria (8)	61
Buxton's Victorian Guest House, Buxton, Derbyshire (4)	62
Camelot Lodge, Eastbourne, E Sussex (0)	64
Carlyon Bay Hotel, St Austell, Cornwall (0)	66
Carnoustie Golf Hotel, Carnoustie, Angus (0)	68
The Cedars, Grantham, Lincolnshire (0)	69
Cherrygarth Cottages, Slingsby, Yorkshire (0)	72
Church Farm Country Cottages, Bradford-on-Avon, Wiltshire (0)	73
Cliff Barns, Narborough, Norfolk (0)	74
Clow Beck House, Darlington, Co Durham (0)	76
The Coach House at Crookham, Cornhill-on-Tweed, Northumberland (0)	78
Cofton Country Holiday Park, nr Dawlish, S Devon (0)	80
Coldbeck House, Kirkby Stephen, Cumbria (12)	82
The Colonnade, W London (0)	83
Compton Pool Farm, Mardlow, Devon (0)	84
Cossington Park, Bridgwater, Somerset (0)	86
The Courthouse Kempinski, W London (5)	88
The Cove, Penzance, Cornwall (0)	89
Cressbrook Hall, Buxton, Derbyshire (0)	90
The Crown Inn, Playhatch, Berkshire (0)	92
Damerons Farm, Ipswich, Suffolk (0)	93
Dannah Farm, Belper, Derbyshire (0)	94
De Grey's Town House, Ludlow, Shropshire (0)	96
Domineys Cottages, Dorchester, Dorset (5)	98
Draycott Hotel, SW London (0)	99
Emsworth House, Bradfield, Essex (0)	101
Eshott Hall, Morpeth, Northumberland (12)	104
Fairfield Garden Guest House, Bowness-on-Windermere, Cumbria (8)	105
Faweather Grange, High Eldwick, Yorkshire (0)	106
The Firs, Bath, Somerset (0)	108
Foxes Reach, nr Tintern, Monmouthshire (4)	109
Foxgloves, Wigton, Cumbria (0)	110
Gallon House, Knaresborough, N Yorkshire (0)	112
Garden Lodge, Folkestone, Kent (0)	113
Glebe House, Chippenham, Wiltshire (0)	114
The Grange, Shanklin, Isle of Wight (0)	117
The Grange Hotel, Newark, Nottinghamshire (0)	118
The Green Hotel, Kinross, Perthshire (0)	119
Green Lawns Hotel, Falmouth, Cornwall (0)	120
Grendon Guest House, Buxton, Derbyshire (varies)	121
Grimblethorpe Hall Country Cottages, nr Louth, Lincolnshire (0)	122
Groomes Country House, Bordon, Hampshire (0)	123
The Hampshire Court, Basingstoke, Hampshire (0)	126
Harbour Heights, Dartmouth, Devon (0)	127
Heatherly Cottage, nr Corsham, Wiltshire (10)	130
Hell Bay, Isles of Scilly (0)	131
Higher Wiscombe, Colyton, Devon (0)	134
Highgate House, Creaton, Northampton (0)	135
Hob Green Hotel, Harrogate, N Yorkshire (0)	136
Holiday Inn Ashford North, Hotfield, Kent (0)	137
Holme House, Hebden Bridge, W Yorkshire (0)	138
Hope Farm House, Alstonefield, Derbyshire (8)	140

\Hornby Hall, Penrith, Cumbria (0) 142
The Island Hotel, Tresco, Isles of Scilly (0) 143
Isle of Eriska Hotel, by Oban, Argyll (0) 144
Jeakes House, Rye, E Sussex (8) 145
Jinlye, Church Stretton, Shropshire (12) 146
Kasbah, Ryde, Isle of Wight (1) 147
Kildonan Lodge Hotel, Edinburgh (1) 148
Kingfisher Barn, Abingdon, Oxfordshire (0) 149
Kingston Estate, Totnes, Devon (0) 150
Lakelovers, Bowness-on-Windermere, Cumbria (0) 155
Langdale Hotel, nr Ambleside, Cumbria (0) 156
Langley Castle Hotel, Hexham,
  Northumberland (0) 157
Linthwaite House Hotel, Windermere, Cumbria (0) 159
Llwyndu Farmhouse, Barmouth, Gwynedd (0) 161
Lonsdale Hotel, Bowness-on-Windermere,
  Cumbria (0) 163
Macdonald Holyrood Hotel, Edinburgh (0) 164
Magnolia House, Canterbury, Kent (12) 165
Manor House Farm, Uttoxeter, Staffordshire (0) 167
Mansefield B&B, Greenlaw, Berwickshire (0) 168
Mansefield House, Arrochar, Argyll and Bute (0) 169
MapleLeaf Middlewick Holiday Cottages & B&B,
  Glastonbury, Somerset (0) 170
Matfen Hall, Matfen, Newcastle upon Tyne (7) 172
Melrose House, SE London (10) 173
Mill of Blackhall, Menmuir, Angus (0) 174
Millness Croft Cottages, Inverness,
  Inverness-shire (0) 175
Millstream Hotel, Chichester, W Sussex (0) 176
Mitchell's of Chester, Chester, Cheshire (0) 177
Nailey Cottages, Bath, Somerset (0) 178
New Inn, Tresco, Isles of Scilly (0) 179
Old Bridge Hotel, Huntingdon,
  Cambridgeshire (0) 183
Old Farm Cottages, Norwich, Norfolk (0) 184
The Old Farmhouse & The Granary, Penzance,
  Cornwall (0) 186
Outchester and Ross Farm Cottages, Bamburgh,
  Northumberland (0) 190
Park Farm, Saxmundham, Suffolk (10) 192
Park Farm Cottages, Saxmundham, Suffolk (0) 193
Park House Hotel, Midhurst, W Sussex (0) 194
The Pheasant Inn, Falstone, Northumberland (0) 198
Raffles, Blackpool, Lancashire (0) 199
The Relish, Folkestone, Kent (0) 201
Hotel Riviera, Sidmouth, Devon (0) 204
Rooke Country Cottages, Wadebridge,
  Cornwall (0) 206
Rothay Manor, Ambleside, Cumbria (0) 208
The Roxburghe Hotel, Edinburgh (0) 209
Royal Lancaster Hotel, W London (0) 212
Rye Lodge, Rye, E Sussex (0) 214
Saunton Sands Hotel, nr Braunton, Devon (0) 216
Sea Tree House, Lyme Regis, Dorset (0) 218

Spanhoe Lodge, Harringworth,
  Northamptonshire (0) 219
The Stables, Shrewsbury, Shropshire (0) 220
Steele's Mill, Penrith, Cumbria (0) 221
The Strathdon, Blackpool, Lancashire (0) 222
Swan Hotel, Lavenham, Suffolk (0) 223
Swinton Park, Masham, N Yorkshire (0) 224
Sychnant Pass Country House, Conwy (0) 227
Ta Mill, Launceston, Cornwall (0) 228
Thirty Two, Cheltenham, Gloucestershire (8) 231
Thornham Hall, Eye, Suffolk (0) 232
Three Chimneys Farm, Goudhurst, Kent (0) 233
Tides Reach Hotel, Salcombe, Devon (8) 234
Tone Dale House, Wellington, Somerset (0) 236
Tower House 1066, St Leonards-on-Sea,
  E Sussex (2) 238
Trafford Bank Guest House, Inverness,
  Inverness-shire (0) 239
Treverbyn Vean Manor, Liskeard, Cornwall (0) 240
The Valley, Truro, Cornwall (0) 243
Venn Farm, Plymouth, S Devon (0) 246
Waitby School, Kirkby Stephen, Cumbria (0) 247
Wallett's Court Country House Hotel, Restaurant
  and Spa, Dover, Kent (0) 248
Waren Lea Hall, Bamburgh, Northumberland (0) 250
The Washington Mayfair, W London (0) 252
Westcott Barton, Barnstaple, N Devon (12) 255
Wethele Manor, nr Leamington Spa,
  Warwickshire (0) 256
Witch Hazel, Wymondham, Norfolk (15) 258
Woodlands Country House, Padstow, Cornwall (0) 260
Woodlands Country House, Ireby, Cumbria (10) 261
Yellowtop Country Park, Foggathorpe, E Yorkshire (0) 262
Yewfield, Ambleside, Cumbria (9) 263
Yorke Lodge, Ambleside, Cumbria (0) 264

Health and/or beauty facilities

	Page
Alliblaster House, Rudgwick, W Sussex	22
Barncastle, Stroud, Gloucestershire (alternative therapies)	38
Beacon Hill Farm, Morpeth, Northumberland	40
Bethany House, Tunbridge Wells, Kent	46
Bruern Stables, Chipping Norton, Oxfordshire	60
Carlyon Bay Hotel, St Austell, Cornwall	66
Carnoustie Golf Hotel, Carnoustie, Angus	68
Cherrygarth Cottages, Slingsby, Yorkshire	72
Church Farm Country Cottages, Bradford-on-Avon, Wiltshire	73
Cliff Barns, Narborough, Norfolk	74
Cossington Park, Bridgwater, Somerset	86
The Courthouse Kempinski, W London	88
The Cove, Penzance, Cornwall	89
Enchanted Manor, Isle of Wight	103

Faweather Grange, High Eldwick, Yorkshire 106
Fern Cottage, Pucklechurch, S Gloucestershire 107
Foxes Reach, nr Tintern, Monmouthshire 109
Garden Lodge, Folkestone, Kent 113
The Grange, Shanklin, Isle of Wight 117
The Green Hotel, Kinross, Perthshire 119
The Hampshire Court, Basingstoke, Hampshire 126
Highcliffe House, Lynton, Devon 133
Isle of Eriska Hotel, by Oban, Argyll 144
Kasbah, Ryde, Isle of Wight 147
Langdale Hotel, nr Ambleside, Cumbria 156
Linthwaite House Hotel, Windermere, Cumbria 159
Macdonald Holyrood Hotel, Edinburgh 164
MapleLeaf Middlewick Holiday Cottages & B&B,
 Glastonbury, Somerset 170
Matfen Hall, Matfen, Newcastle upon Tyne 172
Nailey Cottages, Bath, Somerset 178
The Old Farmhouse & The Granary, Penzance,
 Cornwall 186
The Residence, Bath, Somerset 202
The Roxburghe Hotel, Edinburgh 209
The Royal Duchy Hotel, Falmouth, Cornwall 210
Saunton Sands Hotel, nr Braunton, Devon 216
Swinton Park, Masham, N Yorkshire 224
Tides Reach Hotel, Salcombe, Devon 234
Tone Dale House, Wellington, Somerset 236
Tower House 1066, St Leonards-on-Sea,
 E Sussex 238
Wallett's Court Country House Hotel, Restaurant
 and Spa, Dover, Kent 248

Hen/stag parties

Page
The Apartments – Oxford, Oxfordshire 28
Barncastle, Stroud, Gloucestershire (hen only) 38
Beech Farm Cottages, Kendal, Cumbria 42
Berkeley House, Tetbury, Gloucestershire (hen only) 45
Cliff Barns, Narborough, Norfolk (hen only) 74
The Courthouse Kempinski, W London 88
The Cove, Penzance, Cornwall 89
Grand Hotel, Kenilworth, Warwickshire 116
The Grange, Shanklin, Isle of Wight 117
The Hampshire Court, Basingstoke, Hampshire 126
Higher Wiscombe, Colyton, Devon 134
Kasbah, Ryde, Isle of Wight 147
Lonsdale Hotel, Bowness-on-Windermere,
 Cumbria 163
Macdonald Holyrood Hotel, Edinburgh 164
Mansefield House, Arrochar, Argyll and Bute 169
Nailey Cottages, Bath, Somerset (hen only) 178
Wallett's Court Country House Hotel,
 Restaurant and Spa, Dover, Kent 248
The Washington Mayfair, W London 252
Woodlands Country House, Padstow, Cornwall 260

Internet access

Page
17 Northgate, Oakham, Rutland 14
33/2 Queen Street, Edinburgh 15
40 York Road, Tunbridge Wells, Kent 16
6 & 15 Stonegate Court, York 17
8 Clarendon Crescent, Leamington Spa,
 Warwickshire 18
Alliblaster House, Rudgwick, W Sussex 22
The Apartments, SW London 27
The Apartments – Oxford, Oxfordshire 28
Artizana Suite, Prestbury, Cheshire 31
Ascot House, York, N Yorkshire 32
Atlantic House, Lizard, Cornwall 33
Barbican House, York, N Yorkshire 36
Barncastle, Stroud, Gloucestershire 38
Battlesteads Hotel, Hexham, Northumberland 39
Beacon Hill Farm, Morpeth, Northumberland 40
Berkeley House, Tetbury, Gloucestershire 45
Black Boys Inn, Hurley, Berkshire 48
Blue Hayes, St Ives, Cornwall 51
Bowling Green Hotel, Plymouth, Devon 54
Brayscroft House, Eastbourne, Sussex 55
Brighton Marina Holiday Apartments, Brighton,
 Sussex (three of four) 56
Broadoaks Country House, Windermere, Cumbria 59
Bruern Stables, Chipping Norton, Oxfordshire 60
Bush Nook Country Guest House, Gilsland,
 Cumbria 61
Camelot Lodge, Eastbourne, E Sussex 64
Carnoustie Golf Hotel, Carnoustie, Angus 68
Chequer Cottage, Horseheath, Cambridgeshire 70
Cheriton House, Huntingdon, Cambridgeshire 71
Cherrygarth Cottages, Slingsby, Yorkshire 72
Church Farm Country Cottages,
 Bradford-on-Avon, Wiltshire 73
Cliff Barns, Narborough, Norfolk 74
The Colonnade, W London 83
Cossington Park, Bridgwater, Somerset 86
The Courthouse Kempinski, W London 88
The Cove, Penzance, Cornwall 89
Cressbrook Hall, Buxton, Derbyshire 90
The Crown Inn, Playhatch, Berkshire 92
Dannah Farm, Belper, Derbyshire 94
Draycott Hotel, SW London 99
Enchanted Manor, Isle of Wight 103
Eshott Hall, Morpeth, Northumberland 104
Fairfield Garden Guest House,
 Bowness-on-Windermere, Cumbria 105
Fern Cottage, Pucklechurch, S Gloucestershire 107
Foxes Reach, nr Tintern, Monmouthshire 109
Garden Lodge, Folkestone, Kent 113
Glebe House, Chippenham, Wiltshire 114
Godshill Park Farmhouse, Godshill, Isle of Wight 115

Grand Hotel, Kenilworth, Warwickshire 116
The Grange, Shanklin, Isle of Wight 117
The Grange Hotel, Newark, Nottinghamshire 118
The Green Hotel, Kinross, Perthshire 119
Green Lawns Hotel, Falmouth, Cornwall 120
Groomes Country House, Bordon, Hampshire 123
Halsteads Barn, nr Lancaster, N Yorkshire 125
The Hampshire Court, Basingstoke,
    Hampshire 126
Hell Bay, Tresco, Isles of Scilly 131
Highcliffe House, Lynton, Devon 133
Highgate House, Creaton, Northampton 135
Holiday Inn Ashford North, Hotfield, Kent 137
Holme House, Hebden Bridge, W Yorkshire 138
Hope Farm House, Alstonefield, Derbyshire 140
The Island Hotel, Tresco, Isles of Scilly 143
Isle of Eriska Hotel, by Oban, Argyll 144
Jinlye, Church Stretton, Shropshire 146
Kasbah, Ryde, Isle of Wight 147
Kildonan Lodge Hotel, Edinburgh 148
Kingfisher Barn, Abingdon, Oxfordshire 149
Kingston Estate, Totnes, Devon 150
Kingston House, Totnes, Devon 152
Langdale Hotel, nr Ambleside, Cumbria 156
Langley Castle Hotel, Hexham, Northumberland 157
The Leconfield, Ventnor, Isle of Wight 158
Linthwaite House Hotel, Windermere, Cumbria 159
Llwyndu Farmhouse, Barmouth, Gwynedd 161
Macdonald Holyrood Hotel, Edinburgh 164
Magnolia House, Canterbury, Kent 165
Mansefield B&B, Greenlaw, Berwickshire 168
Mansefield House, Arrochar, Argyll and Bute 169
MapleLeaf Middlewick Holiday Cottages & B&B,
    Glastonbury, Somerset 170
Marlborough House, Bath, Somerset 171
Melrose House, SE London 173
Millness Croft Cottages, Inverness, Inverness-shire 175
Millstream Hotel, Chichester, W Sussex 176
Mitchell's of Chester, Chester, Cheshire 177
Nailey Cottages, Bath, Somerset 178
New Inn, Tresco, Isles of Scilly 179
Oak Farm Barn, Bury St Edmunds, Suffolk 180
Ocklynge Manor, Eastbourne, East Sussex 182
Old Bridge Hotel, Huntingdon, Cambridgeshire 183
The Old Vicarage, Pickering, N Yorkshire 189
Park House Hotel, Midhurst, W Sussex 194
Pelham House, Lewes, E Sussex 196
Pentre Mawr Country House, Llandrynog,
    Denbigh 197
The Relish, Folkestone, Kent 201
The Residence, Bath, Somerset 202
Rooke Country Cottages, Wadebridge, Cornwall 206
The Roxburghe Hotel, Edinburgh 209
Royal Lancaster Hotel, W London 212
The Royal Oak, Chichester, W Sussex 213

Rye Lodge, Rye, E Sussex 214
Sea Tree House, Lyme Regis, Dorset 218
Spanhoe Lodge, Harringworth,
    Northamptonshire 219
Steele's Mill, Penrith, Cumbria 221
Swan Hotel, Lavenham, Suffolk 223
Sychnant Pass Country House, Conwy 227
Tall Ships, Charlestown, Cornwall 230
Thirty Two, Cheltenham, Gloucestershire 231
Thornham Hall, Eye, Suffolk 232
Three Chimneys Farm, Goudhurst, Kent 233
Tides Reach Hotel, Salcombe, Devon 234
Tom's Barn, Ashbourne, Derbyshire 235
Tower House 1066, St Leonards-on-Sea,
    E Sussex 238
Trafford Bank Guest House, Inverness,
    Inverness-shire 239
Treverbyn Vean Manor, Liskeard, Cornwall 240
Ty'n Rhos Country House, Caernarfon, Gwynedd 241
Vanilla Cottage, nr Usk, Monmouthshire 244
Waitby School, Kirkby Stephen, Cumbria 247
Wallett's Court Country House Hotel,
    Restaurant and Spa, Dover, Kent 248
The Washington Mayfair, W London 252
Wethele Manor, nr Leamington Spa,
    Warwickshire 256
Witch Hazel, Wymondham, Norfolk 258
Woodlands Country House, Padstow, Cornwall 260
Woodlands Country House, Ireby, Cumbria 261
Yellowtop Country Park, Foggathorpe, E Yorkshire 262
Yewfield, Ambleside, Cumbria 263
Yorke Lodge, Ambleside, Cumbria 264

Large parties

	Page
Abbey Court, Shrewsbury, Shropshire	21
The Apartments – Oxford, Oxfordshire	28
Barncastle, Stroud, Gloucestershire	38
Berkeley House, Tetbury, Gloucestershire	45
Bidwell Farm Cottages, Upottery, Devon	47
The Blue Rooms, York, N Yorkshire (in restaurant)	52
Broadoaks Country House, Windermere, Cumbria	59
Bruern Stables, Chipping Norton, Oxfordshire	60
Carnoustie Golf Hotel, Carnoustie, Angus	68
Cherrygarth Cottages, Slingsby, Yorkshire	72
Church Farm Country Cottages,	
Bradford-on-Avon, Wiltshire	73
Cliff Barns, Narborough, Norfolk	74
Cossington Park, Bridgwater, Somerset	86
The Cove, Penzance, Cornwall	89
Cressbrook Hall, Buxton, Derbyshire	90
The Crown Inn, Playhatch, Berkshire	92
Dannah Farm, Belper, Derbyshire	94
De Grey's Town House, Ludlow, Shropshire	96

Eshott Hall, Morpeth, Northumberland   104
Fairfield Garden Guest House,
    Bowness-on-Windermere, Cumbria   105
Grand Hotel, Kenilworth, Warwickshire   116
The Grange, Shanklin, Isle of Wight   117
The Grange Hotel, Newark, Nottinghamshire   118
Green Lawns Hotel, Falmouth, Cornwall   120
Groomes Country House, Bordon, Hampshire   123
The Hampshire Court, Basingstoke,
    Hampshire   126
Harbour Heights, Dartmouth, Devon   127
Higher Wiscombe, Colyton, Devon   134
Highgate House, Creaton, Northampton   135
Holiday Inn Ashford North, Hotfield, Kent   137
Hornby Hall, Penrith, Cumbria   142
Jinlye, Church Stretton, Shropshire   146
Kasbah, Ryde, Isle of Wight   147
Kingston Estate, Totnes, Devon   150
Kingston House, Totnes, Devon   152
Langdale Hotel, nr Ambleside, Cumbria   156
Linthwaite House Hotel, Windermere,
    Cumbria   159
Llwyndu Farmhouse, Barmouth, Gwynedd
    (14-20 people)   161
Lonsdale Hotel, Bowness-on-Windermere,
    Cumbria   163
Macdonald Holyrood Hotel, Edinburgh   164
Mansefield House, Arrochar, Argyll and Bute   169
MapleLeaf Middlewick Holiday Cottages & B&B,
    Glastonbury, Somerset   170
Melrose House, SE London   173
Nailey Cottages, Bath, Somerset   178
Old Bridge Hotel, Huntingdon, Cambridgeshire   183
Old Farm Cottages, Norwich, Norfolk   184
Park House Hotel, Midhurst, W Sussex   194
The Relish, Folkestone, Kent   201
Rothay Manor, Ambleside, Cumbria   208
The Roxburghe Hotel, Edinburgh   209
Royal Lancaster Hotel, W London   212
Spanhoe Lodge, Harringworth,
    Northamptonshire   219
Swan Hotel, Lavenham, Suffolk   223
Ta Mill, Launceston, Cornwall   228
Thornham Hall, Eye, Suffolk   232
Tone Dale House, Wellington, Somerset   236
Tower House 1066, St Leonards-on-Sea,
    E Sussex   238
Trafford Bank Guest House, Inverness,
    Inverness-shire (up to 15 people)   239
The Valley, Truro, Cornwall   243
Wallett's Court Country House Hotel,
    Restaurant and Spa, Dover, Kent   248
Waren Lea Hall, Bamburgh, Northumberland   250
Wethele Manor, nr Leamington Spa,
    Warwickshire   256

Leisure/sporting facilities

                                                Page
Beacon Hill Farm, Morpeth, Northumberland   40
Broadoaks Country House, Windermere, Cumbria   59
Bruern Stables, Chipping Norton, Oxfordshire   60
Carlyon Bay Hotel, St Austell, Cornwall   66
Carnoustie Golf Hotel, Carnoustie, Angus   68
Cherrygarth Cottages, Slingsby, Yorkshire   72
Church Farm Country Cottages,
    Bradford-on-Avon, Wiltshire   73
Cliff Barns, Narborough, Norfolk   74
Cofton Country Holidays, nr Dawlish, S Devon   80
Compton Pool Farm, Mardlow, Devon   84
The Cove, Penzance, Cornwall   89
Cressbrook Hall, Buxton, Derbyshire   90
Damerons Farm, Ipswich, Suffolk   93
Enchanted Manor, Isle of Wight   103
Faweather Grange, High Eldwick, Yorkshire   106
Garden Lodge, Folkestone, Kent   113
The Grange, Shanklin, Isle of Wight   117
The Green Hotel, Kinross, Perthshire   119
Green Lawns Hotel, Falmouth, Cornwall   120
Groomes Country House, Bordon, Hampshire   123
The Hampshire Court, Basingstoke, Hampshire   126
Hell Bay, Tresco, Isles of Scilly   131
Higher Wiscombe, Colyton, Devon   134
Highgate House, Creaton, Northampton   135
The Island Hotel, Tresco, Isles of Scilly   143
Isle of Eriska Hotel, by Oban, Argyll   144
Kingston Estate, Totnes, Devon   150
Kingston House, Totnes, Devon   152
Langdale Hotel, nr Ambleside, Cumbria   156
Linthwaite House Hotel, Windermere, Cumbria   159
Macdonald Holyrood Hotel, Edinburgh   164
MapleLeaf Middlewick Holiday Cottages & B&B,
    Glastonbury, Somerset   170
Matfen Hall, Matfen, Newcastle upon Tyne   172
New Inn, Tresco, Isles of Scilly   179
Old Farm Cottages, Norwich, Norfolk   184
Park House Hotel, Midhurst, W Sussex   194
Pentre Mawr Country House, Llandrynog,
    Denbigh   197
The Residence, Bath, Somerset   202
The Roxburghe Hotel, Edinburgh   209
Royal Duchy Hotel, Falmouth, Cornwall   210
Saunton Sands Hotel, nr Braunton, Devon   216
Steele's Mill, Penrith, Cumbria   221
Swinton Park, Masham, N Yorkshire   224
Sychnant Pass Country House, Conwy   227
Ta Mill, Launceston, Cornwall   228
Three Chimneys Farm, Goudhurst, Kent   233
Tides Reach Hotel, Salcombe, Devon   234
Tone Dale House, Wellington, Somerset   236
Treverbyn Vean Manor, Liskeard, Cornwall   240

Ty'n Rhos, Caernarfon, Gwynedd	241	
The Valley, Truro, Cornwall	243	
Wallett's Court Country House Hotel, Restaurant and Spa, Dover, Kent	248	
Waren Lea Hall, Bamburgh, Northumberland	250	

Perfect for reunions

	Page
17 Northgate, Oakham, Rutland	14
33/2 Queen Street, Edinburgh	15
Abbey Court, Shrewsbury, Shropshire	21
The Apartments – Oxford, Oxfordshire	28
Armsyde, Padstow, Cornwall	30
Ascot House, York, N Yorkshire	32
Atlantic House, Lizard, Cornwall	33
Barbican House, York, N Yorkshire	36
Barncastle, Stroud, Gloucestershire	38
Beacon Hill Farm, Morpeth, Northumberland	40
Beech Farm Cottages, Kendal, Cumbria	42
Berkeley House, Tetbury, Gloucestershire	45
Bidwell Farm Cottages, Upottery, Devon	47
Blenheim Lodge, Bowness-on-Windermere, Cumbria	50
Bowling Green Hotel, Plymouth, Devon	54
Broadoaks Country House, Windermere, Cumbria	59
Bruern Stables, Chipping Norton, Oxfordshire	60
Bush Nook Country Guest House, Gilsland, Cumbria	61
Camelot Lodge, Eastbourne, E Sussex	64
Carnoustie Golf Hotel, Carnoustie, Angus	68
Cherrygarth Cottages, Slingsby, Yorkshire	72
Church Farm Country Cottages, Bradford-on-Avon, Wiltshire	73
Cliff Barns, Narborough, Norfolk	74
Coldbeck House, Kirkby Stephen, Cumbria	82
Cossington Park, Bridgwater, Somerset	86
The Courthouse Kempinski, W London	88
The Cove, Penzance, Cornwall	89
Cressbrook Hall, Buxton, Derbyshire	90
The Crown Inn, Playhatch, Berkshire	92
Dannah Farm Country House, Belper, Derbyshire	94
De Grey's Town House, Ludlow, Shropshire	96
Eshott Hall, Morpeth, Northumberland	104
Fairfield Garden Guest House, Bowness-on-Windermere, Cumbria	105
Fern Cottage, Pucklechurch, S Gloucestershire	107
Foxes Reach, nr Tintern, Monmouthshire	109
Grand Hotel, Kenilworth, Warwickshire	116
The Grange, Shanklin, Isle of Wight	117
The Grange Hotel, Newark, Nottinghamshire	118
Green Lawns Hotel, Falmouth, Cornwall	120
Groomes Country House, Bordon, Hampshire	123
The Hampshire Court, Basingstoke, Hampshire	126
Harbour Heights, Dartmouth, Devon	127
Higher Wiscombe, Colyton, Devon	134
Highgate House, Creaton, Northampton	135
Hob Green Hotel, Harrogate, N Yorkshire	136
Holiday Inn Ashford North, Hotfield, Kent	137
Holme House, Hebden Bridge, W Yorkshire	138
Hope Farm House, Alstonefield, Derbyshire	140
Hornby Hall, Penrith, Cumbria	142
Isle of Eriska Hotel, by Oban, Argyll	144
Jinlye, Church Stretton, Shropshire	146
Kasbah, Ryde, Isle of Wight	147
Kildonan Lodge Hotel, Edinburgh	148
Kingfisher Barn, Abingdon, Oxfordshire	149
Kingston Estate, Totnes, Devon	150
Kingston House, Totnes, Devon	152
Langdale Hotel, nr Ambleside, Cumbria	156
Langley Castle Hotel, Hexham, Northumberland	157
Linthwaite House Hotel, Windermere, Cumbria	159
Lonsdale Hotel, Bowness-on-Windermere, Cumbria	163
Macdonald Holyrood Hotel, Edinburgh	164
Manor House Farm, Uttoxeter, Staffordshire	167
Mansefield House, Arrochar, Argyll and Bute	169
MapleLeaf Middlewick Holiday Cottages & B&B, Glastonbury, Somerset	170
Marlborough House, Bath, Somerset	171
Melrose House, SE London	173
Nailey Cottages, Bath, Somerset	178
Old Bridge Hotel, Huntingdon, Cambridgeshire	183
Old Farm Cottages, Norwich, Norfolk	184
Park Farm Cottages, Saxmundham, Suffolk	193
Park House Hotel, Midhurst, W Sussex	194
Pelham House, Lewes, E Sussex	196
Pentre Mawr Country House, Llandrynog, Denbigh	197
The Pheasant Inn, Falstone, Northumberland	198
Raffles, Blackpool, Lancashire	199
The Relish, Folkestone, Kent	201
Hotel Riviera, Sidmouth, Devon	204
Rothay Manor, Ambleside, Cumbria	208
The Roxburghe Hotel, Edinburgh	209
Royal Lancaster Hotel, W London	212
Spanhoe Lodge, Harringworth, Northamptonshire	219
The Stables, Shrewsbury, Shropshire	220
Swan Hotel, Lavenham, Suffolk	223
Sychnant Pass Country House, Conwy	227
Ta Mill, Launceston, Cornwall	228
Thornham Hall, Eye, Suffolk	232
Three Chimneys Farm, Goudhurst, Kent	233
Tone Dale House, Wellington, Somerset	236
Tower House 1066, St Leonards-on-Sea, E Sussex	238
Underleigh House, Hope Valley, Derbyshire	242
Wallett's Court Country House Hotel, Restaurant and Spa, Dover, Kent	248
Waren Lea Hall, Bamburgh, Northumberland	250

The Washington Mayfair, W London 252
Wethele Manor, nr Leamington Spa,
  Warwickshire 256
Woodlands Country House, Padstow, Cornwall 260
Woodlands Country House, Ireby, Cumbria 261

Weddings catered for

Page

Battlesteads Hotel, Hexham, Northumberland 39
Berkeley House, Tetbury, Gloucestershire 45
The Blue Rooms, York, N Yorkshire 52
Broadoaks Country House, Windermere, Cumbria 59
Camelot Lodge, Eastbourne, E Sussex 64
Carnoustie Golf Hotel, Carnoustie, Angus 68
Cliff Barns, Narborough, Norfolk 74
The Courthouse Kempinski, W London 88
The Cove, Penzance, Cornwall 89
Cressbrook Hall, Buxton, Derbyshire 90
The Crown Inn, Playhatch, Berkshire 92
De Grey's Town House, Ludlow, Shropshire 96
Enchanted Manor, Isle of Wight 103
Eshott Hall, Morpeth, Northumberland 104
Garden Lodge, Folkestone, Kent 113
The Grange Hotel, Newark, Nottinghamshire 118
Green Lawns Hotel, Falmouth, Cornwall 120
Groomes Country House, Bordon, Hampshire 123
Highgate House, Creaton, Northampton 135
Hob Green Hotel, Harrogate, N Yorkshire 136
Holiday Inn Ashford North, Hotfield, Kent 137
Isle of Eriska Hotel, by Oban, Argyll 144
Jinlye, Church Stretton, Shropshire 146
Kasbah, Ryde, Isle of Wight 147
Kildonan Lodge Hotel, Edinburgh 148
Kingston Estate, Totnes, Devon 150
Kingston House, Totnes, Devon 152
Langdale Hotel, nr Ambleside, Cumbria 156
Langley Castle Hotel, Hexham,
  Northumberland 157
Linthwaite House Hotel, Windermere, Cumbria 159
Macdonald Holyrood Hotel, Edinburgh 164
MapleLeaf Middlewick Holiday Cottages & B&B,
  Glastonbury, Somerset 170
Millstream Hotel, Chichester, W Sussex 176
Nailey Cottages, Bath, Somerset 178
Old Bridge Hotel, Huntingdon, Cambridgeshire 183
Park House Hotel, Midhurst, W Sussex 194
Pelham House, Lewes, E Sussex 196
Raffles, Blackpool, Lancashire 199
Hotel Riviera, Sidmouth, Devon 204
The Roxburghe Hotel, Edinburgh 209
Royal Lancaster Hotel, W London 212
Spanhoe Lodge, Harringworth,
  Northamptonshire 219
Swan Hotel, Lavenham, Suffolk 223

Swinton Park, Masham, N Yorkshire 224
Sychnant Pass Country House, Conwy 227
Thornham Hall, Eye, Suffolk 232
Tone Dale House, Wellington, Somerset 236
Tower House 1066, St Leonards-on-Sea,
  E Sussex 238
Wallett's Court Country House Hotel,
  Restaurant and Spa, Dover, Kent 248
Waren Lea Hall, Bamburgh, Northumberland 250
Wethele Manor, nr Leamington Spa,
  Warwickshire 256

Wedding ceremonies

Page

Beech Farm Cottages, Kendal, Cumbria 42
Broadoaks Country House, Windermere,
  Cumbria 59
Carnoustie Golf Hotel, Carnoustie, Angus 68
Cliff Barns, Narborough, Norfolk 74
The Courthouse Kempinski, W London 88
The Cove, Penzance, Cornwall 89
Cressbrook Hall, Buxton, Derbyshire 90
Dannah Farm Country House, Belper,
  Derbyshire 94
De Grey's Town House, Ludlow, Shropshire 96
Eshott Hall, Morpeth, Northumberland 104
Grand Hotel, Kenilworth, Warwickshire 116
Green Lawns Hotel, Falmouth, Cornwall 120
Groomes Country House, Bordon, Hampshire 123
Highgate House, Creaton, Northampton 135
Hob Green Hotel, Harrogate, N Yorkshire 136
Holiday Inn Ashford North, Hotfield, Kent 137
Isle of Eriska Hotel, by Oban, Argyll 144
Kingston Estate, Totnes, Devon 150
Kingston House, Totnes, Devon 152
Langdale Hotel, nr Ambleside, Cumbria 156
Langley Castle Hotel, Hexham,
  Northumberland 157
Linthwaite House Hotel, Windermere, Cumbria 159
Macdonald Holyrood Hotel, Edinburgh 164
Manor House Farm, Uttoxeter, Staffordshire 167
Millstream Hotel, Chichester, W Sussex 176
Old Bridge Hotel, Huntingdon, Cambridgeshire 183
Park House Hotel, Midhurst, W Sussex 194
Pelham House, Lewes, E Sussex 196
The Roxburghe Hotel, Edinburgh 209
Royal Duchy Hotel, Falmouth, Cornwall 210
Swan Hotel, Lavenham, Suffolk 223
Swinton Park, Masham, N Yorkshire 224
Sychnant Pass Country House, Conwy 227
Thornham Hall, Eye, Suffolk 232
Tone Dale House, Wellington, Somerset 236
Wethele Manor, nr Leamington Spa,
  Warwickshire 256